ROUTLEDGE LIBRARY EDITIONS:
WOMEN, FEMINISM AND LITERATURE

GENDER, GENRE AND NARRATIVE PLEASURE

GENDER, GENRE AND NARRATIVE PLEASURE

Edited by
DEREK LONGHURST

Volume 9

Routledge
Taylor & Francis Group

LONDON AND NEW YORK

First published in 1989

This edition first published in 2012
by Routledge
2 Park Square, Milton Park, Abingdon, Oxfordshire OX14 4RN

Simultaneously published in the USA and Canada
by Routledge
711 Third Avenue, New York, NY 10017

First issued in paperback 2014

Routledge is an imprint of the Taylor and Francis Group, an informa company

British Library Cataloguing in Publication Data
A catalogue record for this book is available from the British Library

ISBN 13: 978-0-415-52326-4 (Volume 9)
ISBN 13: 978-0-415-75234-3 (pbk)

Publisher's Note
The publisher has gone to great lengths to ensure the quality of this reprint but
points out that some imperfections in the original copies may be apparent.

Disclaimer
The publisher has made every effort to trace copyright holders and would
welcome correspondence from those they have been unable to trace.

Reading Popular Fiction

GENDER, GENRE AND NARRATIVE PLEASURE

Edited by
DEREK LONGHURST

London
UNWIN HYMAN
Boston   Sydney   Wellington

© Derek Longhurst and contributors, 1989

This book is copyright under the Berne Convention. No reproduction without permission. All rights reserved.

Published by the Academic Division of
Unwin Hyman Ltd
15/17 Broadwick Street, London W1V 1FP, UK

Unwin Hyman Inc.,
8 Winchester Place, Winchester, Mass. 01890, USA

Allen & Unwin (Australia) Ltd,
8 Napier Street, North Sydney, NSW 2060, Australia

Allen & Unwin (New Zealand) Ltd, in association with the Port Nicholson Press Ltd,
60 Cambridge Terrace, Wellington, New Zealand

First published in 1989

British Library Cataloguing in Publication Data

Gender, genre and narrative pleasure. —
   (Popular fiction and social relations).
   1. Popular fiction in English. Sociocultural aspects
   I. Longhurst, Derek II. Series
   306′.488

   ISBN 0-04-445008-7
   ISBN 0-04-445009-5 Pbk

Library of Congress Cataloging in Publication Data
Library data applied for.

Typeset in 10/11 point Plantin
and printed in Great Britain by
Billing and Son, London and Worcester

Contents

General Editor's Preface

IT IS now widely recognized that the study of popular fiction plays an important part in cultural analysis. No longer is reading popular fiction generally considered to be an activity akin to a secret vice to which one should admit shamefacedly. Nor can popular narrative be adequately understood as merely narcotic and its readers as unenlightened junkies. Thankfully, the field of critical study is now typified by provocative and stimulating debates rooted in cross-disciplinary inquiry and addressing key questions concerning social groups and their relation to the culture which they inhabit. For instance, how do the institutions and processes involved in the production of popular fictions shape the ways in which texts and genres, meanings and ideological values are distributed and circulated? How does British popular culture interact with other cultures, especially American? How do popular fictions 'address' their readership in terms of class, race, gender, age, regionalism, national identities? Under what material conditions does reading as a social practice take place? What do readers draw upon in order to *make sense* of a popular narrative? And so on.

This series is designed to provide a context for such debates and as a resource for readers, students and teachers fascinated by the pleasures of popular fiction in all their ambivalence, tension and contradiction. Drawing in an accessible way upon contemporary critical theory, the series will investigate production contexts, genres in their historical diversity and fluid boundaries, texts and the formation of identities or subjectivities, readerships and the historical conditions which shape the production and reproduction of re-readings. Clearly, too, it will be necessary to offer accounts of how the various media of publishing, cinema, radio and television, each with its own determinants and specificities, also interact in complementary and contrasting modes.

Consequently the series is committed to investigate the terrain of the production, reproduction and reception of popular fiction as a matter of historical, cultural and political concern. The tired, old dichotomy of 'high' vs 'low' literature can no longer provide (if it ever could!) an adequate basis upon which to build satisfactory accounts of how narratives impinge upon the lives and experiences of their readers, interacting with widespread social meaning systems. Certainly this is not a matter of constructing an alternative 'canon' but of confronting the negotiations between popular fictions, social discourses and the desires and fantasies, aspirations and identities of heterogeneous readerships.

A large project, indeed, but one that is profoundly worthwhile.

Derek Longhurst

Acknowledgements

I WOULD like to thank Wolfson College, Oxford, for the award of the Charter Fellowship in English Language and Literature. This was encouraging support from a number of points of view and it enabled me to complete the editorial work on this book.

I would also like to acknowledge the commitment and constant support this project has received from Jane Harris Matthews of Unwin Hyman. It has been a genuine pleasure to work with her.

Finally, I must pay public tribute to the enthusiasm and interest of Dee Dine. Without her, the thick and thin of public sector education in Britain in the 1980s would have been even more difficult to endure.

GENDER, GENRE AND NARRATIVE PLEASURE

Introduction

DEREK LONGHURST

RECENT years have witnessed important new initiatives in the study of popular fictional modes of writing. At one time the field could have been described with reasonable accuracy as fenced around by two traditions. On the one hand, deriving out of sociological investigation, there was some concern to analyse the production and distribution of popular fictions as commodities. A central problem here, however, was the tendency to *assume* that 'effects', commonly seen as escapist and (therefore?) ideological, followed on from the nature of what was, essentially, a capitalist enterprise, an assumption in other words that consumption could be predicated upon analysis of the modes of production and distribution. On the other hand, across the common room, the 'Eng. Lit.' corner was dominated by those who regarded popular fiction as the negative which offered high definition to the exposure of the positive which was, of course, the 'great' canonic literary tradition. (A few mildly eccentric figures emerged in the evenings from their concordances of *Beowulf* to engage in a little slumming with SF or detective fiction.) Generally, then, popular fictions were to be 'evaluated' according to the institutionalized norms which had been established as common sense practice around literary studies, a range of largely formalist strategies designed to demonstrate that unlike 'literature', popular fiction was standardized and formulaic, a debased coinage, of little 'moral' value, distorting the truths of 'lived experience', time-bound rather than addressing the transhistorical and universal territory of the 'human condition'.[1] Both academic traditions shared a tendency to base their analysis upon rescuing *other*, less enlightened readers from the predatory tentacles of the pleasures of popular fiction, either in the interests of demystifying false consciousness of the socio-economic power structures of capitalism or of preserving the liberal-humanist values fostered within élite culture as the only viable bastion against the trivializing experiences of 'mass' culture. And, finally, it is worth noting that both traditions are ethnocentric in critical orientation (e.g. 'Englishness' as 'universal') and male-dominated. As such, this sheds an interesting perspective upon the tendency to stress the pleasures of rational cognition and the controlled expression of emotion in opposition to the pleasures of the body and the 'baser instincts' of mankind [*sic*].

The decade of the 1970s ushered in a bewildering range of theoretical debates which impinged very significantly upon literary studies in particular. Panic-stricken academics were heard to inquire in some desperation, 'What is structuralism?' This cultural disturbance in the corridors of Higher Education even made it on to the pages of the quality press (it wasn't quite salacious enough for the tabloids). Suddenly, the 'Eng. Lit.' corner found itself encircled and even invaded by voices discussing critical methodology, Marxism, semiotics, narratology, feminism, psychoanalysis, structuralism, post-structuralism and even popular film and television! One defensive response was crusty old boy dismissiveness – a load of 'jargon', certainly not for 'me' in comparison to the dark mysteries of the human soul (no jargon here, of course) plumbed in Lawrence's prose. Not totally unconnected was the institutional response of appropriation as, after all, no academic course would be entirely secure in the market terms of the 1980s without its token critical theorist (and/or feminist?).

Clearly there is *some* danger here of caricature and it can certainly be agreed that the processes, determinants and consequences of this 'sea change' in the Humanities disciplines were – and are – complex and manifold. For the study of popular fiction, however, the crucial gain in Britain was perhaps the establishment of interdisciplinary courses in communication, cultural and media studies providing a network of contexts within which serious analysis could evolve and progress. Much of this development has taken place within the public sector of Higher Education, through CNAA-validated[2] degree courses in the Polytechnics and Colleges rather than in the Universities, although it should be noted that research centres such as the Centre for Contemporary Cultural Studies at Birmingham University or Leicester's Centre for Mass Communication Research were important influences and generated productive theoretical methodologies allied to empirical work.

The agendas which have been constructed gradually around the critical study of popular fiction are complex and varied but there were some rather simple starting points: the desire to challenge the literary canon as 'given' rather than as produced and reproduced in specific historical formations; dissatisfaction with critical practices which (a) endorsed the simplistic dichotomy of 'major' vs. 'minor' literature, (b) assumed as self-evident the category of 'literature', (c) constituted historical formations as mere 'background' to the literary text within which meanings were intrinsic rather than produced. All in all, the critical project needed to be redefined around a more dialectical relation between writing, history and ideology.

Initially, perhaps, the most influential theoretical model within literary studies was provided by the early work of Pierre Macherey whose analysis of Jules Verne[3] suggested that a text could be defined by its 'absences' or silences, ideological contradictions which its author could not *consciously* confront but which the textual production of 'magical resolutions' to such conflicts cannot completely conceal. Thus, critical reading of a narrative can offer access into the ideological tensions and contradictions of a specific historical formation. There are a number of problems in such an approach and characteristically it constituted a highly authoritative critical practice. Once again the Marxist academic critic was located in the powerful position of unearthing history and ideology for other readers through his (usually) skill in reading the text and 'possession' of theory.

More significant in the domain of cultural studies was the influence of Gramsci and his delineation of the concept of hegemony and of the complex cultural processes by which the ruling class maintained its dominance not only through coercion but through the *consent* of the subordinate classes. Here, the most productive feature was Gramsci's sense of culture as a site of constant struggle and conflict, of *negotiation* between dominant culture and the 'resistances' within popular culture.[4] Thus, for Gramsci there is always the potentiality for oppositional responses to dominant culture and this has led to considerable debate about the extent to which all cultural texts are open to a range of readings, negotiated between text and reader in relation to social experience.

Characteristically in the field of cultural studies emphasis was initially placed on the influence of class and social status upon readers but empirical research into media audiences by David Morley and others suggested that such categories were too general and simplistic for delineating the range of potential meanings and readings which could be generated by a text.[5] Consequently recent work has turned to discourse theory to provide a more open and flexible methodology. In cultural analysis, discourse means more than just language and must be distinguished from discourse analysis in linguistics; rather it refers to all of the processes of signification, to the production and *framing* of meanings around social experience and their circulation throughout a range of institutional power structures. Thus, a text is constituted around a discourse or even multiple discourses and readers *make sense* of it in relation to the discourses (of age, race, gender, class, region and so on) through which their consciousness makes sense of social reality and through which they are constituted as subjectivities. It will be seen that this theoretical field informs some of the contributions to this collection of essays.[6]

Finally, the most fundamental challenges and questions for cultural studies have been developed from within feminism. It does not seem overly polemical, however, to argue that, in the field of popular fiction, male critics have clearly felt more at ease ploughing their furrows with the sharp edges of contemporary Marxist paradigms while gender can be 'left to the women' preparing the picnic of romance over by the hedge. One primary objective of this collection is to undermine this dichotomy and to propose that all narrative and its reading are intrinsically inflected by sexual politics.

Such a bold statement is easy enough to make; how to address the problems it raises is quite a different matter, as the various approaches represented here will demonstrate. For one thing, confrontation of the gendered pleasures of reading draws us into territory which is frequently at the edges of cognitive security and definition, an exploration of the sources of fantasy and desire and power, the 'recognition' (and misrecognition) of tensions and contradictions between what we may regard as our consciously held beliefs and 'attitudes' on the one hand and deeply felt, less articulated aspirations and insecurities on the other. Obviously these are interactive in the social processes of reading – as in social experience more generally – and constitute a necessary factor in any debates about popular fiction and its attendant, socially-inscribed pleasures.

Following on from this, it is not the intention that the contributions by male writers to this collection should be seen as 'men doing feminist work'. Such a strategy is a contradiction in terms and one which frequently registers that characteristic masculine practice of appropriation and even in its more bizarre manifestations the most extraordinary arrogance of 'setting women right', 'correcting' the 'errors' of feminism. Rather, the objective is to begin to frame, describe and unearth the notion of 'men as readers' as a *project* rather than as the usual, unquestioned normative procedure. Clearly, this raises questions about self, sexuality and identity within specific social and historical formations. It should also be agreed that the readings and arguments set forth here are inflected by our generation (we are in the main of that generation who entered secondary and higher education in the 1960s) and by our ethnicity (all of the contributors are white English or American women and men).

Drawing eclectically upon Marxist, psychoanalytic and discourse theory – and influenced by an engagement, both personal and political, with feminism – the essays in this collection set out readings of popular texts and genres, not in the spirit of these being the *only* readings or of exhausting the potentiality of meanings generated by a text or group of texts but rather in the pursuit of engaging other readers of popular fiction in debates, some polemical, others more tentative and exploratory. The emphasis, then, is upon reading 'textuality' rather than upon the reading of self-contained texts.

One important feature of popular genres is that they are not rigidly self-contained categories (e.g. *Hill Street Blues*) but evolve interactively and in relation to specific historical formations. In the opening essay Jane Tompkins polemically challenges existing 'histories' of the Western, indicating how those masculine 'histories' share the assumptions of the genre they are claiming to describe. She argues that the Western '*answers* the domestic novel' and can also be seen as a response to women's participation in a range of *antebellum* reform activities. In the secular environment of the Western, man confronts death and nature in ways which marginalize and displace women as subjects, constructing a fictional world of masculine bonding or competition in which women are either distractions or objects to be rescued, reformed or won.

Where the domestic novel of the nineteenth century, referred to by Tompkins, offers potential for readings which stress women as strong, even heroic, E. Ann Kaplan addresses the operations of a prime example of another tradition, the sentimental novel, which registers the more pathetic sides to mothering and the unconscious fears and frustrations of women's experience within patriarchy. Mrs Henry Wood's *East Lynne* was originally published in 1861 and was hugely popular both in Britain and America well into the twentieth century. The narrative concerns Lady Isabel, a wife and mother, who deserts her husband and children for another man, a vile seducer. Tortured by her losses, she returns as governess, unrecognized, to her family and has to endure the spectacle of her husband's remarriage. Finally, she dies, repentant, and is forgiven her transgression. Drawing upon Lacanian psychoanalytic theory, Ann Kaplan explores a central drama playing at the heart of the novel, an interaction of political and psychoanalytic discourses which suggests that erotic fantasy for the lost mother object, displaced into the terrain of passionate heterosexual romance, disturbs the norms of the bourgeois capitalist social order and must therefore be repressed, curtailed and punished.

While the first decade of the twentieth century witnessed the rise of the Western as a cultural force in American society, the final decade of the nineteenth ushered in detective fiction as the overwhelmingly popular genre for Victorian society. Unlike the exclusively masculine genre of the Western, however, crime fiction immediately proved 'open' to men and women both as writers and readers. In my own essay on the first cycle of Sherlock Holmes narratives (*Adventures* and *Memoirs*) I try to suggest ways in which the formal structures of the genre are inflected not only by positivism and social Darwinism but also by discourses of class alignment, masculinity and white supremacy. A central objective here is, quite simply, to assert that formalist accounts of the phenomenal popularity of the narratives do not seem to be very satisfactory unless they are located in some analysis of the discursive formations within which the cultural myth of the 'great detective' has been produced and, indeed, reproduced.

David Glover's essay provides a valuable and cautionary qualification of this approach by suggesting that there is some danger in assuming that 'pleasure just is ideology'. In debates about crime fiction pleasure has tended to be inadequately theorized and this essay examines how 'histories' of the genre have disregarded sexual difference as a significant factor. Glover challenges such approaches, argues for a gendered history of crime fiction and concludes with a comparison between two novels which 'address' prostitution, Robert B. Parker's *Ceremony* and Barbara Wilson's *Sisters of the Road*.

The issues surrounding pleasure and gender are taken up by Peter Humm and Paul Stigant in their reflections upon William McIlvanney's crime novels and the problems in developing 'masculinist' criticism (as opposed to phallic criticism). Clearly, such a criticism has to address not only masculinity and patriarchy but also heterosexuality as a dominant perspective through which 'deviance' is commonly defined. While this essay seeks to draw out the significance of heterosexuality in shaping 'readings', the one which follows by Roger Bromley examines what happens to the genre of crime fiction when the central figure of the detective is represented as gay. A major focus of Bromley's argument is to locate Joseph Hansen's series of Dave Brandstetter novels in relation to the evolution of gay culture and politics since the 1960s.

Until comparatively recent years the political thriller has been predominantly a male genre and Tony Davies's essay considers that 'history' in relation to the (re)production of historically differentiated masculinities involving male power in confrontation but also paranoid and insecure. Here, Freudian theory is articulated not as universal and ahistorical but in relation to a series of historical 'moments' since the turn of the century. A contrasting approach to the genre is offered in Barry Taylor's essay which seeks to unpick some of the signifying strategies of *Gorky Park*, the earliest and most successful of a sub-genre which has developed in Reagan's America and which represents the corrupt soviet system, pre-*Glasnost*, as the 'evil empire' potentially subvertible by masculine individualism (Tom Clancy's *The Hunt for Red October*), which can even lead ultimately to wholesale social combustion (Robert Moss's *Moscow Rules*). Taylor offers a 'reading' of *Gorky Park* in terms of how the fiction draws upon American cultural signifiers in constituting the alienated, male individual vs the system and soviet ideology. Crucially, he then reflects upon his own critical discourse and the 'exclusions' of the reading he has produced.

The final group of essays offers readings of 'Horror' and science fiction. Verena Lovett argues that Stephen King's *Carrie*, distinctively amongst his *oeuvre*, can be appropriated for a 'progressive' representation of female energy through its symbolic modes and interdiscursive narrative techniques. Clearly, this has a significance beyond the confines of the text itself as Lovett's argument makes clear.

While the Horror genre has commonly served some very dubious purposes in its signification of women and 'otherness', science fiction has proved to be a genre attractive to women writers, especially since the 1960s. Sarah Lefanu investigates why this is so and reflects particularly upon the work of Ursula Le Guin, Marge Piercy and Joanna Russ. She comments that much male-authored SF renders women as absent or peripheral (versions of the Western?), commonly representing technological futures in ways which reconstitute the social relations and power structures of patriarchy. My own final essay takes up this question and tries to isolate some of the ways in which several male-authored 'cult' science fictions, mainly published originally in the 1960s but subsequently reprinted continuously, may now be read as producing discourses of gender relations and identities which orientate their textuality predominantly towards white, male heterosexual readers. The pleasures generated around the genre's typical obsession with the alien, with 'otherness', need to be located, then, in relation to the pleasures of 'recognition' of male power and of the displacement, finally, of threats to male subjectivity.

This collection of essays is offered, then, as a contribution to the critical study of popular fiction in the interests of provoking, in every sense, other readers who are tantalized, excited and fascinated by reading popular narratives. If it also succeeds in rendering such critical debate as unthinkable without gender as a central concern, then a useful objective will have been served.

Notes

1   See, for instance, John G. Cawelti's *Adventure, Mystery and Romance* (Chicago: University of Chicago Press, 1976) for an account which is

limited by this notion of popular fiction as formulaic and consensual compared to 'mimetic' literature.

2 The Council for National Academic Awards was (and is) a national body established to validate and monitor academic courses in the public sector of Higher Education in Britain. It is often argued that CNAA set standards for course design that many University departments would have done well to emulate.

3 Pierre Macherey, 'Jules Verne: the Faulty Narrative' in *A Theory of Literary Production* trans. G. Wall (London: Routledge & Kegan Paul, 1978), pp. 159–248.

4 The even more recent 'recovery' of Mikhail Bakhtin's work, produced in the context of the repressive regime of Stalinism, has lent further support to approaches which stress the fluidity of the 'boundaries' between popular culture and élite culture. For Bakhtin, like Gramsci, culture was always political; there is evidence that some contemporary 'versions' of his work would like to dispense with this crucial principle or at least reduce it to vacuousness.

5 David Morley, *The 'Nationwide' Audience: Structure and Decoding* (London: British Film Institute, 1980). See also David Morley, *Family Television: Cultural Power and Domestic Leisure* (London: Comedia, 1986) and Dorothy Hobson, *'Crossroads': The Drama of a Soap Opera* (London: Methuen, 1982).

6 Morley's empirical study of different social groups and their responses, as 'audiences', for a television text have been invaluable in media studies. There is an urgent need for comparable research on readerships for popular fiction to supplement the limited but useful insights provided in Janice Radway's *Reading the Romance: Women, Patriarchy and Popular Literature* (Chapel Hill: University of N. Carolina Press, 1984). Unfortunately this kind of research needs material support of a kind which it is increasingly difficult to obtain, certainly in Britain, but it is hoped that this series of books will provide a basis for such initiatives.

1

West of everything

JANE TOMPKINS

THIS essay is part of a longer work on Westerns which is just beginning to take shape. It offers an explanation of why Westerns (novels and movies) arose when they did, taking other explanations to task in the process. My account departs from a single question and pushes its way forward, asking the questions implied by the answers it arrives at, until it comes to a major depot, rather like the trains that make their way across the plains in Western films, moving on from one forsaken little station to the next. Unlike the trains that chug harmlessly into the desert, and more like the gun battles with which Westerns normally conclude, the essay is polemical. But the conclusions it offers – the results of a first foray into unfamiliar territory – are meant to provoke discussion rather than to close it off.

Near the beginning of *Hondo* (1953), one of Louis L'Amour's best-known novels, the hero discovers the remains of a fight between a band of Apaches and a company of US cavalrymen.

> Atop the hill he drew up, looking around. He saw all that remained of Company C, the naked bodies of the dead, fallen in their blood and their glory as fighting men should.[1]

Hondo muses on the scene of battle, reconstructing what must have happened, noting those whom the Indians had left unmutilated as a mark of respect for their courage, admiring old Pete Britton, the scout 'who had held out at least an hour longer than the others. On his hard old face . . . a taunting, wolfish grin. He had defeated his ancient fears of loneliness, sickness and poverty.'[2]

Hondo continues on his way, taking shelter from a storm in a dug-out on the side of a hill. He settles down for the night, thinking of the woman he has just begun to love, and then L'Amour writes this paragraph:

> Somewhere along the tangled train of his thoughts he dropped off and slept, and while he slept the rain roared on, tracks were washed out, and the bodies of the silent men of Company C lay wide-eyed to the rain and bare-chested to the wind, but the blood and the dust washed away, and the stark features of Lieutenant Creyton C. Davis, graduate of West Point, veteran of the Civil Wars and the Indian wars, darling of Richmond dance floors, hero of a Washington romance, dead now in the long grass on a lonely hill, west of everything.[3]

This passage makes explicit a movement towards death which marks the Western and sets it off from other genres. Death is portrayed here as transfiguration and fulfilment – 'the silent men of Company C lay wide-eyed to the rain and bare-chested to the wind', purified and made beautiful by death – as the apotheosis of personal achievement – Pete Britton has defeated his ancient fears, the others have fallen 'in their blood and their glory as fighting men should' – and as a comradely condition – Lieutenant Davis lies next to Clanahan, the drunkard ('Hondo could picture the scene . . . the Lieutenant giving the bottle to the man he had several times sent to the guardhouse for drunken brawling, but a man who had died well beside an officer he understood').[4] And, faintly shadowed in the preceding passage but more explicit later on, death is figured as the fulfilment of sexual desire. As Hondo falls asleep, thinking of the woman he will eventually marry, L'Amour cuts to Lieutenant Davis, darling of Richmond dance floors and hero of a Washington romance, who 'in the long grass on a lonely hill, west of everything' has already met and embraced his bride.

To go west, to go as far west as you can go, west of everything, is to die. And death in the Western is double: glory, transfiguration, fulfilment and, at the same time, annihilation. For the Western rejects the notion of an afterlife and announces itself as determinedly secular, valuing the strength and skill required to stay alive above the glory of sacrificial defeat. The hero, who always defeats death by killing his adversaries, plays a game in which survival is everything. And this means that we ourselves do not have to face death, as we watch the movie or read the novel, but continually escape it, along with the protagonist. Thus, death is repressed in the Western because figured only as what happens to someone else.

At the same time, death is continually courted, flirted with, risked and finally imposed – on others: Indians, villains, 'Company C', cowards, the protagonist's relatives and friends. In fact, death is everywhere in this genre. Not just in the scores of bodies that pile up towards the narrative's close, but, even more compellingly, in the desert landscape with which the bodies of the gunned-down eventually merge. The classical Western landscape is barren and hostile, a tableau of towering rock and stretching sand where nothing lives. Its aura of death, both parodied and insisted on in place-names like Deadwood and Tombstone, exerts a strong attraction. For although to die is to lose the game – Lieutenant Davis's apotheosis is only a small landmark along the trail of Hondo's victorious struggle to live – there is a strange play of irony in this. All the lieutenant's dreams and expectations have ended on a lonely hill, suggesting faintly that there was something unrealistic about them, turning the joke on him. And yet, the pure glory of his death makes Hondo's survival look momentarily banal. The sense of consummation L'Amour's description of Company C conveys, their transfiguration in death, while it puts them out of play, also seals their perfection.

The ubiquity of death – it hangs over everything and everybody – and its doubleness, both glory and annihilation, are among the genre's most salient features, features which we tend to take for granted, as if there had always been stories about men who shoot each other down in the dusty main street of a desert town. But these stories came into being only shortly after the towns themselves did, and although the shooting stopped a few years later, American culture has been obsessed by that particular scene of violence ever since. In trying to understand the Western as a narrative type that was speaking to and for the culture as a whole, one has to ask why, at a certain moment in history, a genre should arise in which death, both as a condition and as an event, should command so much attention.[5]

In a pithy article called 'Origins of the Western', drawing on the work of several other scholars, Richard Etulain has argued that Westerns came to prominence because of the circumstances surrounding the year 1900, which he summarizes roughly as follows:

1   revival of interest in the historical novel, signalling a need to recapture the past;
2   increased interest in the west;
3   the ethos of 'the strenuous age' characterized by the virile, out-of-doors fiction of Jack London and Harold Bell Wright, coinciding with the Spanish-American War, Teddy Roosevelt and militant Anglo-Saxonism;
4   the disappearance of the dime novel;
5   the strength of the melodramatic tradition as a feature associated with Western literature;
6   the mentality of the Progressive Era which precipitated conflict between the New Nationalists – optimistic reformers led by Teddy Roosevelt – and those nostalgic for a pre-industrial America who wanted to break up the power of the large corporations, represented by Woodrow Wilson.[6]

Etulain concludes that 'the conflict between industrial and agricultural America and the resultant nostalgia for the past' were crucial to the rise of the Western and reminds us that 'the origins of a new popular idea or genre are usually tied to specific occurrences in the mind and experience of the era that produces them'.[7] This is certainly true. But I believe that the occurrences Etulain and the scholars he relies on use to account for the Western's popularity, while convincing as long as they are considered from a certain point of view, function less as explanations of the mentality the Western represents than as extensions of it. Located *within* the mind and experience formed by the Western, Etulain has been able to discuss the genre only in terms which the genre itself has made available.

Etulain and the historians he cites in his footnotes emphasize wars as important turning-points in human history (the Spanish-American War), reflecting a preoccupation with death and conflict in the public space; omit women from the historical record entirely (none of them imagines that women's roles in this period could have anything to do with the rise of the Western), demonstrating an unconscious antifeminism; deny the relevance of religious or spiritual experience to understanding human events (none of them notes Christianity's striking absence from the genre in an era of religious revival) and so betray their secular, positivist mentality; and, in focusing on 'great men' (Teddy Roosevelt, Woodrow Wilson) and in assuming that both fiction and history naturally *are* about men, show the phallocentric bias of their thought. Rather than providing a perspective on the Western, these historians simply act it out.[8]

For the Western is secular, positivist and antifeminist; it focuses on conflict in the public space, is obsessed by death and worships the phallus. Etulain and company do not question the Western's exhibition of these characteristics because they were formed by a culture that exhibits them as well. Thus, in explaining why the Western arose when it did, Etulain does not ask why it is a narrative of male violence, for that is what he already takes for granted, but focuses instead on something his assumptions have not already naturalized, the narrative setting. The question his account of the Western's origin is always implicitly answering is, why does the Western take place in the west? This question cannot be answered by referring to 'increased interest in the west' and the popularity of 'virile, out-of-doors fiction', answers which only repeat the question; but it can be dealt with by returning to the question I have already posed: what accounts, at the beginning of the twentieth century, for the rise of a genre pervaded by death and the threat of death? If you hold this question in mind while examining the popular fiction that immediately preceded the Western's rise to prominence, its preoccupation with death begins to make sense.

In 1896, Charles M. Sheldon, minister of the Central Congregational Church in Topeka, Kansas, began reading a story out loud to his young people on Sunday evenings. It was about a minister who, while preparing his sermon one morning, is disturbed by a ringing doorbell. He finds on his doorstep a young man in shabby clothes, hat between his hands, an air of dejection about him. The man says he has been out of work for a long time and wonders if the minister could help him find a job. The minister says he is very sorry, that he knows of no jobs, that he is very busy, and wishes the man luck. After closing the door he catches a glimpse of this homeless, forsaken figure making his way down the walk, heaves a sigh and returns to his sermon on following the teachings and example of Christ.

This sermon, delivered the following Sunday, is a great success, but just before the service ends, the figure of the shabbily dressed man appears in the back of the church. He makes his way forward and asks to speak, assuring the congregation that he is neither drunk nor crazy. He tells them that he has been out of work for ten months and has been tramping the country looking for a job. His wife has been dead for four months and their little girl is staying with friends. There are a great many other people like him who are out of work because machines are now doing the jobs men were trained for, and though he doesn't expect people to go out of their way to find jobs for others, he wonders what the minister's sermon about 'following the teachings and example of Christ' means to them. He quotes the hymns they've been singing: 'Jesus, I my cross have taken, all to leave and follow Thee', 'All for Jesus, all for Jesus' and 'I'll go with him, with him all the way'. He suggests in a quiet, reasonable voice that if the people who sang those hymns went out and lived them, the world might be a different place. What would Jesus do, he asks, about the men and women who die in tenements in drunkenness and misery? At this point, the man keels over, faint from hunger. The minister takes him home, but the man dies during the course of the week.

The next Sunday the minister arrives in church a changed person. He tells the congregation that he has taken a vow for the next year to ask before he does anything 'What would Jesus do?' and to try to act as he believes Jesus would in that situation. He invites members of his congregation who feel moved to take a similar vow to meet with him after the service. The rest of the story, which Sheldon called *In His Steps*, concerns what happens to these people as a result.[9]

There is no way to know even within several hundred thousand how many copies *In His Steps* sold because, through a publisher's error, it was never copyrighted. As soon as it appeared, it was pirated by sixteen publishers in the United States and fifty in Europe and Australia (it was translated into twenty-one languages). Sheldon reports in a 1936 foreword to the novel that according to *Publisher's Weekly* it had sold more copies than any other book except the Bible.[10] Exactly how many copies *In His Steps* sold doesn't matter. It was stupendously popular. And, as a type, it resembled the other most popular novels of the end of the nineteenth century: Lew Wallace's *Ben-Hur* (1880), Mrs Humphry Ward's *Robert Ellesmere* (1888) and Henryk Sienkiewicz's *Quo Vadis?* (1896), novels which not only share its Christian frame of reference, but make Christian heroism their explicit theme.[11]

I have spent some time sketching in the opening of Sheldon's novel because I want you to understand the kind of book it is and the nature of its appeal. Even today, without a supporting context, you can sense the enormous power it must have had. My point is that only six years after *In His Steps* came out and sold like wildfire, Owen Wister's *The Virginian* initiated a narrative tradition so different from the one to which Sheldon's novel belonged that the two seem to have virtually nothing in common. The juxtaposition, I think, helps to explain a great deal about the purpose and meaning of Westerns, and, among other things, begins to explain the Western's preoccupation with death.

Death in late-nineteenth-century religious novels is neither a problem nor a focus. Whereas in *The Virginian* five characters die and the hero almost does more than once, in Sheldon's novel no one even comes close. The main problem for his characters is not facing death but facing themselves, for, if you believe in the immortality of the soul, what you fear most is not death but sin. Avoiding sin means, for Sheldon and other advocates of the social gospel, following Christ's example by reforming the evils of the world. His characters strive for the moral and social courage necessary to defy convention, and so, instead of risking death, risk losing their friends, the affection of their families, their money, their jobs and their social position. In these stories, facing death is never the challenge or the problem; it's what you do with your life before you die that counts. In Westerns, the two become conflated; facing death and doing something with your life become one and the same thing. For once you no longer believe you are eternal spirit, risking death becomes the supreme form of heroism. The newly secular hero *must* pursue death in order to show what he is made of because risking death is the bravest thing he can do.

The Western plot therefore turns not on struggles to conquer sin but on external conflicts in which men prove their courage to themselves and to the world by facing their own annihilation, a form of heroism that has consequences for the kind of world the Western hero inhabits. When life itself is at stake, everything else seems trivial by comparison. Events that would normally loom large – birth, marriage, embarking on a career – become peripheral and the activities and preoccupations of everyday life seem almost absurd. The Western's concentration on death puts life on hold, empties the canvas of its details, while placing unnatural emphasis on a few extraordinary moments – the hold-up, the jail-break, the shoot-out. The story that results, stripped down, ritualistic, suspenseful, seems to be telling a universal truth about the human condition. But the picture of the human condition from which its truth is drawn leaves nearly everything out of account.

If focusing on death is a consequence of the Western's rejection of Christianity, this raises the question of how and why the rejection came about. Given the tremendous vogue of novels like Sheldon's, it is clear that two thousand years of custom and belief didn't just naturally fade from the cultural consciousness. The Western shows us, among other things, that Christianity had to be forcibly ejected. When the genre first appears on the national scene, one might say it defines itself by struggling to get rid of Christianity's enormous cultural weight.

You can see that struggle dramatized fully and explicitly in *Riders of the Purple Sage* (1912), whose opening scene enacts the passage from a sacred to a secular dispensation.[12] The heroine, Jane Withersteen, a young Mormon woman who owns a large ranch the Mormon power structure covets, is about to watch her best rider, Bern Venters, be whipped by the Mormon elders because he is a Gentile.

Once more her strained gaze sought the sage-slopes. Jane Withersteen loved that wild and purple wilderness. In times of sorrow it had been her strength, in happiness its beauty was her continual delight. In her extremity she found herself murmuring, 'Whence cometh my help!' It was a prayer, as if forth from those lonely purple reaches and walls so red and clefts of blue might ride a fearless man, neither creed-bound nor creed-mad, who would hold up a restraining hand in the faces of her ruthless people.

The next thing we know, someone is pointing to the west:

'Look' said one . . . 'A rider!' Jane Withersteen wheeled and saw a horseman, silhouetted against the western sky, come riding out of the sage . . . An answer to her prayer.

He wears black leather and a black sombrero and he packs 'two black-butted guns – low down'.

'A gun-man,' whispered another.[13]

In her hour of need, the heroine, a Christian woman who dresses in white, loves children and preaches against violence, turns her eyes to the hills; Zane Grey deliberately invokes the biblical reference and just as deliberately rejects it. Instead of help coming from the Lord who made heaven and earth, as in the psalm, it arrives in the form of 'a horseman, silhouetted against the western sky, come riding out of the sage'. An emanation of the desert, this redeemer is not from heaven but from earth, connected to the natural world by his horse and to the world of men by his black dress and black-butted guns. He is Lassiter, a famous gunman whom everyone fears, a death-dealer – the saviour as anti-Christ.

The person whom he arrives in time to save – Bern Venters – represents an emasculated common man who has given in to the enfeebling doctrines of Christianity. Afraid that Bern would kill one of the Mormon elders, Jane Withersteen had taken his guns away, but after Lassiter saves him, Venters asks for them back in an exchange that advertises the phallic nature of the regime Lassiter represents:

'Jane, I must be off soon,' said Venters. 'Give me my guns. If I'd had my guns – '
'Either my friend or the Elder of my church would be lying dead . . . Oh, you fierce-blooded, savage youth! Can't I teach you forbearance, mercy? Bern, it's divine to forgive your enemies. "Let not the sun go down upon thy wrath." '

'Hush! talk to me no more of mercy or religion – after to-day. To-day this strange coming of Lassiter left me still a man, and now I'll die a man! . . . Give me my guns.'[14]

In Venters, American men are taking their manhood back from the Christian women who have been holding it in thrall. Mercy and religion, as preached by women and the clergy, have stood in manhood's way too long, and now men are finally rebelling. But 'manhood', in this scenario, does not express itself sexually. Even though the gun is obviously a symbol for the penis, sexual activity is not what ensues when men get guns. What breaks out is violence. 'Now I'll die a man,' says Venters, when he gets his pistols back. Which is to say, now that I can risk death in a gunfight, I can be a man.

When Christianity is no longer the frame of reference – that is, when Lassiter arrives – manhood can prove itself only through risking death. At the moment this shift occurs, the gospel of peace and charity becomes manhood's nemesis, depriving men of the chance to demonstrate their courage in the face of mortal danger. In place of the gospel of forgiveness, Lassiter installs the reign of an eye for an eye. 'Mercy and goodness,' he says to Jane at the end,

such as is in you, though they're the grand things in human nature, can't be lived up to on this Utah border. Life's hell out here. Jane, you think – or you used to think – that your religion made this life heaven. Mebbe them scales on your eyes has dropped now.[15]

The speech reads like an answer to *In His Steps*. Where Sheldon told people that if they lived like Christians they'd see it could transform their lives, this book insists that you can't live by Christian love because if you do you'll be destroyed. The truth the novel asserts is that Jane Withersteen's goodness and mercy and the twenty-third psalm from which the phrase comes and the whole Judaeo-Christian tradition it represents won't work when the chips are down. Only brute force will, because 'life's hell out here' and all the religion in the world isn't going to change it.

Lassiter's doctrine and the actions that support it signal a major shift in cultural orientation. When he comes riding out of the purple hills in place of the Lord, Lassiter prepares the way not only for a long line of Western heroes played by Gary Cooper and Jimmy Stewart, but for Hemingway's Jake Barnes and Albert Camus's Stranger as well. The transfer of power from Jane Withersteen to Lassiter entails a shift from a reliance on unseen spiritual entities ('My help cometh from the Lord') to faith in the ultimate reality of matter ('Give me my guns'), a shift which will manifest itself in the twentieth century's overwhelming commitment to science and technology and a decline in the prestige of religious and humanistic discourse. In Lassiter, godless, armed and invincible, 'man', through his domination of nature, truly becomes the measure of all things, and scientific knowledge replaces religion as the *doxa* that will save us.

Although Westerns do not follow the course of modern history by setting technology and science in the place of Christian dogma, the genre does embrace matter, physical facts and physical force, especially deadly force, as the ultimate truth of human existence. As late as 1976, in the opening scene of *The Outlaw Josey Wales*, the Western film is still carrying on the fight against Christianity. When Clint Eastwood sees the home-made cross he has put on the grave of his son fall over, he picks up a gun from the charred ruins of his house (which has just been burnt down by the people who killed his wife and children) and starts shooting maniacally at a tree, one two three four five six seven eight nine ten times, every shot ramming home his rejection of Christian forgiveness as a way of dealing with injury, and promising the audience more violence to come.

Exchanging the cross for the gun is a theme replayed countless times in Western films as part of an ongoing guerrilla war against the church as an institution. Church congregations often appear, literally, on the margins of the screen, or just off camera, in the form of small revival meetings whose only trace is the sound of a hymn – always 'Shall We Gather at the River?' to which the answer is always implicitly: no. Sometimes a church building (or the *thought* of one) is present as the backdrop to a wedding celebration. In *Warlock*, the music we hear wafting our way from a wedding is not even a hymn but 'Beautiful Dreamer', and all we see of the wedding is a reception where Henry Fonda, playing the new marshal, meets the church organist (Dolores Michaels), who, though she opposes the violence he stands for, ends up by falling in love with him. Thus the church is peripheral even to the matters over which it presides, and these, in turn, are peripheral to the hero's business – in the example cited, Wyatt Earp's vendetta against the Clanton gang. In *High Noon*, which begins in church, the movement of the entire film – as if to compensate – is away from the sacramental moment of the protagonist's marriage and towards the apocalyptic moment of his shoot-out: the sacrament the Western substitutes for matrimony. But in ridding itself of the authority of organized religion and the belief structure it represents, the Western elaborates its own set of counter-rituals and beliefs.

The need to dispose of the corpses which the genre's love affair with death generates affords opportunities for some of its more laconic put-downs of Christianity, incidents which seem innocent enough, but are riddled with metaphysical intent. In *Red River*, as the tyrannical leader of a cattle drive (John Wayne) mutters, with obvious disrelish, an ever more perfunctory 'the Lord giveth, the Lord taketh away' over the bodies of men he has killed on the trail, we are supposed to perceive the ridiculousness of believing in a divine Providence which has obviously had no part in deciding the fate of these poor chumps, and to recognize instead the power of one strong-willed, almost superhuman man. This message about the bootlessness of belief in 'the Lord' becomes even more succinct in *Cowboy*, where Glenn Ford, another cattle-drive leader, about to bury a man who has been killed accidentally, asks 'Does anybody know the proper words?' – and no one replies.

These casual graveside episodes aren't just burying Christianity, they are putting something else in its place. When Glenn Ford speaks over the grave of the fallen cowhand, he makes no reference to a deity or an afterlife, or to religious notions of any kind. His speech is deliberately prosaic and uninspired; he says he doesn't know why the man died when he did – it could have come in some other way, a Comanche, or his horse stepping in a prairie dog hole at night. 'But', he concludes, 'he was a good man with cattle and he always did the best job he could. I hope they can say as much for me some day.'

As a substitute for Christian burial, these words convey a straightforward meaning: there is no such thing as God (or if there is, we don't know anything about him). What is real are objects in the physical world (cattle) and what counts is how good one is at dealing with them ('he was a good man with cattle') – not just in any situation, but in the workplace, which is *the* place for doing one's best ('and he always did the best job he could'). In the movie's crucial scene, Jack Lemmon, a tenderfoot who wants to become a cowboy, proves himself by going alone into a cattle-car where the cattle are trampling each other and risks his life to pull them upright again. He is joined by Glenn Ford (the cowboy), who proves his loyalty to his comrade in doing so. A gloss on the burial episode, the incident shows both characters being good men with cattle and doing the best job they can, but it adds something more: the idea of comradeship. As a wise old codger has said earlier in the film: 'A man has to have somethin' besides a gun and a saddle. You just can't make it all by yourself.' The ethic which the graveside and cattle-car scenes represent would take a long time to unfold; they are laconic – Westerns don't trust language – but they speak volumes. *Cowboy* posits a world without God, without 'ideas', without institutions, without what is commonly recognized as culture, a world of men and things, where male adults in the prime of life find ultimate meaning in doing their best together on the job.

By this point it is clear that in getting rid of Christianity, the Western was ridding itself of a great deal else as well. If we recall the opening of *In His Steps*, the minister in his third-floor study, the shabbily dressed man looking for work, the congregation of rich, important people, the main characters' inner struggles, it all contrasts as sharply as possible with the scenes I have been discussing: Company C dead in the long grass, Lassiter riding out of the hills, Venters getting back his guns, perfunctory prairie funerals. Why does the Western leave so much behind? Why does it welcome violence so much? Above all, why does it jettison the country's most pervasive, deep and sustaining framework of beliefs? The clue, I think, lies further back in the nineteenth century, in the domestic 'sentimental' novels that for so long dominated the cultural scene. The dispensation which the Western sets itself against is represented not so much by Sheldon and his contemporaries, who mark an era of transition, but by the writers who set the stage for them: Harriet Beecher Stowe, Susan Warner, Maria Cummins and the dozens of other women whose work had such a profound effect on American values and mores before and after the Civil War.

In their books, a woman is always the main character, usually a young orphan girl, with several other of the main characters being women too. Most of the action takes place in private spaces, at home, indoors, in kitchens, parlours and upstairs chambers. And most of it concerns the interior struggles of the heroine to live up to an ideal of Christian virtue – usually involving uncomplaining submission to difficult and painful circumstances, learning to quell rebellious instincts and dedicating her life to the service of God through serving others. In these struggles, women give one another a great deal of emotional and material support, and have close relationships verging on what today we would identify as homosocial or homoerotic. There's a lot of Bible reading, praying, hymn-singing and drinking of tea. Emotions are expressed very freely and openly. Often, there are long-drawn-out death scenes, in which a saintly woman dies a natural death at home.

The elements of the typical Western plot arrange themselves in stark opposition to this pattern not just vaguely and generally, but point for point. First of all, Westerns are always written by men. The main character is always a full-grown adult male, and almost all the other characters are men. The action takes place either out of doors – on the prairie, on the main street – or in public places – the saloon, the sheriff's office, the barber shop, the livery stable. The action concerns physical struggles between the hero and a rival or rivals, always culminating in a fight to the death with guns. In the course of these struggles the hero frequently forms a bond with another man – sometimes his rival, more often a comrade – a bond which is more important than any relationship he has with a woman and is frequently tinged with homoeroticism. There is very little free expression of the emotions. The hero is a man of few words who expresses himself through physical action – usually fighting. And when death occurs it is never at home in bed but always sudden death, usually murder. Finally, nature, which has played only a small role in the domestic novel where it is always pastoral and benign, looms very large in the Western, where it is grand, monumental, dwarfing the human figure with its majesty, the only divinity worshipped in this genre, other than manhood itself.

This point for point contrast between a major popular form of the twentieth century and the major popular form of the nineteenth is not accidental. The Western *answers* the domestic novel. It is the antithesis of the cult of domesticity that dominated American Victorian culture. The Western hero, who seems to ride in out of nowhere, in fact comes riding in out of the nineteenth century. And every piece of baggage he doesn't have, every word he doesn't say, every creed in which he doesn't believe has been deliberately jettisoned. What isn't there in the Western hasn't disappeared by accident; it isn't there because it has been repudiated or repressed. The surface cleanness and simplicity of the landscape, the story-line, the characters, derive from the genre's will to sweep the board clear of encumbrances. And of some encumbrances more than others. If the Western deliberately rejects evangelical Protestantism and pointedly repudiates the cult of domesticity, it is because it seeks to marginalize and suppress the figure who stood for those ideals.

If you look back over the scenes I have cited, there are no women present in any of them, except the one from *Riders of the Purple Sage* which openly dramatizes what most Western novels and movies have already accomplished and repressed: the destruction of female authority. Repeating the pattern of the domestic novels in reverse, Westerns either push women out of the picture completely or assign them roles in which they exist only to serve the needs of men.

At first, a woman will often seem independent, as in *Gunfight at the OK Corral* (1957), where Rhonda Fleming plays a lady gambler (Laura Dembo), daring, clever, vaguely aristocratic, whom Burt Lancaster (Wyatt Earp) wants to get rid of because she's trouble. He ends up courting her, lukewarmly, as, in the course of the film, she becomes more and more demure – as is suitable for the marshal's future consort. But in the end, when she asks him to stay with her, he can't; he has to go help his brother, a marshal who's having trouble in another town.

The love affair never goes anywhere and occupies only a small part of the footage because the person Wyatt Earp really loves is Doc Holliday, another gambler and troublemaker, whom he had also tried to get rid of at the beginning of the movie. Thus, the Laura Dembo character is both an extension of Wyatt Earp (as she starts to wear high-necked, long-sleeved blouses she gets more and

more like him, a straight-arrow, letter-of-the-law type); yet at the
same time, as gambler and troublemaker, she is a screen for Doc
Holliday, an alibi the movie supplies Wyatt Earp with so that his
love for Doc won't mark him as 'queer'. Either way, she's the
shadow of a more important male. Female 'screen' characters, who
are really extensions of the men they are paired with, perform this
alibi function all the time, masking the fact that what the men
are really interested in is one another. Western novels and movies
not only tell stories that stem from the positions men occupy in
the social structure, and tell them from the man's point of view,
they concentrate on male–male relationships, downplaying or omit-
ting altogether those areas and times of life when women are
important in men's lives.

In doing so, they also suppress what women stand for ideologically. Near the beginning of *The Searchers* (1956), after a
woman and her older daughter have been raped and murdered and
a younger daughter carried off by Indians, Ethan Edwards (John
Wayne), who is heading up the search party, is addressed by an
older woman, who says: 'Don't let the boys waste their lives in
vengeance.' He doesn't even dignify her words with an answer, and
the movie chronicles the seven years he and his adopted nephew
spend looking for the lost girl. In this story, as in many Westerns,
women are both the motive for male activity (it's women who are
being avenged, it's a woman the men are trying to rescue) and at the
same time what women stand for – love and forgiveness in place of
vengeance – is precisely what that activity denies. Time after time,
the Western hero commits murder, usually multiple murders, in
the name of making his town/ranch/mining-claim safe for women
and children. But the discourse of love and peace which women
articulate is never listened to (sometimes the woman who represents
it is actually a Quaker, as in *High Noon* and *Cheyenne Autumn*), for
it belongs to the Christian world-view the Western is at pains to
eradicate. Indeed, the viewpoint women represent is introduced *in
order* to be swept aside, crushed, or dramatically invalidated. Far
from being nugatory or peripheral, women's discourse, or some sign
of it, is a necessary and enabling condition of most Western novels
and films. The genre's ideological plot depends upon an antithetical
world of love and reconciliation both as a source of meaning – it
defines the male code of violent heroism by opposition – and as a

source of legitimation. The women and children cowering in the background of Indian wars, range wars, battles between outlaws and posses, good gunmen and bad, legitimize the violence men practise in order to protect them.

Yet at the same time, precious though they presumably are since so much blood is shed to save them, their lives are devalued by the narrative, which focuses exclusively on what men do. Westerns pay practically no attention to women's experience. Nor could they. When women wrote about the west, the stories they told did not look anything like what we know as 'the Western'. Their experience as well as their dreams had another shape entirely, as scholars like Annette Kolodny have begun to show.[16]

Now, the question is, why should this de-authorization of women have occurred? Why are Westerns so adamantly opposed to anything female? What, in the history of the country at the turn of the century, could have caused this massive pushing away of the female, domestic, Christian version of reality?

The answer to this question must lie partly in a story of counterviolence, a story I will not be telling here: in the violence of women towards men, in whatever suppression of male desire and devaluation of male experience followed from women's occupying the moral high ground of American culture for most of the previous century. The discourse of Christian domesticity – of Jesus, the Bible, salvation, the heart, the home – had spread from horizon to horizon in the decades preceding the Western's rise to fame. And so, just as the women's novels which captured the literary market-place at mid-century had privileged the female realm of spiritual power, inward struggle, homosociality and sacramental household ritual, Westerns, in a reaction that looks very much like literary gender war, privilege the male realm of public power, physical ordeal, homosociality and the rituals of the duel.

But Westerns arise in response to phenomena that are not only cultural and literary. During the period immediately preceding their emergence on the national scene, the role and status of women in American society was changing rapidly. In the decades after the Civil War, there was a massive movement of women out of the home and into public life. Aptly termed 'social home-making', the movement was inspired by women's participation in *antebellum* reform activities, which had been centred on church and home.

We hear 'A woman's place is at home' [wrote Carry Nation, one of
the great reformers of the post-Civil War era]. That is true but what
and where is home? Not the walls of a house. Not furniture, food
or clothes. Home is where the heart is, where our loved ones are.
If my son is in a drinking place, my place is there. If my daughter,
or the daughter of anyone else, my family or any other family, is
in trouble, my place is there. [A woman would be either selfish or
cowardly if she] would refuse to leave her home to relieve suffering
or trouble. Jesus said, 'Go out into the highways and hedges'. He
said this to women, as well as men.[17]

During the reform era, millions of women involved themselves
in socially improving activities outside the home.

Among the issues they addressed were prohibition of alcoholic
beverages; ending prostitution; sterilization of criminals; improvement
of prisons; physical education for girls and boys; sex education as
a means of ending 'vice'; pure food laws and the cleaning up of
food-processing plants; child labor; public sewers; antitrust laws;
tax reform; public utilities; wiping out political machines; vocational
training for girls and boys; good nutrition; free libraries; parks and
recreation; protecting historical landmarks; public transportation,
and peace.[18]

This list may seem exhaustive but to it can be added: working
with the immigrant populations in the inner city (Jane Addams
and the Settlement House movement); agitation for Indian rights;
the founding of schools of higher education for women (this was
the era when the women's Ivy League colleges were established);
the women's labour movement – the forming of women's groups
within already existing unions and the founding of the garment
workers union, the ILGWU; and, of course, most famous of all,
the suffrage movement which in the United States ended in 1920
with women getting the vote.

Among the factors that allowed for this greater activity in the
public sphere were a decrease in the birth rate and changes in the
technology of housekeeping which made an enormous difference
in the amount of time and energy women had available for work
outside the home.[19] While it is true that the industrialization and
urbanization responsible for these improvements also created the
conditions of overcrowding and dehumanized labour that men

wanted to escape by dreaming of a home on the range, and that a huge and ethnically diverse population badly split along class lines needed a classless male hero who could stand for 'everyone', and while it is also true that the militarism excited by the war with Spain, and the popularity of survival-of-the-fittest philosophies, could be said to have produced the impetus for the Western, these standard notions of where Westerns came from do not recognize that the circumstances they cite refer almost exclusively to men and men's experience. What I want to argue for specifically here is the idea that the Western owes its essential character to the dominance of a women's culture in the nineteenth century and to women's invasion of the public sphere between 1880 and 1920.

For most of the nineteenth century the two places that women could call their own in the social structure were the church and the home. The Western contains neither. It is set in a period and in an environment where few women are to be found and where conditions are the worst possible for their acquiring any social power: a technology and a code of justice both of which required physical strength in order to survive. Given the pervasiveness and power of women's discourse in the nineteenth century, I think it is no accident that men gravitated in imagination towards a womanless milieu, a set of rituals featuring physical combat and physical endurance, a *mise-en-scène* that, when it did not reject culture itself, featured, prominently, whisky, gambling and prostitution – three main targets of women's reform in the later years of the nineteenth century. Given the enormous publicity and fervour of the Women's Christian Temperance Union crusade, can it be an accident that the characteristic indoor setting for Westerns is the saloon?

Most historians explain the fact that Westerns take place in the west as the result of the culture's desire to escape the problems of civilization. They see it as a return to the concept of America as a frontier wilderness and as a re-enactment of the American dialectic between civilization and nature. My answer to the question, why does the Western take place in the west, is, the west was a place where technology was primitive, physical conditions harsh, the social infrastructure non-existent, and the power and presence of women proportionately reduced. The Western doesn't have anything to do with the west as such. It isn't about the encounter between civilization and the frontier. It is about men's fear of losing their hegemony and hence their identity, both of which the Western tirelessly reinvents.

Notes

1   Louis L'Amour, *Hondo* (New York: Bantam, 1953), p. 56.
2   ibid.
3   ibid., p. 59.
4   ibid., p. 56.
5   It is a mistake, I think, to try to assimilate novels by Zane Grey and Louis L'Amour, and movies starring John Wayne and Clint Eastwood, to a literary 'Leatherstocking tradition' starting with Cooper and ending with *Lonesome Dove*. Western novels as we now know them – not dime novels but the kind that sold as books – became best-sellers at the beginning of the twentieth century, at the same moment when Western movies began to be shown in theatres. While the novels of James Fenimore Cooper, the dime novels of the 1860s and 1870s and the novels of Charles King in the 1880s had some elements in common – rescue plots, for example, and frontier settings – the earlier forms had nothing like the consistency that marks popular Western novels and movies since the turn of the century. The Western as a cultural force makes its appearance with the publication of Owen Wister's *The Virginian* in 1902 and the screening of Edwin S. Porter's *The Great Train Robbery* in 1903. At this moment, from being one among many popular forms, it becomes central. And it disappears, for all practical purposes, at another moment – some time in the mid-to-late 1970s, when Westerns were supplanted at the box office (though not yet at the bookstands) by horror and science fiction movies. The fact that the 75-year period during which Westerns flourished coincides with the United States' dominance as a world power suggests that the genre is intimately tied to the country's sense of itself, both politically and psychologically.
6   Richard W. Etulain, 'Origins of the Western', in William T. Pilkington (ed.), *Critical Essays on the Western American Novel* (Boston: Hall, 1980), pp. 56–60.
7   ibid., p. 59.
8   It is not really fair to single out Etulain for holding such attitudes; nor do all the historians he cites in his notes share them equally. I am using his essay to demonstrate that there is more than a superficial similarity between the values the Western promotes, on the one hand, and those that historians assume, on the other.

9   Charles M. Sheldon, *In His Steps* (New York: Grosset & Dunlap, 1981 printing).
10   ibid., p. vi.
11   James D. Hart, *The Popular Book: A History of America's Literary Taste* (Berkeley, Calif.: University of California Press, 1950), pp. 162–9.
12   Although *The Virginian*, which appeared ten years earlier, satirizes the church in its devastating portrait of a self-important clergyman, the novel never really takes Christianity seriously, as though its hash had already been settled.
13   Zane Grey, *Riders of the Purple Sage* (New York: Pocket Books, 1912, 1940), pp. 6–7.
14   ibid., p. 17.
15   ibid., p. 301.
16   See Annette Kolodny, *The Land Before Her: Fantasy and Experience of the Frontier* (Chapel Hill, NC: University of North Carolina Press, 1984).
17   As quoted in Carl Degler, *At Odds: Women and the Family in America from the Revolution to the Present* (New York: Oxford University Press, 1980).
18   Carol Hymowitz and Michaele Weissman, *A History of Women in America* (New York: Bantam, 1978), p. 219.
19   ibid., pp. 220–1; on this and on social home-making in general see Julia Matthaei, *An Economic History of Women in America: Women's Work, the Sexual Division of Labor, and the Development of Capitalism* (New York: Schocken, 1982), pp. 152–93.

2

The political unconscious in the maternal melodrama:

Ellen Wood's *East Lynne* (1861)

E. ANN KAPLAN

THIS essay deals with a woman's popular novel, *East Lynne*, taken as 'representative' of certain imaginary fascinations which had broad appeal in the mid-nineteenth and early twentieth centuries. The novel was immediately successful and its themes repeatedly rehearsed over the next sixty years or more. I situate the text in the interlocking theoretical frameworks of mothering theory and female subjectivity. Representations in a text like this are always multi-determined, emerging from the complex interaction of authorial gender; historical gender discourses at the time of writing (including the broader familial discourse); codes of class and race produced by a culture's particular industrial/technological stage; the psychoanalytic discourse (which can be inferred in texts existing before that discourse became explicit and public); and, finally, intertextual discourses, having to do with aesthetic and formal conventions as well as specific influences. In this case, melodrama (as a generalized aesthetic mode, embodying a particular type of imagination and set of codes) provides a governing framework.[1]

Obviously, full treatment of all of these determinations is impossible in the scope of this essay; my main focus will be the psychoanalytic discourse and an attempt to situate the originating text in the discourses crucial to its production. In this novel, erotic fantasy for the lost mother object – a fantasy itself produced by woman's patriarchal psychic positioning – is displaced into the terrain of passionate heterosexual romance and love for child that patriarchy prefers. But even this is seen to threaten the new capitalist social order and must be curtailed. I am interested in the political uses of melodrama as well as in the way gender ideology constrains (or shapes representations of) unconscious psychic processes having to do with the relationship to the mother in patriarchy.

Representations of pre-Symbolic bondings[2] take different forms in texts, depending on whether or not there is identification with the mother figure. When such identification is present, the mother-sacrifice paradigm may expose the oppressive aspects of the patriarchal positioning of the mother; the text may reveal how the mother so constructed strives to gain unmet gratifications for herself by establishing a fusional relationship with her child; this may take the form of the over-invested mother or the powerful 'phallic' one.[3]

When there is no identification with the mother figure, the paradigm looks very different: the ideal, self-sacrificing mother threatens to collapse into the phallic one (always seen as evil from the patriarchal viewpoint), who is perhaps being defended against in the idealized 'sacrifice' image. (For instance, unconscious fear of being devoured by the maternal may lead to fantasies in which the opposite happens, namely where the mother is excessively devoted to the child.)[4] Or the ideal figure may be made object of the text's sadistic urges against her. (That is, she is frequently excessively punished for slight deviation from her maternal role as in, for example, Alexander Bisson's *Madame X*, and its many subsequent film versions.) Often, as in *East Lynne*, the ideal figure is associated with death and destruction, not only of herself but also her child.

The maternal sacrifice pattern may appeal in different ways to both male and female readers, depending on differences in the complex ways that each patriarchally constructed gender deals with the need for individuation – with, that is, the culturally necessary separation from the mother. The melodrama is precisely the form geared towards expression of such unconscious processes, concerned as it is, in Brooks's words, to make sense of aspects of experience not represented in other genres.[5] However, even the melodrama represses woman's pleasure in mothering for its own sake, i.e. not as a way to fulfil unmet needs or to please patriarchal law.

Careful examination of the representation of the mother and of pre-Symbolic longings in melodrama may help us to understand some of the discrepancies in male and female fantasies, and how cultural gender ideology not only inflects unconscious desire, but also the *political* uses of the fallen woman story;[6] in this story, an innocent (often but not necessarily working-class) young girl is sexually abused and destroyed by an unscrupulous, lascivious, aristocratic male.

A novel like Ellen Wood's *East Lynne* (1861) obviously provides evidence for only one of many possible mythic, mother-victim heroines, with its accompanying political implications. But this form, addressing primarily the middle-class reader, was a frequent type. Working-class victim-mothers are evidently infrequent in the 1860s, although the seduction of the young innocent working-class girl is a familiar figure in literary and, as Judy Walkowitz has shown, also in extra-literary discourses.[7] When the victimized working-class mother did appear, it was in the context of 'temperance' melodramas – didactic polemics against the evil effects of alcohol on the family. Focus on working-class mother paradigms in America only arises towards the end of the century with the social purity and eugenics movements, when the middle classes were suddenly concerned about the so-called 'degeneration' of the race through poverty and the growing slum conditions that began to parallel those long familiar from Europe. These movements coincided with the invention of film, and thus we find in early film a focus on working-class subjects as a way both of addressing working-class spectators (always one film audience) and of educating the middle-class film audience (increasingly being appealed to in the second decade of the century) about their social responsibilities.[8]

Before the social purity and eugenics movements, there would presumably have been little appeal in the surface narrative figuring the working class; novel readers were presumed to be largely female and middle-class, and plots were shaped accordingly. The working-class plot in *East Lynne* is merely a device for underscoring the political discourse (see below). Unlike many middle-class figures (who are given a certain psychic depth), the working-class characters are one-dimensional stereotypes.

Aside from the specific political implications of the mother-victim pattern in *East Lynne*, the repetition of this pattern, more or less in its basic Victorian and Christian form, over at least one hundred years suggests that it had enormous appeal. It is precisely the basis for that appeal, which could be utilized for multiple political purposes, that I hope to illuminate through a psychoanalytic reading of the text. I will then discuss the political implications of the melodramatic structures outlined.

In *East Lynne*, it is the double-pronged unconscious desire for the lost mother object combined with sadistic urges towards the same object, along with unconscious fantasies about father-daughter incest, that the text articulates as a powerful field to engage the reader. *East Lynne* stands interestingly at the juncture of the melodramatic pattern that showed the family as threatened from the outside (by dangerous, usually male, figures, often aristocrats or men in authority abusing their power) and the later melodramas that explore the sexual dangers and problems *within* the nuclear family – a trend that accelerates after Freud's 'discoveries' of sexual desire between parents and children. The previous focus on the evil seducer from outside the family may then be seen as a displacement of what was all the time an internal problem. Nevertheless, the shift in focus has important political ramifications since where the blame for destabilization is placed depends on what social reorderings are either economically necessary or are under way for other reasons (e.g. new technological discoveries necessitating changes in work patterns; or the demands of a war situation requiring new gender arrangements).

In the examination of potential psychoanalytic readings to be drawn from *East Lynne*, we will see that the text offers a multiplicity of possible positions for reader identification in satisfying unconscious desire; but ultimately the discourses are hierarchically ordered in the fictional resolution of ideological, patriarchal and political tensions.

East Lynne is particularly interesting in that it moves from the romance to the maternal sacrifice pattern, and exposes similarities between the psychic aspects of romance and of mothering. Fascinating here is the tension between a view of woman's psychology strikingly similar to the constructs of Helene Deutsch, the well-known neo-Freudian psychoanalyst, and the excess desire remaining from the pre-Symbolic mother-child relation that breaks through the narrative and must be contained in the end. Although *East Lynne* was written about thirty years before Freud initiated the psychoanalytic discourse, it embodies a conception of woman's psychology that Freud's female followers particularly were to develop. I am interested in how the social/historical constitution of the bourgeois family produced a certain set of psychic constructs evident before Freud's articulations.

According to Helene Deutsch, the child becomes for the mother the ego-ideal (i.e. the father) from which a cathexis to the sexual partner had also been drawn; the complete process of sublimation is only affected for the woman in giving birth to the child. In so doing, Deutsch notes, the woman returns to 'that primal condition . . . in which there was as yet no distinction between ego-libido and object-libido'.[9] But the woman is supposed to move on from this 'primal condition' (a sort of narcissism) to 'object-love' (which implies the establishment of proper boundaries), although, as Deutsch already realized, the distinction is a difficult one. Deutsch follows Freud in paying insufficient attention to the pre-Oedipal attachment to the Mother that is arguably the source of all subsequent desire.

It is Isabel's failure to make the correct kind of sublimation through what Deutsch calls 'the maternal function of the vagina' – her holding on to the cathexis with the sexual partner in the attraction to Levison – that brings on her tragedy. She learns painfully that literal fulfilment of erotic desire is impossible (Levison cannot match her fantasies), but she still does not understand 'object-love' or the sublimation that culture demands. Instead, she displaces her erotic desire into the boy-child, for which she must be further punished. In contrast to Isabel, the text holds up the middle-class Barbara Hare as the ideal model – as the one embodying the correct relation to husband and child.

The novel usefully contains, in the sub-plot, a representation of the 'bad' mother paradigm in both her husband Carlyle's 'surrogate' mother, Cornelia (his sister), and in Mrs Vane, the heroine's aunt, thus permitting comparison between the two fusional paradigms (i.e. symbiosis with the child through negation of self and through controlling and possessive behaviour) that Monique Plaza outlines.[10] As in so many nineteenth-century romances by women, the true, 'good' mothers are dead, absent, or ill. In *East Lynne*, both the heroine and hero, Isabel and Carlyle, are orphaned but only Isabel lacks the protecting surrogate mother figure. As is frequent in the romance, the heroine's dilemma is presented in explicitly Christian terms, particularly in the imagery that links Isabel to the figure of Eve in the Garden of Eden pursued by the 'snake' Levison, and in references to Isabel's mother.

The saintly nature of Isabel's dead mother is indicated in the young woman's devoted memories and in her being linked to holiness through Isabel's cherished necklace with the cross on it. It is this necklace that Levison ominously breaks on his first meeting with Isabel. Isabel's distress comes from the fact that her mother gave her the cross as she was dying, telling the child to let it be a talisman to guide her when in need of counsel (p. 13). Its breaking signals Isabel's aloneness and vulnerability to the 'snake' Levison ready to step into the gap left by her mother's death.

That the breaking of the cross indicates a link between the lover and the mother is clear later on, when we are told that Isabel's thoughts were 'running on many things', moving from thoughts of her mother 'with whom she was last at East Lynne', via thoughts of her father's illness, to thoughts of Levison – 'even as she thought of him, a thrill quickened her veins' (p. 55). I will be arguing that it is something akin to the symbiosis with her mother that Isabel is represented as seeking both in a male lover and in her relation to her children. We see here that woman in patriarchy must, like the male, reject the mother and turn towards the Father so as to enter the Symbolic. She desires the Father because the mother desires him and because it is only in that way that she has a place and a function. But the pre-Symbolic yearning for the mother remains, nevertheless. Thus, woman seeks in the male satisfaction both of the desire for symbiosis (the pre-Symbolic mother-relation) and of a place in relation to the Law (the Symbolic Father-relation). The pre-Symbolic yearning evokes contradictory responses from the patriarchal system that produces it.

From the start, Isabel experiences a merging sensation with Levison but not with Carlyle. Her marriage to Carlyle, admittedly one of convenience, is nevertheless idyllically happy to begin with, mainly because of Carlyle's stance as protective father. Upon marrying, Isabel regresses to dependency and childishness, wanting only to be by Carlyle. Bored, listless and empty without Carlyle, Isabel gives no evidence of a subjectivity outside of him. As the marriage progresses, emptiness becomes her normal state; she still yearns for the embraces and kisses that Carlyle has outgrown, knowing only how to express a desire to be desired. She becomes aware of her own desire only in relation first to the children and then, later, in renewing her relationship with Levison.

Passion for children in the world of *East Lynne* is a 'safe' location of female desire, although the text ultimately seeks also to confine such love within suitable bounds. (Child-care discourses of the period deplored the over-indulgent mother and praised the one who kept her distance and imposed strict obedience.)[11] The narrating voice manifests sympathy for Isabel's yearnings to merge with her love-objects – be they her mother, Levison, or her children – but finally shows that such desire is excessive: the system simply has no room for this kind of female passion. Like Helene Deutsch, the narrator would turn Isabel towards the Father and away from the mother: the ego ideal is 'correct' when taking the Father-relationship for the model and 'incorrect' (or dangerous) when taking the mother-daughter bonding as the model. But excessive love displaced into the child is socially preferable, of course, to taking a lover.

That Isabel realizes this herself is evident at a crucial juncture, when she is to leave for France; she begs Carlyle to let her take the children, exposing here her emotional need for them and her fear of separation, individuation, emotional autonomy. Cornelia's impatience with Isabel's desire suggest that it is seen as excessive; yet the narration makes it clear that Isabel is vulnerable to erotic desire if separated from her children; the text wishes to constrain Isabel's erotic desire, and to reward her attempts to fulfil the proper 'maternal function'.

Isabel is persuaded not to take the children, and the gap in her emotional life is soon filled by passion for Levison who steps into the breach. Isabel's desire forces itself upon her *physically*, in a way rare in fictional representations of female characters. Because the novel locates Isabel within the power relations of patriarchy, she cannot consciously accept herself as a desiring subject; desire is thus forced to find expression through her body. 'What was it', the narrator asks, 'that caused every nerve in her frame to vibrate, every pulse to quicken . . . changing the monotony of her mind into tumult?' (p. 171). The 'cause' is Levison's approach, of course.

Interestingly, both the narrator and Isabel see her desire as evil – Isabel prays for strength to overcome 'this dangerous foe that was creeping on in guise so insidious' (p. 176). Although the desire for lover and children has similar origins, love for the children provides a kind of defence against the passion for Levison because (despite its symbiotic nature) the former love is to a degree socially sanctioned.

Note that Isabel asks her husband anxiously about the children as she feels Levison's effects (p. 176).

What Isabel seeks both in the children and the men in her life is the satisfaction of a passionate, merged feeling. This desire for loss of self in the Other images the impossible desire for unity with the mother left over from childhood and, in nineteenth-century patriarchy, not permitted sublimation in women in the public sphere. While Carlyle's calm, distanced, rational style prohibits collusion in this sort of merging, Levison's seductiveness and his own desire to possess make such projection easy. Just because Carlyle has set himself up as the wise, intimidating father figure, Isabel cannot confide in 'the strong arm of shelter round her, a powerful pillar of protection, he upon whom she leaned' (p. 188). We see here how the text limits its representations of masculinity to two modes, both unsatisfactory for woman – those of the good but morally awesome father (his standards are so high) and of the duplicitous lover.

But the text cannot accommodate Isabel's *erotic* desire. In fact, there is simply no more place in this system than in Deutsch's for Isabel as subject of erotic desire. Even the limited action and power of the domestic role is denied her by her class privilege (maids take care of everything for her, including the children); Isabel is left indeed in the position of lack, object of the male gaze (Levison, Carlyle), and of the jealous female gaze/identification (Barbara, Cornelia). She 'completes' Carlyle's world but is herself quite incomplete.

Female jealousy, possessiveness and competition are the product of woman's 'incompleteness', her positioning in patriarchy as object, not subject. Cornelia's role runs counter to Barbara Hare and Isabel in terms of her response to this positioning. Surrogate mother to Carlyle (his stepsister), Cornelia is a mild, semi-comic version of the 'bad' mother type – tyrannical, possessive, controlling and not above deceit. But Cornelia's jealousy indicates the incestuous mother-son dynamic that is rarely so explicitly addressed. Anticipating Freudian theory again, the text suggests that Cornelia's repressed erotic love for her brother has made her adopt a masculine identification with her brother.

Barbara Hare's story runs parallel to Isabel's, providing another example of a young woman's vulnerabilities and emotional dependencies through lack of a strong mother figure; the angelic Mother, Mrs Hare, is present, but so sickly and confined as to be unable to help her daughter. Most of the interaction between Mrs Hare and her daughter actually has to do with the mutually loved son/brother, who is self-described as 'spoiled' (essentially 'feminized') by his mother. One of the purposes of the Richard Hare plot is to bring Carlyle and Barbara together (around their secret project to redeem Richard from a false murder charge), arousing Isabel's jealousy so intensely that she runs off with Levison on impulse.

Like Isabel, Barbara yearns for Carlyle's love and protection; for Barbara like Isabel lacks the kindliness of the fantasized ideal Father (although living, Mr Hare is the harsh, domineering father-type). Arguably, when the mother provides such nurturing and bonds closely with her daughter, such qualities in the Father are less essential; but in the absence of the autonomous and nurturing mother, the daughter searches even more for the Father's love and protection. As will be clear later on, Carlyle emerges as the only father figure to carry out his responsibilities in the ideal way that culture requires: Mr Hallijohn is an inarticulate bully; Mr Hare is insensitive and unduly severe; Lord Mount Severn is incapable of running his affairs, and anyway invalided before his death; Levison, not a 'literal' father, cannot live up to the role in any of its forms. And thus, it is left to Carlyle to embody the figure that the Father-husband should be.

It is significant that the experiences of both women are represented in *physical* terms – that is, in relation to the effects of perceptions on their *bodies*. They do not 'think' about what they see or even about what they feel. The text implies a bodily sensation direct from the perception, without any mediation. Only when it is all over for her, i.e. when all her mistakes are made, her situation irreversible, is Isabel granted the capacity to *reflect* on her emotions and her actions.

These representations embody the modern male/female dichotomy that Rousseau first fully articulated in his *Emile* (1762) and that was taken up later in Europe and then America; Rousseau reinscribes in culture a division of labour necessary for the development of modern capitalism.[12] He theorizes the public (male), private (female) split that structures the separate spheres in the nineteenth and early twentieth centuries. Classic in Rousseau is the ascribing to 'nature' of what is already cultural, and the assumption that the middle-class ethic is to be taken as the norm. In the new version of the division, the very survival of the human race depends on the woman's function in cementing the family through her skills in emotions and relationships, while equally important are the male's capacities for rational thought devoid of unreliable feelings.

Hence, in *East Lynne*, woman is shown as delicate, sensitive, prone to jealousy and distrust, easily intimidated, insecure; and the male (in the classic Rousseauian style) as uncomplicated, sensible, rational, cautious, moderate, a good citizen, kindly and involved in his work. The narrator almost never describes Carlyle in terms of bodily sensations; the one exception is on his reading of Isabel's farewell note, when, we are told, 'Though a calm man, one who had his emotions under control, he was no stoic, and his fingers shook as he broke the seal' (p. 235).

When the seduction finally happens, the text refuses the reader the satisfaction of being witness to the consummation of Isabel's erotic desire for Levison. The two come together now in ugliness, Isabel goaded only by furious feelings of jealousy and revenge on seeing Carlyle and Barbara Hare together in the dark (in fact, waiting innocently enough to meet with Richard Hare). Her jealousy fuelled by Levison, Isabel breaks into bitter sobs: 'Alas! Alas!' she moans; but, the narrator tells us, 'Francis Levison applied himself to soothe her with all the sweet and dangerous sophistry of his crafty nature' (p. 227).

Once Isabel is repositioned in her own home, incognito, as the governess, she becomes the voyeur; she is able to look and grieve, but unable to have the gaze of recognition blaze back on herself. In the first half of *East Lynne*, Isabel is inside the circle; she is the lucky, successful heroine; her 'sin' makes for a fall, allowing the 'good' sister to take her place in the family unit. But Isabel now has to endure living out the childhood family romance; she is positioned as governess on the periphery, but is able to watch the goings-on, like the child peeking in at the parents through the bedroom keyhole. The narrator ostensibly holds up Barbara as the one to copy, Isabel as the dangerous warning about the results of desire; in reality, however, we are given vicarious satisfaction in the passionate and sensational life that Isabel lives. Her intense emotionality captures our interest, while Barbara ceases to have much appeal once happily married. The device permits all kinds of comparisons between the two heroines.

Barbara (having apparently read all the right child-care manuals) makes it clear that a mother should not be too much with her children, and also that being a mother comes second to being a wife. She makes a point of criticizing, not those mothers who neglect their children out of a selfish desire for their own pleasure – such mothers are not worth talking about - but those who dote too much on their children, who 'are never happy but when with their children' (p. 341). Barbara makes a distinction between the physical and mental needs of children, arguing that the former should always be supplied by the nurse, the latter by the mother.

Isabel apparently assents to these views and, indeed, inwardly notes that this was more or less 'her system' when first in East Lynne. However, Isabel seems surprised by Barbara's second point about putting wifehood before motherhood. 'You would not stay indoors for the baby, then?' she asks; and the round reply is 'Certainly not. If I and Mr. Carlyle have to be out in the evening baby gives way, I should never give up my husband for my baby; never, dearly as I love him' (p. 343). And, indeed, Barbara is mainly described in terms of her desire for Carlyle. The blame here, however, finally rests on Isabel for leaving the children in the first place; no one apparently expects a stepmother to care much. Only at the very end of the novel does Barbara admit that she has harboured jealous feelings for Carlyle's children because Isabel was their mother and had been his wife (p. 525).

Reading against the grain, we can see the contradictory demands that are placed on the patriarchal mother; she has at once always to be available to the husband – always sexually attractive and alluring (as Barbara points out, if a wife fails in this, her husband will seek amusements elsewhere), and at the same time a devoted mother, taking care of her children's slightest needs. The slippage from erotic energy in the service of the husband and in the service of the children seems endemic to the mother's construction in patriarchy. Both psychic sets involve a desire to re-experience the original illusory oneness with the mother, and embody a desire for merging, for loss of self in Other. In other words, given her positioning as 'lack' in the patriarchal Symbolic order, women are represented as seeking for identity/wholeness either via romantic love or via identification with children – both of which evidence an attempt to refind the lost mother. Like Isabel, women seek such 'wholeness' in the men they marry; but husbands, socialized à la Rousseau to perform rationally, in the service of the state, often refuse such symbiosis.

For Isabel on her return only the children are available. Yet it is significant that (at least on the conscious level) it was the longing for the children, not Carlyle, that tempted Isabel to take the dangerous route of returning as governess to East Lynne.

But the children now displace by necessity her only other possible love (her 'correct' love all along, had she but known it), namely Carlyle. Isabel has more passion for Carlyle now that he is unavailable than when they were married; her passion is perhaps spurred by the Oedipal configuration of her situation, positioned as she is as the child to Carlyle and Barbara (cf. discussion above). But (more importantly) she has learned the 'proper' libidinal relations that culture demands. It is Carlyle's recognition and forgiveness that she now 'correctly' (according to the Freudian model outlined by Deutsch) desires and finally receives on her deathbed. Meanwhile, Carlyle's saintly goodness, his protective function, remain until the end; he is capable both of sending Isabel satisfied to her death, and, immediately afterwards, of convincing Barbara of his undying love for her.

East Lynne thus exposes the unconscious 'family romance' processes (first articulated as such by Freud in his famous essay) that structure cultural relationships in the bourgeois imaginary. The novel shows Isabel's necessary turning away from the lost mother object towards the Father – a direction she learned only through painful experience. It is significant that the only truly intersubjective figure in the novel is discovered in a male, namely Carlyle. All the mother figures fail in some way or another, either too merged with their children (Isabel), too 'cool' to them (Barbara), or too controlling (Cornelia). The text exposes the psychic underpinnings of the feminine as constructed in patriarchy, concluding that this 'feminine' is not adequate to excellent mothering; it calls in the services of the male to fill the functional gap. The novel's end, however, suggests that Barbara Hare will become the Ideal Mother, once she is secure with Carlyle and has overcome her jealous feelings for Isabel. Barbara thus embodies the 'correct' turn from the Mother to the Father that Deutsch outlined.

In this regard then the novel underscores notions of women's weaknesses and vulnerabilities, their need of the male. Nevertheless, the novel earlier violated Deutsch's model in showing how it is desire for the mother that operates in young girls' sexuality; and how, at least for Isabel, the child does not represent the Father but the Mother. In exposing this, the novel is transgressive. Although Isabel suffers for her transgressions (the novel in that sense supports the patriarchal law), the very articulation of the difficulties of women's lives, of the constraints that hemmed them in, of the lack of any place in the system for female desire, of the contradictory demands made upon women, surely gave some satisfaction to female readers.

Now what of the appeal to the hypothetical male reader? How could a male identify in a text like this one clearly addressing a female audience (viz. the narrator's 'lectures' to her addressees)? It is possible that males largely 'consumed' the narrative via its many play versions (and I cannot deal with those here).[13] But we know something of the response of the male literary establishment to the novel: according to Sally Mitchell, Samuel Lucas loved the novel but felt that he shouldn't, while other critics focused on its literary flaws (cf. Mitchell introduction, p. vii). Both kinds of response may be useful in theorizing how the novel appealed to the average middle-class male reader.

Both the defensiveness of the critics searching for literary flaws and the suggestion in Lucas's comment that he experienced some illicit pleasure in the novel indicate that the novel touched the male unconscious. It is possible that the narrative addressed unresolved Oedipal wishes of some male readers. The longing of the lovely Lady Isabel for her absent children (two are sons), her affection for them when present, her dedicated devotion for the dying William, all address repressed male longings to win the Mother away from the Father and to possess her love. The second half of the novel, indeed, enacts the male child's fantasy of having 'won' the Mother from the Father, given that here the children become Isabel's total concern. (The fantasy is somewhat protected by having the children ignorant of the fact that their governess is their mother.) The mythic pattern positions the male both as the one capable of being in control, even when abandoned, and as the focus of the mother's adoring affection and desire. The myth attends to the double-sided male desire for an Ideal Imago while also being object of the maternal gaze.

On a less obvious level, the melodrama may have addressed the powerful, unconscious, Father-daughter incest wishes evident in patriarchal discourses. For, once married, Carlyle's feelings are those of a doting father towards his little girl. When he finds Isabel sleeping on the grass, we are told that 'she looked like a lovely child, her lips open, her cheeks flushed and her beautiful hair falling around. It was an exquisite picture, and his heart beat quicker within him *as he felt that it was his own*' (p. 124, emphasis mine). In a rare mention of any physical reactions on the part of Carlyle, it is *possession* that creates the sensations in place of the unmediated desire that thrills Isabel's veins. As the years go on, however, even this level of passion dwindles in Carlyle to a 'calmness' which, we are told, 'may look like indifference or coldness' (p. 166) but which the narrator warns is unavoidable. Already preparing for the later 'lectures' about enduring a boring marriage already mentioned, the narrator tells us that all this is inevitable and in the 'nature' of man.

But perhaps there was a more cognitive level on which the novel appealed to men, namely in its political implications. One obvious point of male identification – so obvious that the figure seems constructed largely for that purpose – is Mr Carlyle. In his solid, respectable manliness, his rationality, his calmness in the face of turmoil, his control in the face of loss and crisis, in his dedication to work and his service to the community, Mr Carlyle stands as the epitome of middle-class values of the time - the very bedrock on which the nation could stand. His authoritative position is emphasized (as so often in repetitions of this mythic paradigm) by having the Father also a man of Law on the literal level, thereby doubly inscribed in the Symbolic, doubly in control of the phallic social order. In addition to all this, Carlyle is handsome and wins the ladies' attentions. Every male reader must have wanted to be a Mr Carlyle. The text's focus on women's needs for dependence on the male, their longing for love and protection, permits the male reader to feel strong and needed through identification with Carlyle.

From the start, Carlyle assumes the position of the Law, the Father, towards Isabel, setting up a distance that alienates her, and yet that establishes precisely his Rousseau-defined 'manliness'. In an early discussion with Lord Mount Severn we see the sort of discourse about marriage in which men engage, focusing on Carlyle's financial capabilities and on how well he can take care of Isabel. When Severn mentions love, Carlyle at first refuses to answer since 'Those are feelings that man rarely acknowledges to man', but finally agrees that he loves Isabel passionately (p. 117). The reader, however, knows that it was Isabel's abandoned situation that provoked the marriage proposal, perhaps out of a desire for power and dominance over a woman he had allowed Cornelia to usurp. Although Cornelia continues to live with Carlyle and his wife, the power relations are reversed, as becomes increasingly obvious. This is something that a male reader might enjoy.

But let me conclude with brief discussion of the text's wider political implications which centre on the figure of Carlyle, turning first to the main plot. This plot, as is evident from the above discussion, is a woman's melodrama enmeshed in pre-Symbolic yearnings and post-Symbolic jealousies and sibling rivalries. The main families involved (i.e. the Carlyles and the Hares) are solidly middle class. Isabel Mount Severn is aristocratic, but her family has been virtually erased as a result of decadent indulgence and squandering of wealth. And she quickly joins the middle classes in marrying Carlyle.

The political implications of this narrative have to do with the depiction of the aristocratic class as wasteful, decadent and sometimes immoral. We have here a specific discourse about class: Lord Mount Severn belongs to the old noble aristocracy, but is unable to continue in a noble manner; his sister, Mrs Vane, and Francis Levison, on the other hand, represent the promiscuous, lascivious, impulsive and morally decadent wing of the dwindling aristocracy. The novel's idealization of the middle class, whose solid families are prey to exploitation from the immoral aristocrats, has to do with the political requirement for a reshuffling of discourses about class as England was becoming more entrenched in the industrial era. Economic realities required that the aristocratic class be dislodged from its privileged status in the political imaginary,[14] and the middle class represented as the new source of morality and the Law.

On the political level, then, Isabel's transgressions symbolize the failure of the aristocracy. Although the novel speaks from her point of view, and the narrator empathizes with her sufferings, Isabel nevertheless has to give way to the middle-class Barbara Hare. Sensible and solidly grounded, Barbara Hare, as we saw, has a more healthy understanding of marital and parental relations than has the aristocratic Isabel.

The narrator serves as a device for articulating the new discourses, which, interestingly enough, look back to Rousseau's *Emile*. This is significant in that, as a (presumed) female voice addressing (clearly) a female reader, the narrator endorses the new middle-class family. She serves patriarchy, further, in her severe critique of female erotic desire. The voice can vividly appreciate the attractions of desire, but self-righteously sets itself against it in the 'lectures' to the reader cited earlier. Like Ellen Wood herself, the narrator cannot think outside of the discourses available within the fictive world and thus cannot conceive of a world in which female desire would not destabilize the entire system. Yet paradoxically (in this novel by a woman author) she registers the power of what has to be repressed in order to secure male dominance.

To the narrator, Carlyle embodies a highly valued puritanical type of middle-class male. Part of this type's value arises precisely from its asceticism; while Carlyle's caution may make him a flat, boring character, the novel sees him as a necessary mode; for the new professional middle class could prosper and obtain solid ground only if they stood opposed to aristocratic waste and self-indulgence.

The novel looks back to *Emile*, again in the adoption of the discourse of sentimental individualism that Rousseau articulated. The sentimental discourse of the family is to replace the hedonistic type of individualism reflected in the declining European aristocracy. Rousseau's text develops a *political* concept of individualism in the sense that the boy's education is specifically to train him to take his part as a responsible citizen. It is a *moral* education, since the boy is to think not only in terms of himself but of the society as a whole; he is part of a political community in which he has particular responsibilities.

In *East Lynne*, the thriller sub-plot provides an opportunity for articulation of some of the middle-class responsibilities. This plot centres on the working-class Hallijohn family, whose promiscuous, sexy daughter, Afy, anxious to upgrade herself, seduces the middle-class Richard Hare, and is seduced in turn by a Captain 'Thorn', really Francis Levison. Richard Hare is falsely accused of murdering Afy's father (it was in fact the lascivious Francis Levison whose aristocratic degeneracy knows no bounds). Barbara Hare convinces Carlyle of Richard's innocence, and Carlyle becomes the major investigator into the crime.

The sub-plot, then, positions the working class as open to temptation and as requiring the middle-class liberal humanist to keep unsuitable passions in control. Carlyle, in true liberal fashion, does not condescend to the working classes, treating them rather with dignity and respect. This is obvious in all his dealings with the working classes in the novel, but a good example is a short interchange between Afy and Carlyle towards the end of the novel when Afy is going to be married to the petty bourgeois Mr Jiffin, owner of the local grocery. Afy thinks herself far above the man, and is setting out to be the 'kept' middle-class lady; but Carlyle insists that Mr Jiffin is 'a very civil, respectable man' (p. 474). He cautions Afy not to spend all Mr Jiffin's hard-earned money.

The novel shows that the only class capable of the correct balance between desire and its release is the middle class. The classes at either end of the spectrum display excess and an inability to control desire that leads to their downfall. Middle-class members, like Richard Hare, who fall prey to seduction or give in to desire inappropriately, also require the services of the liberal humanist for unravelling the disasters contingent upon such behaviour. Thus, the thriller sub-plot provides the opportunity for both excoriation of passionate excesses, and for demonstration of the liberal humanist Carlyle's rationality, decorum, moderation and dedication to the larger social community.

We can now begin to see the interconnections between the psychoanalytic and the social levels of the novel: the novel's overall project is to show the necessity for control of a socially inscribed desire – a desire that has to do with the very formation of the social order, or Lacan's Symbolic. It is specifically female desire that is the problem and that must be brought under control; in the case of both Isabel and Afy Hallijohn – situated as each is at either end of the class spectrum – *their* desire brings about disaster; Levison is merely the willing and available vessel for evoking and then receiving their sexual desire. The middle-class Barbara Hare is impervious to such an excess as both Isabel and Afy engage in. The ideology of the family in its class relations is to repress and control threats to its security from above and below – an alliance against illicit passions and excessive, 'degenerate' desire.

The novel demonstrates that erotic fantasy, particularly that which arises from desire for the lost mother object, displaced into passionate heterosexual romance, threatens the new capitalist and patriarchal social order and must be severely curtailed. The ego-ideal for both sexes must be the Father, not the Mother, if desire is to be properly subject to the patriarchal Law. The new liberal humanist couple – Barbara Hare and Carlyle – emerge as the ideal towards which the reader should aspire. They embody the new middle class, envisaged already by Rousseau, that will enable the proper functioning of the industrial order. Although this order is barely evident in the novel, it hovers on the margins of the small world of East Lynne. The old aristocratic social order has to be dismantled, and political discourses changed, in order for industrial capitalism to get fully under way: this is the central, underlying theme of Ellen Wood's novel.

Notes

1 Melodrama, *per se*, has been much discussed in feminist film theory over the past five years or so. For summary and furthering of the debate, cf. E. Ann Kaplan, *Motherhood and Representation, 1830 to 1960* (London and New York: Methuen, forthcoming [1988]). For introduction to many issues, cf. E. Ann Kaplan, 'The maternal melodrama, 1910–1940', in Christine Gledhill (ed.), *Home Is Where the Heart Is: Studies in Melodrama and The Woman's Film* (London: British Film Institute, 1987). This book contains an analysis of play and film adaptations of *East Lynne* (pp. 113–37).

2 I am using 'pre-Symbolic' explicitly to refer to the Lacanian psycho-analytic model. Lacan distinguishes the level of the 'Imaginary' (basically, the period before the child learns language and 'I'/'You' positions – the period of illusory oneness with the Mother) from that of the 'Symbolic', which happens with acquisition of language and the onset of the much-discussed 'mirror phase'. At this point, the child acquires a split subjectivity as it misrecognizes an Ideal 'mirror' self as itself. The level of the Imaginary continues after the entry into the Symbolic and the intervention of the Father (the third term) into the mother-child dyad. Much of what I discuss in the essay has to do with the persistence of desire born in the Imaginary phase in the adult psyche. While both Mother and Father have Symbolic functions (that of the Mother of course subservient to the Father), there is no pre-Symbolic Father. The significant Mother relation is the pre-Symbolic one: the Mother in

the Symbolic has very specific, patriarchally defined roles. See below and note 3 for more on mothering theory.

3 For full discussion of this phenomenon, cf. Monique Plaza, 'The mother the same: hatred of the mother in psychoanalysis', *Feminist Issues*, vol. 2, no. 1 (Spring 1982), pp. 75–99. Mothering theory has been extensively discussed in feminist and other writing by women. A chapter in my forthcoming book surveys the debates. Key texts include Dorothy Dinnerstein, *The Mermaid and the Minotaur: Sexual Arrangements and Human Malaise* (New York: Harper & Row, 1976); Adrienne Rich, *Of Woman Born: Motherhood as Experience and Institution* (New York: Norton, 1976); Nancy Chodorow, *The Reproduction of Mothering and the Sociology of Gender* (Berkeley, Calif.: University of California Press, 1978); Luce Irigaray, *This Sex Which Is Not One*, trans. Catherine Porter with Carolyn Burke (Ithaca, NY: Cornell University Press, 1985). A useful collection that looks at some of the debates is Hester Eisenstein and Alice Jardine (eds), *The Future of Difference* (New Brunswick, NJ: Rutgers University Press, 1985). For full bibliography of texts relevant to mothering theory, cf. Kaplan, *Motherhood and Representation*.

4 cf. narratives in some texts which themselves expose links between the mother types; for example, the mother in Basil Deardon's 1947 film, *Frieda*, whose good-natured efforts in fact betray a desire to control her son's life; Harriet Beecher Stowe's *Uncle Tom's Cabin* actually explodes the patriarchal mother paradigms in the figure of Cassy, the much-abused mulatto. The text shows how it is the brutality of patriarchy towards mother-child relations that drives Cassy to murderous excess.

5 Peter Brooks, *The Melodramatic Imagination: Balzac, Henry James and the Mode of Excess* (New Haven, Conn.: Yale University Press, 1976). For treatment of similar issues more specifically related to the Hollywood film, cf. Thomas Elsaesser, 'Tales of love and fury: observations on the family melodrama', *Monogram*, no. 4 (1972), pp. 2–15.

6 cf. a forthcoming book by Judy Walkowitz which deals with the relationship between melodrama and professional Samaritans like Josephine Butler or self-stylized, muck-raking journalists, like Stead who exposed the brothel and underworld London life of the nineteenth century.

7 The forthcoming book by Judy Walkowitz includes discussion of these discourses. Her paper, 'Melodrama, sexual scandals, and Victorian political culture', read at a New York Institute for the Humanities seminar in May 1986, is a draft version of parts of the forthcoming book.

8 cf. in this connection especially Miriam Hansen, 'Early cinema: whose public sphere?', *New German Critique*, no. 29 (1983), pp. 147–84.

9 cf. Helene Deutsch, 'The psychology of women in relation to the functions of reproduction', *International Journal of Psychoanalysis*, vol. 6 (1926), p. 414. Page nos refer to this edition.

10 cf. Plaza, 'The mother/the same'.

11 For full discussion of these child-care discourses, cf. Kaplan, *Motherhood and Representation*, chs 2 and 4.

12 cf. ibid., for more discussion of Rousseau and for relevant bibliography.

13 cf. Sally Mitchell, 'Introduction' to her edition of *East Lynne* (New Brunswick, NJ: Rutgers University Press, 1984), p. xiv.

14 I am here using this phrase in the senses first developed by Louis Althusser and also by Deleuze and Guattari in *The Anti-Oedipus*. For Althusser, 'ideology is a representation of the imaginary relationship of individuals to their real conditions of existence' ('Ideological state apparatuses', *Lenin and Philosophy*, p. 162). It is the way in which the subject is constituted through the Lacanian mirror phase that renders him/her vulnerable to being 'hailed' (as Althusser puts it) by ideology, and made into *ideological* subjects (necessarily – there is no being outside of ideology). But the specific *kinds* of ideal imagos (of, that is, fantasy political relations) will vary from one cultural context and historical period to another. And they will change as, on a level of which the individual is not aware, his/her 'real' conditions of existence change. cf. for full discussion of many of these matters, Fredric Jameson, *The Political Unconscious: Narrative as a Socially Symbolic Act* (Ithaca, NY: Cornell University Press, 1981).

3

Sherlock Holmes: Adventures of an English gentleman 1887–1894

DEREK LONGHURST

> Sherlock Holmes, the immortal character of fiction created by Sir Arthur Conan Doyle, is ageless, invincible and unchanging.
> Solving significant problems of the present day, he remains – as ever – the supreme master of deductive reasoning.
>
> (Opening frame, *The Voice of Terror*, 1942)

MANY critics of crime fiction have emphasized the innovative contributions of Poe and Doyle to the genre in terms of formulaic narrative structures. To do so, however, is to abstract rather too neatly the significance of those structures and to disregard the extent to which genres, as Fredric Jameson has pointed out, are 'literary *institutions*, or social contracts between a writer and a specific public'.[1] One might wish to substitute cultural for literary here and, moreover, stress that genres, as with any other institutions of social communication, are subject to the dynamics of historical change and cross-institutional relations. Hence, it is surely possible to argue that the common critical assertion that the 'history' of crime fiction has its point of 'origin' in the work of Poe and Doyle is based upon the formalist abstraction of certain conventions, and this neglects to offer much account of how those conventions may have developed in response to both pre-existing fictional representations of crime and to widespread social definitions of criminality.

Dickens's preoccupation with crime is well known. His fictions constantly worry at the contradictions between the preservation of order and the pervasiveness of fraudulence, hypocrisy and a double standard of morality within Victorian society. Everywhere in Dickens, criminal acts whether of violence or, crucially, of the fraudulent exploitation of the power of money, are integrated into an awareness of social injustice and the social causes of crime located in the contradictions between 'human' needs and social constraints. Various forms of criminality are represented in relation to the class system and in particular to the tensions induced by the pressure towards upward social mobility.

In his fictions Dickens can resolve such conflicts only by the imposition of 'magical' narrative conclusions – acts of benevolence, the long-lost heir, the comic man's eccentric ploys, the domestic retreat – and as such he shares a deep affinity with the dominant structures of popular theatrical melodrama. The point to make, however, is that Dickens and others of his generation are registering a preoccupation with crime amongst the middle class and upper layers of the working class at a crucial transitional stage. On the one hand there is the widespread fear of social unrest, associated with the Chartist movement, and on the other the social reality that the most common form of crime in the period involves fraud or bankruptcy. Thus, the forces of law and order are represented in the period in a very ambivalent manner; necessary for state control in the public domain but agents of state interference in the 'private' domain of a *laissez-faire* market economy. Inspectors Bucket and Cuff are such notable exceptions that their presence in *Bleak House* and *The Moonstone* makes the point. In the fictional representation of criminality of the mid-Victorian period, the detection and resolution of crime is frequently constructed out of a 'natural' or 'providential' turn of events – an ideological commitment to the 'natural laws' of *human* relations *and* of the economy (Merdle, Veneering).

When we turn to Conan Doyle's work some twenty years later, the significant shift to an emphasis on *detection* has been completed. Unlike the mass circulation newspapers and popular broadsheets, Conan Doyle consciously decentres the lurid details of acts of criminality in the interest of fictionalizing the processes through which crime is detected, resolved and even, in some cases, prevented. By the 1880s the middle class has achieved economic and social ascendancy within institutional power structures and no longer are the police, for instance, viewed entirely as plodding morons. It is important, however, that in fictional representation they are registered as members of the lower middle or upper working classes while criminal acts, especially those involving attacks on private property, have become 'individualized', the result either of the brilliantly perverted mind (Moriarty) or of an unethical pursuit of greed. Hence, the criminalization of attacks on private property makes it possible to turn these attacks themselves into ideological supports of the sanctity of private property. So, too, the criminal exploitation of women in terms of their exchange value within marital relations operates ultimately to justify patriarchal structures of power and the moral virtues of 'innocent' marriage. I shall return to these issues later.

The period from the 1880s onward is notable, of course, for the work of social investigators, such as Charles Booth – the first volumes of his *Life and Labour of the People in London* appeared in 1889 and 1891 and are exactly contemporaneous therefore with the first cycle of Holmes's *Adventures* and *Memoirs*. Booth and novelists like Gissing, Walter Besant and Arthur Morrison (also a detective story writer) are seen as 'discovering' and representing 'outcast' London in the East End, to middle-class Victorians a fearful underworld of crime, vice, poverty, domestic violence and degradation. Here lay the potential for a volcanic eruption of mob violence – as in 1886 and 1887 – in a context which also witnessed the growth of the socialist movement claiming to represent politically the interests of the working class, thus reinforcing the spectre of a radical challenge to bourgeois hegemony.

Published in the *Strand* magazine, the first cycle of Holmes narratives contains and dispels such fears for its middle-class readership. Placed in a context of 'interviews' with celebrated opera singers or composers (Madame Armani, W. S. Gilbert) or pen-portraits and drawings of royalty and nobility, the 'pleasures' offered by Conan Doyle's stories are those of the satisfactory resolution of 'mystery' in place of any sense of crime as a social practice. The individualization of criminal acts finds its ideological location within middle- and lower-middle-class deviance, 'commonly' revolving around two dominant narrative structures. First, there are the mysteries associated with the contradictions of the marriage market in which women are represented as gullible or virtually passive damsels in distress rescued from a 'Gothic' world by Holmes the chivalrous knight errant. Secondly, there is a consistent interest in the gradual revelation of a guilty, usually colonial, past history.

So, then, Holmes, in his inexorable pursuit of the 'truth' of the reality which lies behind mystifying appearances, constitutes a figure of scientific and, it is suggested, 'imaginative' rationality who provides a sense of security, power and reassurance not only for his clients but also for his readers. That many of 'his' readers construed the fictional figure as 'real', addressing their appeals for assistance to the non-existent 221B Baker Street, is hardly surprising in that Holmes's 'authority' is equally mystified, lying outside the normal institutions of society as a final court of appeal when all else has failed.

The mode of representation of this mastery of deductive reasoning is also crucial in achieving this effect of slippage between fiction and reality. It has become commonplace to identify the ascendancy of the middle class and the aesthetic form of realism as a shared ideological commitment to a positivist world-view – a sense of an empirical reality to be observed and analysed, ordered in logical and sequential fashion through scientific and rational processes of thought, available to direct 'representation'. Above all, perhaps, there is the necessity of closure, resolution. Clearly such conventions are not only central to the Holmes-Watson narratives but they are 'present' in supremely undisguised form in that they are integral to the very processes which Holmes employs in the 'solution' of crime. In addition, Watson as narrative point of view, the crucial linking perspective between reader and 'mystery', consistently locates the 'fantastic', 'unique', or even Gothic aspects of the 'Adventures' in relation to the 'commonplace'. Holmes is given a rather different position:

'My dear fellow,' said Sherlock Holmes as we sat on either side of the fire in his lodgings at Baker Street, 'Life is infinitely stranger than anything which the mind of man could invent. We would not dare to conceive the things which are really mere commonplaces of existence. If we could fly out of that window hand in hand, hover over this great city, gently remove the roofs, and peep in at the queer things which are going on, the strange coincidences, the plannings, the cross purposes, the wonderful chain of events, working through generations, and leading to the most *outré* results, it would make all fiction with its conventionalities and foreseen conclusions most stale and unprofitable.'

(Conan Doyle, 1981, 'A Case of Identity', pp. 190–1)

The banal platitude – 'Life is stranger than fiction' – serves, of course, a disingenuous purpose in *this* fiction but it is also interesting in that Holmes's commitment to a strange and mysterious reality – the Peter Pan fantasy for Victorian adults is important – is located both in the sense of a teeming urban world of London out of human control while simultaneously imposing the concluding Darwinian frame of a 'chain of events, working through generations'. Elsewhere Holmes offers an even more clearly Darwinian account of human character as forged out of family ancestry. Fundamental to his 'methods' is the application of the processes of investigation associated with the natural sciences to the understanding of human society, seen specifically in class terms:

> Like all other arts, the science of Deduction and Analysis is one which can only be acquired by long and patient study. Before turning to those moral and mental aspects of the matter which present the greatest difficulties, let the inquirer begin by mastering more elementary problems. Let him, on meeting a fellow mortal, learn at a glance to distinguish the history of the man, and the trade or profession to which he belongs. Puerile as such an exercise may seem, it sharpens the faculties of observation and teaches one where to look and what to look for. By a man's fingernails, by his coat sleeve, by his boot, by his trouser knees, by the callosities of his forefinger and thumb, by his shirt-cuffs – by each of these things a man's calling is plainly revealed.
> (Conan Doyle, 1981, *A Study in Scarlet*, p. 23)

This appeal to the exercise of the power of analytical intelligence was – and remained – the crucial definition of rationality permeating the Holmes narratives. Associated with the Victorian sense of scientific, industrial and technological 'progress', Conan Doyle effectively negotiated a transference of such analytical powers to the domain of society and in particular to the ideological resolution of that which was regarded as 'mystery', the fear of the socially disruptive.

Holmes's 'methods', then, are those of the realist story-teller. To return to our fireside chat, Watson is not satisfied with Holmes's sense of the strangeness of the commonplace:

> 'And yet I am not convinced of it', I answered. 'The cases which come to light in the papers are, as a rule, bald enough, and vulgar

enough. We have in our police reports realism pushed to its extreme limits, and yet the result is, it must be confessed, neither fascinating nor artistic.'

'A certain selection and discretion must be used in producing a realistic effect,' remarked Holmes. 'This is wanting in the police report, where more stress is laid, perhaps, upon the platitudes of the magistrate than upon the details, which to an observer contain the vital essence of the whole matter. Depend upon it, there is nothing so unnatural as the commonplace.'

(Conan Doyle, 1981, 'A Case of Identity', p. 191)

This is an initial note which is consistently struck in Watson's 'chronicles' of the 'history' of Sherlock Holmes; the generally secure, very male environment of Baker Street into which puzzled, anxious and threatened clients of the lower middle, middle and, very occasionally, aristocratic classes bring their narratives of bizarre events and *from* which Holmes 'selects' the essential, sallying forth (predominantly) into a strangely sketchy and, therefore, I would argue, ideologically mystified environment of the capital of the empire in order to render the inexplicable as commonplace. It is important that he offers this service 'for the love of his art [rather] than for the acquirement of wealth' (Conan Doyle, 1981, p. 257). This class position operates as a crucial defining centre within the narratives and is resonant of an insistent strand within English culture – the sense of the gentleman-amateur imbued with that 'natural' superiority of *Englishness*, rooted in its class system and 'above' vulgar professionalism. Thus, crime investigated by the 'official' police force is, indeed, 'vulgar' as are most of the force's lower-class representatives – Lestrade is a 'lean, ferret-like man, furtive and sly-looking' (Conan Doyle, 1981, p. 207) – while the Holmes narratives seek to establish their 'superior' realism compared to documentary police and newspaper reports, from which Holmes, of course, excludes himself as a gentleman once the crime is resolved.

Even Holmes's asceticism, his unconventional eccentricities and habits are contributory to his – and the narrative's – class orientations. While tobacco and music operate as stimulants to his unusual thought-processes, opium is merely an occasional resort in the very early stories when Holmes is languishing in some obscurity because 'society' is failing to provide him with objectives upon which he can exercise his talents. His asceticism is also specifically that of the male intellectual, his powers dependent on an abnormal degree of detachment and capacity for abstraction while women are, with the one early exception of Irene Adler, debarred by 'nature' from the exercise of rationality and analytical, logical deduction. It is precisely the function of Holmes's selectively idiosyncratic 'bohemianism' to provide him with the necessary 'knowledges' to control the mysterious world which surrounds his clients and readers, thereby serving ultimately in the interest of his class allegiances.

It is he – certainly not the reader or client – who *knows* 'London', especially its dens of vice and criminal beggary, as in 'The Man with the Twisted Lip' which centres on the Victorian preoccupation with the separation between suburban domesticity and 'city' business, that fragmentation of identity whose most famous exemplar is Wemmick in *Great Expectations*. It is also notable that Holmes's impenetrable disguises are always dependent on a 'downward' change of social class, or gender, or, occasionally, both:

> He hurried to his chamber, and was down again in a few minutes dressed as a *common* loafer. With his collar turned up, his shiny, seedy coat, his red cravat, and his worn boots, *he was a perfect sample of the class.*
> (Conan Doyle, 1981, 'The Beryl Coronet', p. 311; my emphases)

Thus, Holmes's methods of logical deduction are not simply located in the much-vaunted science of forensic observation and analysis but also derive out of his 'knowledge' of London and all of the social classes contained therein:

> He loved to lie in the very centre of five millions of people, with his filament stretching out and running through them, responsive to every little rumour or suspicion of unsolved crime.
> (Conan Doyle, 1981, 'The Resident Patient', p. 423)

While viewing the British workman as 'a token of evil', Holmes's web of relationships includes bands of 'street arabs', cab drivers and so on who materialize at his command.

So, too, Conan Doyle's location of Holmes's social origins within a family of country gentry is of some significance. The second half of the nineteenth century is notable not only for the gentrification of the Victorian middle classes but also for the rise of the modern professions. Lawyers, doctors (Doyle's original profession), men of letters [sic] as social groups both expanded in numbers and achieved enhanced status through the restructuring of their professions to emphasize specialist expertise while maintaining an allegiance to traditional gentry values. As Matthew Arnold in 1868 had commented, 'in no country . . . do the professions so naturally and generally share the cast of ideas of the aristocracy as in England'.[2] In comparison to Conan Doyle's representation of Holmes as combining the values of science and the cultured gentleman-amateur, Arnold's view of the consequence of the processes of gentrification was

> a middle class cut in two and in a way unexampled anywhere else; of a professional class brought up on the first plane, with fine and governing qualities, but without the idea of science; while that immense business class, which is becoming so important a power in all countries, on which the future so much depends . . . is in England brought up on the second plane, but cut off from the aristocracy and professions, and without governing qualities.[3]

Throughout the century the traditional aristocracy either had to adjust to the realities of an industrial economy through investment or marriage, or find themselves bought out by those capitalists who wished to purchase land in order to acquire social status. English social critics and cultural commentators repeatedly held trade and industry in some suspicion while expressing an ideological commitment to the ownership of land as the true measure of social position and the respectable status of gentlemen. Through this process middle-class industrialists who had made their wealth through trade or colonial speculation were enabled to mask the 'vulgar' source of their wealth and hence achieve class alliance with the traditional aristocracy whose economic adjustments had been forced to operate in the reverse direction in order to maintain their social power.

It is worth noting that the disruptive figure of Moriarty – and the Irish name may be significant at a time of crisis in the Home Rule struggle – appears as a criminal master-mind towards the end of the cycle. As Holmes's ruthless opponent, he is stripped of two central identities – the status of an English gentleman and the mental and moral capacities for cultured imagination. Moriarty, we are informed by Holmes, had had his brilliant mind perverted by science, by the abstract study of pure mathematics. As such, he may be located in relation to that 'immense business class without governing qualities' so distressing to Arnold. The competitive rivalry for power and dominance in society, waged between Holmes and Moriarty, becomes foregrounded gradually, allowing the development of a Manichaean confrontation between the values of 'Englishness' struggling 'manfully' against the deceit and perniciousness of the alien criminal mind. This is a conflict which is accentuated in the later cinematic narratives, especially in the context of the Second World War, and the most striking characteristic of its representation is the evident fear of an organized network, an underground which might be rendered powerfully threatening to the social organism through the ruthless leadership of the deviant individualist.[4]

The location for this drama is, of course, London with occasional forays into the depths of the 'Home' counties ('The Stock-Broker's Clerk', an interesting exception, occasions a trip to Birmingham to investigate a fraud) and otherwise represses all sense of an industrial or money economy. Watson's narrative glides easily over such discursive statements as

> Our visitor bore every mark of being an average commonplace British tradesman, obese, pompous and slow.
> (Conan Doyle, 1981, 'The Red-Headed League", p. 177)

Indeed the narrative hangs very largely on the greed and absurd gullibility of Mr Jabez Wilson whose 'otherness' is completed by his evident Jewishness. By contrast, the representatives of the 'new' scientific professions – a GP in 'The Resident Patient' or an engineer in 'The Engineer's Thumb' – are 'young' gentlemen like 'Mr Victor Hatherley, hydraulic engineer' who is 'quietly dressed in a suit of heather tweed . . . with a strong, masculine face' (Conan Doyle, 1981, p. 274). Deriving perhaps out of Doyle's own experience as a struggling young GP, all of these professional gentlemen are initially having difficulty in making their way in Victorian society, suffering a sense of frustration which, the narratives suggest, renders them prey to ruthless exploitation. Victor Hatherley, for instance, is inveigled into servicing machinery which is being used to counterfeit English coinage by a 'gang' whose murderous leader is German.

The preservation of values associated with the integrity of 'Englishness' is fundamental to the Holmes narratives transcending class boundaries in the representation of the ethnically 'other'. The King of Bohemia, for instance, is decidedly 'foreign' in the dishonesty of his sexual-marital ethics registered not only in his appearance

> His dress was rich with a richness which would, in England, be looked upon as akin to bad taste.
> (Conan Doyle, 1981, 'A Scandal in Bohemia', p. 164)

but also in his language. As a German, he is 'uncourteous to his verbs' whereas the cultured command of the English language is always a valorized norm of social status. In the case of the traditional English aristocracy Watson's narrative voice mediates a note of ambivalence about the class through the metaphor of the power of the body: Lord Robert St Simon is

> a gentleman . . . with a pleasant, cultured face, high nosed and pale with something perhaps of petulance about the mouth, and with the steady, well-opened eye of a man whose pleasant lot it had ever been to command and to be obeyed . . . his general appearance gave an undue impression of age, for he had a slight forward stoop and a little bend of the knees as he walked . . . As to his dress, it was careful to the point of foppishness.
> (Conan Doyle, 1981, 'The Adventure of the Noble Bachelor', p. 291)

Holmes has already learnt of Lord Robert's marriage to Miss Hatty Doran, a young Jamesian heiress whose 'education has come from Nature' – she is American – and who is possessed of a 'graceful figure and striking face' allied to a 'dowry . . . [of] six figures'. Lord Robert's family has been forced to sell some of their 'pictures', symbols of traditional heritage, but the emergence of the United States as an economic competitor to Britain is rewoven in Doyle's newspaper report into the exchange value of women as 'products':

> There will soon be a call for protection in the marriage market, for the present free-trade principle appears to tell heavily against our

home product. One by one the management of the noble houses of Great Britain is passing into the hands of our fair cousins from across the Atlantic. An important addition has been made during the last week to the list of the prizes which have been borne away by these charming invaders.

(Conan Doyle, 1981, p. 289)

Holmes reveals that Miss Doran has been 'rescued' on the morning of this marriage of social and economic convenience by her former 'natural' husband whom she had presumed dead as he had been 'a prisoner among the Apaches'.

America, then, is a source of innocent young women – and of a mysterious criminality around such secret societies as the Mormons (*A Study in Scarlet*) or the Ku Klux Klan ('The Five Orange Pips'), or around the possibilities of miscegenation ('The Yellow Face'). All of this is rooted in a very English sense of the alien quality of American society with its origins in immigrant populations. Simultaneously, however, the expansion of the power and influence of the United States is also negotiated through Holmes's (and Doyle's) sense of a 'special relationship'.

The colonies of Australia and India provide a rather different but equally recurrent source of mystery and criminality. Here the focus is always on a tainted, specifically male, past history. The best-known of these narratives is the early *Sign of Four* with its 'unhallowed dwarf' Tongan whose 'features [are] so deeply marked with all bestiality and cruelty', a 'devilish native' whose 'small eyes glowed and burned with a sombre light, and his thick lips were writhed back from his teeth, which grinned and chattered at us with half-animal fury' (Conan Doyle, 1981, p. 138). As such, he shares a racial affinity with the 'black devils', 'hundreds of the black fiends', 'fanatics and fierce devil worshippers of all sorts' who, in Jonathan Small's narrative-within-the-narrative, took part in the Indian Mutiny. The defining perspective on the mutiny is that

It was a fight of the millions against the hundreds; and the cruellest part of it was that these men that we fought against, foot, horse and gunners, were *our own* picked troops, whom *we had taught and trained*, handling *our own* weapons and blowing *our own* bugle calls.

(Conan Doyle, 1981, p. 146; my emphases)

Providing the context for Small's initial act of betrayal in entering into a pact with the native Sikhs, the history of the Indian mutiny against British imperialist power is registered as unbridled 'torture and murder and outrage', an act of mass betrayal with the native population taking unfair advantage, in a very un-English fashion, of their superiority in numbers.

Drawing the line at any kind of military betrayal, Small's guilty past is that he succumbed ignobly to the Sikhs' appeal to act as an individual in a way which, to them, mirrors colonial power:

> We only ask you to do that which your countrymen come to this land for. We ask you to be rich.
>
> (Conan Doyle, 1981, p. 147)

Small's betrayal of the highest standards of what Conrad called 'the idea' of British imperialism forges the first vital link in a chain of further treachery by white men, Sholto and Morstan, which leads ultimately back to England itself as the homeland, while their fanatical and almost psychotic desire to possess *in order* to 'conceal' the treasure leads inexorably to their deaths. Finally, the treasure of Agra lies irretrievably concealed, buried in the mud of the Thames – a note oddly resonant of Conrad's *Heart of Darkness*, a slightly later narrative of imperialism which brings together the Congo and the Thames around symbolic images of the dichotomy of primitivism and civilization.

The informing principle in both Doyle and Conrad would appear to be that late Victorian preoccupation with the moral responsibility of specifically English imperialism, the inculcation of missionary rather than purely economic purposes – an attitude of mind markedly registered in Conan Doyle's subsequent, swingeing critique of the devastating exploitation of the Congo by the Belgians. Thus, these narratives can be seen to lock into the dominant ideology which cloaked British imperialism and policies of annexation in the later nineteenth century, registering its contradictions within a discourse constituted around the terms of ethical/ethnic homogeneity and power mediated as 'progress' towards civilization. The class orientation of this 'naturally' superior imperial English culture is revealed in the confidence with which a Government Report asserts in 1884 that

The culture that men got at Oxford and Cambridge was of the greatest importance in dealing with the natives.[5]

The gentrification, then, of professional colonial administrators provides the context of English imperialism within which deviant acts of betrayal can take place. In each of the Holmes cases involving the colonies ('The Boscombe Valley Mystery', 'The Speckled Band', 'The Gloria Scott', even 'The Crooked Man' in its way) the crime hangs on a tainted 'past', the acquisition of wealth, return to the home country bringing forth the gradual revelation of guilt which registers the *nouveaux riches* status of the criminal:

> among the crowds who were gathered [in Australia] from all nations, we had no difficulty in losing our former identities. *The rest I need not relate.* We prospered, we travelled, we came back as rich colonials to England, and we bought country estates.
> (Conan Doyle, 1981, 'The Gloria Scott', p. 385; my emphasis)

Thus we come, full circle, to that central context of the English class system, to the ownership of the land as the badge of status, while criminality is attached to those who have artificially and unnaturally acquired the external prerequisites without the 'real', 'natural' and profoundly English social qualifications to belong.

In 'The Crooked Man' the 'wealth' gained illicitly is a wife. Just as the narrative structures of Doyle's fiction are informed by discourses of social class and of imperialism and 'Englishness', so, too, gender is central, AS we have already seen, to these 'texts' of criminality. The male bonding of the relations between Holmes and Watson is only one facet, a bonding which excludes and eventually kills off Watson's wife (Miss Morstan) whose main function is to shadow in his heterosexual and romantic inclinations so that Watson may comment occasionally on Holmes's 'asexuality':

> My friend Holmes, rather to my disappointment, manifested no further interest in her once she had ceased to be the centre of one of his problems.
> (Conan Doyle, 1981, 'The Adventure of the Copper Beeches', p. 332)

In fact, Holmes's masculinity is the source of his intellectual detachment and perception resulting in a chivalrous misogyny which denies women as beings except in so far as they are anxious victims of outlandishly Gothic plots. Hence, women are, with a few exceptions, clients who are absurdly gullible and shoddy like Mary Sutherland, of lower-middle-class 'trade' status, or respectably genteel young women such as Violet Hunter – and there are a number of not-quite-shrinking Violets – who 'has the brisk manner of a woman who has had her own way to make in the world' (Conan Doyle, 1981, p. 318). This 'Adventure of the Copper Beeches' is particularly notable for its Gothic quality of the isolated country house, the taciturn or drunken servants, the villainous stepfather who, in the effort to retain control of his stepdaughter's independent income, drives her to a brain-fever in which her hair has to be cut off, eventually locking her, like the mad woman, in the attic to prevent her marriage. As in 'The Speckled Band' with its similar setting, 'colonial' animals and motivation, retribution arrives when the vicious mastiff turns on its master.

While many of these marital 'crimes' focus around issues of identity and the 'economy' of marriage, their Gothic elements dally with the sexual prurience common to the form. In some cases ('A Scandal in Bohemia', 'The Noble Bachelor', 'The Beryl Coronet', 'Silver Blaze', 'The Greek Interpreter', 'The Musgrave Ritual'), woman's sexuality is simultaneously motivating and rendered absent: in 'A Scandal in Bohemia', 'foreign' morganatic wife becomes respectable wife of a young, handsome English lawyer; in 'The Beryl Coronet', Doyle comes close to exploiting that dual male image of woman as madonna and whore in the kind and innocent niece revealed as deceitfully engaged in a degraded sexual liaison which will, we are assured, eventually provide its own retribution. Meanwhile the foreign young woman in 'The Greek Interpreter' who has eloped, nevertheless remains 'clad in some sort of loose *white* gown'; she ultimately wreaks proper justice on her financial and sexual exploiters. Finally, sexual and class relations are intricately interwoven into 'The Musgrave Ritual' in which the philandering butler, actually a schoolmaster who has chosen to work *beneath* his 'true' class position in order to crack the aristocratic 'code' of the Musgrave family passed down through generations, is murdered, at the very moment of his success, in a fit of demented hysteria by the sexually infatuated – and betrayed – maid! A just revenge for unconstrained and unnatural sociosexual desires?

The obvious point to make is that women in these narratives are rendered as essentially passive – the objects of action – while gender difference is constituted in 'nature'. Amongst Holmes's 'logical' deductions are such rational links as 'Women are naturally secretive' (Conan Doyle, 1981, p. 171), or 'A married woman grabs at her baby; and an unmarried one reaches for her jewel-box' (Conan Doyle, 1981, p. 173). Watson's narrative refers consistently to a woman's 'natural reserve' or 'a woman's quick intuition', those instinctual feminine qualities which are valued from the superior power position of the Male Rationalists who are the active agents in the rescue of these supplicants.

The fact that women are so circumscribed in these narratives both as the agents and victims of criminality suggests the nature of the 'social contract' between Doyle and his 'specific public'. He was a well-known opponent, for instance, of the suffrage movement, arguing in chivalrous terms that while divorce law reform might be necessary, only those women who paid their taxes should be 'given' the vote. Otherwise, he berated the movement for its criminal acts against property and offered the opinion that in this exceptional case he was in favour of lynching![6] Other 'exclusions' from the world of Sherlock Holmes and Dr Watson are worth passing mention. Two of the most notorious and much-publicized trials of 1886 and 1889, for instance, were those of Adelaide Bartlett and Florence Maybrick (from Alabama); both criminal investigations involved the alleged use of poison and highlighted the difficulty for contemporary medical science of offering precisely the kind of forensic evidence, especially for domestic crime, so frequently provided by Holmes. And both trials drew into the public domain the motivations of women as sexual beings. Meanwhile, the five most celebrated victims of male violence were those of 'Jack the Ripper' in Whitechapel in 1888.[7]

The point here is not to draw crass comparisons between fiction and social reality but it may be suggested that one of the fundamental pleasures of the Holmes narratives is to construct a tension between the inexplicably enigmatic and the reassurance of total closure. As such, they are 'magical' narratives – to use Jameson's phrase – which play into and upon dominant ideologies at a time when, at the very least, fissures are appearing in bourgeois hegemony, patriarchy and imperial power. There *are* threatening forces gathering in the 1890s against and within Victorian society but the Holmes narratives mediate such political and economic conflicts into a moral discourse with co-ordinates of class, gender and white supremacy, subject either to individual reform or to the ministrations of the English gentlemen of 221B Baker Street.

It was – and remained – a powerfully attractive social narrative which could be adapted and reproduced in subsequent historical formations. But that is another story. And far from elementary.

Notes

All references to the Sherlock Holmes stories are drawn from *The Penguin Complete Adventures of Sherlock Holmes* (Harmondsworth, 1981).

1   Fredric Jameson, *The Political Unconscious* (London: Methuen, 1981), p. 106.
2   Matthew Arnold, *Schools and Universities on the Continent*, edited by R. H. Super (Ann Arbor, Mich.: 1964), pp. 308–9.
3   ibid.
4   This is not to accept Franco Moretti's overly simplistic thesis that the criminal can be equated with individualism while Holmes 'abandons the individualistic ethic'. Franco Moretti, *Signs Taken for Wonders* (London: New Left Books, 1983), p. 142.
5   Cited in Chris Baldick, *The Social Mission of English Criticism 1848–1932* (Oxford: Oxford University Press, 1983), p. 71.
6   Cited in Pierre Nordon, *Conan Doyle: A Biography* (New York: John Murray, 1969), pp. 64, 82.
7   These murders provide the basis for John Hopkins's screenplay for one of the most interesting of later versions of 'Holmes', *Murder by Decree* (dir. Bob Clark) with Christopher Plummer and James Mason. Here the Victorian detective once again confronts a 'network' but in this case it is the system organized to protect the rich and powerful. It is also worth noting that there was a concerted effort to define the 'ripper' murders as un-English which led to racial harassment of the Jewish community of Spitalfields. The *Daily News*, for instance, described the murders as 'foreign to the English style in crime'. Cited in Paul Gilroy, *There Ain't No Black in the Union Jack* (London: Hutchinson, 1987) p. 77.

4

The stuff that dreams are made of:

Masculinity, femininity and the thriller

DAVID GLOVER

LIKE ALL Golden Ages, the Golden Age of detective fiction embodies a myth. Not because it never happened, but because its proponents
turned it into one: the myth that the crime story has an essential
Platonic form, perfected during the 1920s and codified into a set
of mock golden rules. To be 'a puzzle pure and complex' (in Julian Symons's apt phrase) it was logically necessary for the detective
novel to forswear such devices as the use of 'new, undiscovered or
undetectable poisons' and for the investigator never to 'wittingly conceal clues or the reasons for his deductions from the reader' (Quayle,
1972, p. 110). Or so the myth goes. And, puzzlingly, even its fiercest
critics have colluded with it. Until Dashiell Hammett 'took murder
out of the Venetian vase and dropped it into the alley', wrote Raymond
Chandler in his scathing attack on Mayhem Parva in 'The simple
art of murder', first published in 1944, crime fiction consisted of
'problems of logic and deduction' with 'puppets and cardboard lovers
and papier-mâché villains and detectives of exquisite and impossible
gentility' (Chandler, 1980, pp. 184–6). Between them, the myth of
the Golden Age and Chandler's potent counter-aesthetic of the hard-
boiled private dick still delimit the terms in which we write the history
and theory of the detective story, disguising some of its most impor
tant features. Roland Barthes once defined myth as 'depoliticized
speech', and in the same spirit I want to argue that what has been lost
is a sense of crime fiction's sexual politics.

I

Most academic studies which puzzle over detective fiction argue that
it is, at root, a literature of social and psychological adjustment. Their
routes to this conclusion are pretty diverse and diverge more often

than they draw together, treading different theoretical paths. At its simplest, no matter how dazzling the pyrotechnics of structuralist and post-structuralist textual analysis, the argument asserts that 'detective novels provide reassurance': mysteries are dissipated, crimes cleared up, evil is punished, order restored, and endings satisfy. The experience of reading is one of recuperation, confirming us in the moral universe we know, 'making the strangeness of the present familiar' (Porter, 1981, pp. 218–20). At the back of this solution is a well-rehearsed public debate about the significance of popular fiction for modernity stretching back as far as the sixteenth century, which continues to echo in our ears to this day. Nearly a hundred years after the Rev. Jonathan Baxter Harrison pronounced to his fellow Bostonians in 1880 that dime novels were but a harmless 'narcotic', the American literary critic Michael Holquist again pointed to the 'narcotizing effect' of detective stories (Denning, 1986, p. 3; Holquist, 1971, p. 155).

Adjustment of a more subtle kind has been advanced by those trying to explain the social history of crime fiction, including its continuing popularity under changing social conditions. Here the stress has been upon ideology, hegemony and cultural power, identifying crime fiction as a literature whose role is to reconcile, consolidate, obtain consent. Marxism has therefore been a major influence, though responses to it have varied considerably, ranging from relative orthodoxy (Ernest Mandel), through ingenious mixing of Marxism with structuralism and Russian formalism (Jerry Palmer), to its outright rejection as overly 'deterministic' (John G. Cawelti). Among these and other critics crime fiction is conceived as an active force in history, an imaginary solvent of social contradictions rather than a comforting diversion. Even Cawelti's avowedly non-Marxist hypothesis that one of the principal 'cultural functions' of popular genres like the thriller is to 'resolve tensions and ambiguities resulting from the conflicting interests of different groups within the culture' looks suspiciously like a theory of ideology (Cawelti, 1976, p. 35). This shared emphasis upon popular writing as a social practice, and consequently upon genres as social relationships – sets of expectations which circulate between producers and their publics to powerful effect – stands in striking contrast to the many (so far mostly undebated) disagreements about how particular crime texts should be interpreted. Thus, whether Sherlock Holmes is held to personify the dominant rational individualism of his age, or whether he is seen as an agent of the system bringing the deviant individuality of the criminal before the law, the basic mode of explanation remains the same (Knight, 1980, ch. 3; Moretti, 1983, ch. 5).

If this all sounds rather grim, it is because the idea of 'murder for pleasure' (to purloin a famous title) has received surprisingly little attention. Where pleasure has been theorized, it usually either duplicates or shores up the various theories of crime fiction as a source of social and psychological adjustment. On the one hand, pleasure has turned out to be a narcotic, a distraction, textually bound (hand and foot). The mystery is pleasurable puzzle or game, albeit a competitive one in which the reader is pitted against the author/detective, seeking the mystery's solution before it is officially announced; or again, pleasure results 'from the repeated postponement of a desired end', 'the excitement of being played by the novel he [*sic*] holds in his hand in the same way that the concertgoer allows himself to be played by the interpreted score' (Porter, 1981, pp. 32 and 230).

On the other hand, pleasure just is ideology. Jerry Palmer's book *Thrillers*, for example, argues that 'excitement and suspense derive from wholeheartedly wanting one person to succeed and fearing setbacks to their projects' (Palmer, 1978, pp. 61–2). According to his 'minimal definition' of the genre, all thrillers are scaffolded upon two invariant and symbiotic elements, 'a mysterious conspiracy' and a hero, in that the story is necessarily told from the point of view of a central figure struggling against 'an opaque, radically uncertain world'. Though each of these two components has its specific ideological origins, once coupled together they operate an ideology of the text peculiarly their own. In this ideology of paranoia or 'intense suspicion' society's enemies are already inside the gates and only the hero can re-establish the rule of law: in sum, we are given a 'recommendation of competitive individualism, and the presentation of society as somewhere that is, in the normal run of events, devoid of conflict'. The reader's pleasure, therefore, assumes complicity in the thriller's strongly conservative deep structure, for, set beside this fundamental politics of the text, any other political message that is overtly at variance with the basic generic formula can only be a mere 'superficial layer' (ibid., pp. 66–7).

I want to make two critical points about these accounts of pleasure. The first is to underline how important the model provided by the classic or analytical detective story with its country houses and locked rooms is to their understanding of the enjoyment to be had from crime fiction as a whole. To be sure, both Dennis Porter and Jerry Palmer have quite a lot to say about that least deductive of heroes, James Bond, but both see Fleming's fiction as structured by an enigma, its reading motivated by a desire to know. For even if the villain's identity is known (as in most Bond books), the exact nature of his dastardly plot is not. Pleasure is held to flow from identification with the hero which is, in turn, a function of the reader's lack of any other source of knowledge within the narrative: thus the Bond thrillers are supposed to be identical to analytical detective fiction because in both cases reader and hero share in suspense through their common ignorance. But this is to minimize the differences between texts, misleadingly flattening out their empirical diversity.

My second point also concerns difference, this time sexual difference. In these versions of pleasure sexual difference seems not to make much difference. Despite his recognition that 'when we read, we allow our body to be played and played upon by a text', Dennis Porter manages to devote an entire chapter to 'the erotics of narrative' without ever once raising the question of sexual politics. Moreover, in a passage of anti-Freudian polemic he suggests that sexuality and criminality are mutually exclusive terms since 'a detective novel may excite on the level of its manifest content of violence without any necessary allusion to a latent sexual signified' (Porter, 1981, pp. 108–11). The trouble with this is that heroes and heroines obviously have gendered identities to which their capacity for action, including their response to violence, is closely linked. As Jerry Palmer notes, since heroism overlaps significantly with machismo, the thriller's hero is quintessentially 'alone, sexy, competitive'. Sexual conquests serve to demonstrate the hero's special qualities, as when James Bond's magnetic sexuality is empowered to overcome frigidity and lesbianism, all the while remaining aloof and finely controlled, alert and unencumbered for the tasks ahead. Yet because sexual episodes are sometimes absent from the thriller – in Ross Macdonald's books, for example – Palmer concludes that sexuality is not one of its basic ingredients. Consequently, in his argument the gender of the hero – particularly *how* the central character is constructed as male or female – mysteriously disappears from view. And, since all readers identify with the hero through the delivery of a knowledge which is textually identical for everyone, no important distinctions between male and female readers are thought to arise. Like the actual politics of a text (including presumably its sexual politics), gender is just another 'superficial layer'.

I would argue that the history of crime fiction suggests otherwise, but not as it has usually been written. Typically that history has taken the classic detective story as the mature form of the genre, tracing its roots back to Godwin, Vidocq and Poe via Conan Doyle, and then has deduced the spy-thriller and the hard-boiled detective story from the classic model as variations on a theme. Dashiell Hammett and Raymond Chandler, it is said, 'knowingly Americanized the detective story in response to the pressures of American life, tastes, and values', substituting a fresh realism for a tiresomely clever formalism (Porter, 1981, p. 128). This is very much Chandler's own authorized version: Hammett 'did not wreck the formal detective story', but simply 'loosened it up a little here, and sharpened it a little there'. Only 'flustered old ladies – of both sexes (or no sex) . . . who like their murders scented with magnolia blossoms' could possibly deny this (Chandler, 1980, pp. 187–8). Yet through his testy caricature Chandler unknowingly invites an alternative, gendered history of these forms of writing which has been missing for far too long.

II

According to John Cawelti the Golden Age aestheticized crime by turning into a game or puzzle. What he fails to make clear is that its focus upon domestic crime also feminized detective fiction, part of a wider change in the production and consumption of popular literature after the First World War. Many of the new cheap commercial 'little libraries' set up by newsagents and stationers during this period 'were used overwhelmingly by women' and the detective stories they stocked 'were written by women, and essentially also *for* women' (Symons, 1985, p. 86). Fittingly, Agatha Christie's first book *The Mysterious Affair at Styles* (1920) has been seen as the Golden Age's founding text, paving the way for other 'queens of crime' like Josephine Tey, Ngaio Marsh, Dorothy L. Sayers and Margery Allingham and for those unflusterable old ladies like Miss Marple whose special feminine talents for cerebration freed the genre from reliance upon masculine prowess. Even Christie's first hero, the vain and faintly ridiculous Hercule Poirot, helped to inflect the detective story 'towards a passive problem-solving that rejects romantic male heroism as a protecting force', and Poirot himself is notably deferential when speaking of the intuitive powers of women's subconscious minds (Knight, 1980, p. 108).

At the same time, it has to be admitted that women occupied a most contradictory position within the crime fiction of the Golden Age. As Cora Kaplan has pointed out, Agatha Christie may have upgraded the village spinster in her depiction of Miss Marple, but in her books women 'out of place' are always suspect(s) because of their sexual or social misdemeanours, a trait still shared by some of Christie's latter-day descendants (Kaplan, 1986). This is intensified into a sort of collective pathology whenever the mystery is set in an all-female institution, the women's college in Dorothy L. Sayers's *Gaudy Night* (1935) standing as a classic warning of the dangers to be faced when women are kept in one another's company too much. Moreover, *Gaudy Night* is 'limited' by its author's 'inability to put all the clichés about deviant women behind her'. Ironically 'in a novel which examines conflicts caused by the intrusion of professional women into a man's world', only a servant, a landlady's daughter, can be capable of the obscenity and violence which shakes the college (Morris, 1983, p. 494). If the book reflects upon women's newly gained citizenship, equality before the law has but a nominal status.

This imbrication of gender and class helps to explain the Golden Age's preoccupation with generic propriety, its pursuit of ascetic golden rules to the point of self-parody. The pseudo-academic preciousness of the classic detective story represented a status-conscious reaction to the earlier, more swashbuckling fiction commonly known as 'thrillers' or 'shockers', a reaction from within the middle classes, particularly amongst intellectuals, against writers of humbler social origins who monopolized the pulp magazines and the popular press. At its height the Golden Age was an attempt to codify a popular cultural canon, in a sense to civilize the popular fiction industry; hence it was felt that the detective puzzle should be ruled by a gentlemanly ethic of fair play observed by writer and reader alike. What was wrong with the thriller, wrote Dorothy L. Sayers in a 1929 essay, was that 'nothing is explained', a clear violation of 'that quiet enjoyment of the logical which we look for in our detective reading'. The thriller was therefore the province of 'the uncritical' rather than 'the modern educated public' (Sayers, 1980, pp. 59–73). Sayers's argument by exclusion was deliberately at odds with the fluid and disordered world of popular literature where genre boundaries were far from fixed and where terms like 'mystery', 'thriller', 'detective story' and 'adventure' were used loosely and interchangeably. This was a world of masculine derring-do, and it is perhaps worth remembering that Sherlock Holmes's influential 'case book' was filled with what Conan Doyle called 'adventures' rather than 'mysteries' or 'cases', and that Holmes and Dr Watson bore firearms in a way that neither Hercule Poirot nor Miss Marple ever did.

In his recent study of American popular fiction in the late nineteenth century, Michael Denning observes that our present-day system of genre categories 'is a relatively recent development, one that emerged only in the 1920s and 1930s' when narrative production started to specialize into distinct markets and *All-Story Magazine* and *Argosy All-Story* were replaced by *Detective Story Magazine* and *Western Story Magazine* (Denning, 1986, pp. 5–7). This is important, but it downplays the extent to which pulp fiction embodied gender-specific forms of address – most crudely in titles like *Action Stories*, *Battle Aces*, or even *Man Stories*. Manliness was equated here with action, speed, combat, confrontation and pursuit, and intelligence was conceived as essentially practical, mental alertness rather than intellectualism. In the pulps masculinity figured in a blur of genres and locales, often with a solid imperialist pedigree. The self-styled 'King of Thrillers', Edgar Wallace, is a case in point. Many of his prewar books were tales of the 'brave' men who ran the British Empire in Africa like *Sanders of the River* (1911) and, appropriately enough, one of his later successes was the film script for *King Kong*. But it was as a prolific author of thrillers that he rose to fame, contributing to the leading American pulps like *Detective Story Magazine*, and responsible for an estimated 'one in every four books printed and sold in Britain during his heyday' (Quayle, 1972, p. 106). His hybrids of detection and adventure broke all the putative golden rules, as in *The Man at the Carlton* (1931), where a rather traditional country-house mystery – strange events in a mist-enveloped Scottish mansion – rapidly gives way to the thrills of an urban chase led by Tiger Tim Jordan, chief of the Rhodesian CID. Wallace was also significant as a vernacular writer, sometimes using police, criminal and racing slang as a vehicle for bluff mockery of the pretensions of scientific deduction.

Seen from this perspective, the rise of the hard-boiled detective was a refurbishing of already existing masculine forms, drawing imperialist credentials from the North American prairies rather than from Africa. True, gentleman detectives in the Sherlock Holmes mould were heavily featured in the pulps, but to these magazines also belonged the Western, Allan Pinkerton's fictionalized detective memoirs, and the white Anglo-Saxon muscularity of boy-sleuth Nick Carter. *Black Mask*, the most famous of the hard-boiled pulps, often contained Westerns or had a Western action scene on its cover, and when it serialized Hammett's *The Maltese Falcon* between 1929 and 1930 its subtitle announced the magazine's contents as 'Western, Detective and Adventure Stories'. In a 1928 letter to his publisher, Hammett referred to his book *Red Harvest* as 'an action-detective novel', and Cawelti has perceptively described it as 'westernlike in its setting and in its violent and chaotic narrative of gang warfare' (Johnson, 1984, p. 69; Cawelti, 1976, p. 162). Hammett's Continental Op stories often contained no element of mystery or detection, only lurid fight scenes, and in 'Corkscrew' (1925) he actually wrote a Western with the Op as its hero. Given their history and their largely male working-class readership, it's not surprising that prior to the 'tough guy' thriller there was always something of a tension in the pulps between the gentleman and the proletarian as hero. And in a series of short stories by Hammett's immediate precursor, Carroll John Daly, we can trace the evolution of an anonymous 'gentleman adventurer' who is 'no knight errant' into Three-Gun Terry Mack, the first hard-boiled private eye (Nolan, 1983, pp. 41–2).

This masculinization of crime fiction effectively repositioned women both as readers and as fictional characters, while excluding them as writers, and forms the sub-text to Chandler's 'The simple art of murder' which sought to elevate the hard-boiled thriller to cultural respectability, a project it shares with his Philip Marlowe novels. It is a fiction premissed upon an ecology of male power 'in which gangsters can rule nations and almost rule cities, in which hotels and apartment houses and celebrated restaurants are owned by men who made their money out of brothels' (Chandler, 1980, p. 188). And in his overblown description of a *Black Mask* contemporary's prose as 'naked action, pounded into tough compactness by staccato, hammer-like writing', Hammett condensed images of violence and labour into a concentrated summation of the new masculine style.

Small wonder, then, that 'after dying out for over a century', female Gothic novels started to revive and gain ground amongst women readers in the late 1930s, resulting in a marked sexual segregation in the market for popular fiction which continues to this day (Modleski, 1984, p. 21).

Rosalind Coward has suggested that such popular narratives serve as public fantasies and her psychoanalytically informed reading of them shows how the pleasures they offer can take male and female forms. For many male readers the kind of stories they enjoy are 'preoccupied with putting the male body through all sorts of ordeals . . . which are ultimately survived'. Not only is this a celebration of risk-taking and aggression, it also represents, she argues, a male victory over the threat of castration, an assertion of dominance, control and invulnerability, and a denial of sexual ambiguity. But, because this is only fantasy, disturbing elements keep breaking through, creating fresh reading possibilities. Dick Francis's racing thrillers, for example, are highly popular with women readers precisely because their play upon male dependency via accident or injury imaginarily cedes immense power to women as carers. In Rosalind Coward's view these fantasies are 'the unconscious preoccupations of a patriarchal culture expressed in an acceptable way' (Coward, 1984, pp. 189–204). But, at a more historically specific level, we can see such male fantasies as social narratives which speak to our modern ideologies of masculinity and individualism, ideologies that are currently in crisis as women have emerged as new civic and social subjects.

One of the long-term preconditions of modernity has been the gradual movement towards greater personal self-restraint and a self-monitoring approach to one's conduct displayed in social practices as varied as the development of table manners and the norms governing warfare. In the case of the latter, the centralization of the state and its monopoly of armed force entailed a disciplining of the male body through moral and political constraints upon the earlier, less stable forms of male violence. Aesthetically, these changes were sublimated into the literary codes of chivalrous romance with their stress upon personal honour and heroic virtue. Fantasies of adventure rooted in this manly ethic of performance have been amongst the principal carriers of an ideological version of masculinity fixated upon exceptional uses of physical violence, the skilled management of the body under conditions of pressure, and upon the reconciliation of these means with some personal or social ideal. Yet as the official face of organized violence has become more and more technocratic, rendering heroism increasingly redundant, the continuing reinvention of the male adventure story has itself come under pressure, perhaps best exemplified by the complex desperation of the Rambo books and films with their remorseless stripping-back of the self to an inviolable bedrock and their noticeable ambivalence towards advanced weaponry and modern chains of command.

Male adventure forms the main stem of the hard-boiled thriller and, compared to earlier crime fiction, the tie between male hero and social structure was stretched to breaking point from the outset. These are Three-Gun Terry Mack's opening words in 1923:

> I ain't a crook, and I ain't a dick; I play the game on the level, in my own way. I'm in the center of a triangle; between the crook and the police and the victim. The police have had an eye on me for some time, but only an eye, never a hand; they don't know what to think until I've put the hooks in them. Sometimes they gun for me, but that ain't a one-sided affair. (quoted in Nolan, 1983, p. 41)

This at once projects a new social space, quite distinct from the mild rule-bending through which Sherlock Holmes occasionally brought miscreants to justice, and just a step away from that move beyond the law into criminal pathology found in the novels of Jim Thompson or Richard Stark. Justice has become a personal matter, the tension between the hero's own code of ethics and the rules of the social order recurring again and again. Cut adrift from any code but his own, violence serves as the *telos* of action for the thriller's hero, that moment when he is tested and thereby comes to know himself most truly.

Now violence is obviously a crucial part of Mayhem Parva too: if there is no body in the library, then there is no mystery. But, in contrast to the hard-boiled thriller, it is a violence that takes place off-stage, present only in its effects, and the narrative seeks to exhume its deepest causes. Hence the classic detective tale's well-known double structure in which the story of the investigation is painstakingly calibrated with the story behind the mystery. The thriller may also have this double structure, but it is always subtly transformed. Fredric Jameson once judged Raymond Chandler's novels to be 'first and foremost descriptions of searches, in which murder is involved', the search and the murder acting as 'alternating centers for our attention' (Jameson, 1970, pp. 645–8). Here the originary violence of the murder is re-enacted, multiplied, compounded: the thriller directly involves the hero in violence which it is typically necessary for him to commit himself. What is at stake, then, is a refiguring of the physicality of violence and symbolic possession of the means of violence: 'what I had was a coat, a hat, and a gun' in Philip Marlowe's immortal words. And although the initial mystery which provides the narrative's pretext may be a domestic, and sometimes a female, crime, the search for a solution is invariably displaced on to a series of confrontations with other men, anticipating the final climax. For the hero pursues his search through predominantly male-segregated milieux of work and leisure, returning obsessively to those public places like clubs and bars where men can enter alone and belong, places of camaraderie but also of danger, networks of knowledge and support where nothing is ever really certain. Such settings provide for recognition of the hero as *primus inter pares*: 'he must be the best man in his world', Raymond Chandler insisted, 'and a good enough man for any world', a risk-taker in word and deed. One consequence of this is to collapse the existing range of socially constructed masculinities into a narrow competitive individualism. In some recent thrillers like Elmore Leonard's *City Primeval: High Noon in Detroit* (1980) the suspense created through physical confrontation supervenes over mystery entirely, as 'the other random violence of the secondary plot' comes to 'contaminate the central murder' (Jameson, 1970, p. 649). Even the most placid of narratives must preserve an air of menace, that 'quality of unacted violence that held the attention' which private eye Lew Archer observes in a gangster adversary in Ross Macdonald's *The Way Some People Die* (1951): the imminent and intimidating prospect of a flashpoint of violence.

III

Coterminous with male adventure, the hard-boiled thriller has for the most part been written across the codes of sexual difference in such a way as to complicate access for women readers and writers, requiring them to negotiate a set of androcentric conventions which are, as I've already implied, deeply troubled. In the thriller male agency is staged as self-determined, active, brutal, while at the same time it is undercut by a profound sense of homosocial unease. The two are indissolubly linked for, given the premium placed upon the endurance and integrity of the male body as the condition of narrative movement, homosexuality represents the ultimate terror: the loss of self-possession and control, a threat of physical degradation through possession by an Other, and of an uncontrollable and irreversible change in sexual status. It is also the very model of failure, as incarnated in the sexual hierarchies of the prison system. Homosexuality remains unfinished business for the thriller's male order and has almost invariably been depicted in uncompromisingly bleak and contemptuous terms.

But just as events like the 1920 US presidential election – the first in which American women voted – formed a significant backdrop to changes occurring in the pages of *Black Mask*, so the accelerating disturbance in gender relations in the 1970s and 1980s has brought forth new subjectivities and new stagings of transgression and desire. In the commercial mainstream (Elmore Leonard, Andrew Coburn, Charles Willeford) we increasingly find split or mobile reader identifications as fractured narratives using multiple points of view create open possibilities for sympathy with the hero's opponents or movement across the thresholds of gender. And problematizations of sexual difference abound, provoking different kinds of confrontation. So, the most ticklish moment in Sara Paretsky's *Indemnity Only* (1982) comes when private eye V. I. Warshawski – 'karate expert, deadly markswoman and a match for twenty thugs' - attends a university women's group meeting, strictly in the line of duty. Because it invokes the concerns of contemporary feminism, while simultaneously distancing itself from them, *Indemnity Only* perhaps evades the barriers to wider acceptance faced by more recent feminist thrillers which self-consciously address themselves to women readers. Though Sara Paretsky's work has been highly acclaimed in the USA, a major problem with *Indemnity Only*, perhaps, is that its references to the specificity of women's experience may be 'concealed' by a narrative strategy which is, arguably, based upon role-reversal. So, then, if feminism is now an uncomfortable part of the thriller's cultural repertoire, it is one which necessarily calls the achievements of Hammett and Chandler into question. Down these mean streets no easy male/female transpositions are possible.

To bring this point out more forcefully, I want to conclude by contrasting a novel by one of the best of American feminist crime writers, Barbara Wilson's *Sisters of the Road*, with a text from today's hard-boiled school, Robert B. Parker's *Ceremony*. The two books have a similarity of structure and content which makes for instructive comparison. In both, what motivates the story is a concern for the fate of a runaway teenage girl, by now a stock device in the post-Chandler thriller. As a consequence, the hero or heroine has to engage with the sordid and dehumanizing world of street prostitution and each has also to deal with discomfiting questions of sexual politics.

In Parker's *Ceremony*, private eye Spenser's search for April Kyle takes him from Boston's red light district to a specialized brothel run by a corrupt educational administrator. True to form, Parker reworks the conventions and techniques of the genre to create a text that is self-referential, witty and yet infused with the author's own particular brand of moral seriousness. With its title lifted from W. B. Yeats, its climactic fight scene reminiscent of Hammett's 'The Big Knockover', *Ceremony* follows a Chandleresque path through interlocking systems of corruption, high and low, moving in and out of different social milieux with ease. The Combat Zone episodes, for example, function both to confirm Spenser's tough-guy credentials and to reveal the silenced sensitivity behind the muscle. Emotionally upset by his contact with 'a world where fifteen-year-old girls are a commodity, like electrified dildos . . . a world devoted to appetite, and commerce', Spenser is unable to drop the case. 'It's what I do', he affirms flatly, even though he knows he can have little impact upon such a world. But his chosen code permits of no exceptions, and his lover Susan Silverman laughingly compares him to the early American Puritan Cotton Mather (Parker, 1987, p. 64).

In Parker's view 'the private eye opposes to a vast and pervasive corruption his own private honour' and consistent with this Spenser takes prostitution to be ultimately an issue of individual integrity (Parker, 1971). Prostitution is 'not a single experience'; metaphorically the kinds are almost limitless', including 'everyone who does things for money instead of pride'. For Spenser, April Kyle 'has a right to be a whore if she wants to be', and given this premiss he opts for what he sees as the least destructive expedient which is to offer her the protection of an upmarket New York brothel (Parker, 1987, pp. 148–9). Interestingly, there are resonances here of the sort of hyper-individualistic rhetoric of self-ownership articulated by contemporary New Right political philosophers (Cohen, 1986). This liberal option is unavailable in Barbara Wilson's *Sisters of the Road* where prostitution is inseparable from the power relations of gender. As one character puts it, all women may not be prostitutes, but 'ain't *no* woman alive who's living her life the way she wants to, the way she *could* be living it' (Wilson, 1987, p. 183). Sisterly solidarity is a precondition of any advance against this regime, and it is therefore a particularly cathartic reversal when Trish, the runaway teenager whom heroine Pam Nilsen has zealously tried to protect throughout the book, turns into Pam's comforter and support in the penultimate chapter.

Sisters of the Road begins with the murder of a black teenage prostitute but, since the key to what happened lies with her companion Trish who disappears, the book characteristically turns into a search narrative. However, because the agency of the search is female, Barbara Wilson's book is structured quite differently to Parker's. And, because she also deliberately eschews any attempt at creating and normalizing a counter-model of female violence, the all-pervasive presence of male violence acts as a brake upon the narrative, a limit upon movement and access, threatening to hold the investigation back by transforming the heroine into a victim, interrogating the meaning of suspense in the process. In the vicious rape at the book's close male violence constitutes a violation so devastating that, despite rescue and recuperation, complete disintegration is near: 'whatever I knew or had known about myself was being crushed out of me, was spinning into fragments like a planet smashed by meteors' (ibid., p. 194). In fact, knowledge is constantly being problematized by this text. To help her to solve the murder Pam reads a diary she finds while searching the runaway prostitute's hotel room, but though 'it struck me that I knew Trish much better than she knew me . . . suddenly I wasn't sure how I could justify any of this, much less use it now' (ibid., p. 165). Pam recognizes that she can only gather information by intruding upon others, sometimes without their consent. And where assistance and information are given freely, questions of trust and vulnerability continue to bubble awkwardly up to the surface. Even a social worker like the character Beth who helps Pam with her inquiries is in 'the caring profession' because she was once 'down and out myself and I understand what the street's about' – something she cannot bring herself to discuss openly, a fear of self-disclosure which has a disastrous effect upon her closest relationships (ibid., p. 169).

In their contrasting ways each of these two thrillers explores the nature of caring relationships under extreme circumstances: in both books a childless hero/heroine tries to come to terms with the difficulties of parenting, and this is played off against the ongoing personal dramas of love and romance. Part of Spenser's appeal, for male and female readers alike, is precisely that he cares about people like April Kyle for whom no one else does, and who do not care about themselves. Moreover, although he is decidedly not, as one interviewer once suggested to the author, 'a bit of a feminist', he does lack the world-weary misogyny of a Philip Marlowe or the shrill self-righteousness of a Mike Hammer.

Nevertheless, it must be clear from my discussion that I find Parker's *Ceremony* to be the less satisfying of the two. This is because the tough-guy persona is of necessity emotionally tight-lipped, and caring has to be acknowledged carefully, obliquely. Parenting for Spenser is truly paternal and there is a marked tendency in Parker's novels for the law to be displayed as the Law of the Father, the dispensation of justice giving way to the instruction of children, their induction into Spenser's own harsh personal code. But, as Parker has observed in interview, 'Spenser can't wholly understand himself in the context of his society and in the culture in which he moves – that is, among other men', and he is therefore dependent upon women in order to make sense of his experience, personified in the emotional back-up provided by the child therapist Susan Silverman (Ponder, 1984, p. 347). Despite being told from a single, muted first person perspective, the Spenser books are divided between a world of men and a world of women, moving restlessly from one to the other. *Sisters of the Road* is also narrated in the first person but, as I've already argued, its grasp and understanding are hesitant and provisional and there are links here with 'the irregularities, insecurities, disconnections, and fragmentations' often noted as distinctive of female autobiography, making for a far more probing and unsettling text (de Courtivron, 1985, p. 48). The final positive image of Pam's body triumphantly conquering personal fear and danger, skydiving over Seattle, isn't enough to dispel the text's disquiet, nor could it be. This uncertainty is reflected in an instability of address which oscillates between speaking to and for women, and a generalized radical discourse; reflected too in Pam Nilsen's move from male to female partners in Barbara Wilson's earlier *Murder in the Collective* (1984). Perhaps, then, the real pleasures of these texts (and those that will follow) do not lie solely in their power to provoke, but rather in the way they allow us to feel identities slide and turn and float, unfolding a new kind of 'adventure in search of a hidden truth', undreamt of by Chandler (Chandler, 1980, p. 190). The stuff that dreams are made of?

Note

I'd like to thank Lenore Greensides, Cora Kaplan, Derek Longhurst and Chris Pawling for helpful discussion of many of the ideas in this essay, and Ros Billington for starting me thinking about it. It's dedicated to Mary Miller.

Bibliography

Cawelti, J. G., *Adventure, Mystery and Romance: Formula Stories as Art and Popular Culture* (Chicago: University of Chicago Press, 1976).

Chandler, R., 'The simple art of murder', in R. Chandler, *Pearls Are a Nuisance* (London: Pan, 1980).

Cohen, G., 'The ideas of Robert Nozick', in *The New Right: Image and Reality* (London: Runnymede Trust, 1986).

Courtivron, I. de, *Violette Leduc* (Boston, Mass.: Twayne, 1985).

Coward, R., *Female Desire: Women's Sexuality Today* (London: Paladin, 1984).

Denning, M., 'Cheap stories: notes on popular fiction and working class culture in nineteenth-century America', *History Workshop Journal*, issue 22 (Autumn 1986), pp. 1–17.

Holquist, M., 'Whodunit and other questions: metaphysical detective stories in post-war fiction', *New Literary History*, vol. 3, no. 1 (Autumn 1971), pp. 135–56.

Jameson, F., 'On Raymond Chandler', *The Southern Review*, vol. 6, no. 3 (July 1970), pp. 624–50.

Johnson, D., *The Life of Dashiell Hammett* (London: Chatto & Windus, 1984).

Kaplan, C., 'An unsuitable genre for a feminist?', *Women's Review*, issue 8 (June 1986), pp. 18–19.

Knight, S., *Form and Ideology in Crime Fiction* (London: Macmillan, 1980).

Mandel, E., *Delightful Murder: A Social History of the Crime Story* (London: Pluto, 1984).

Modleski, T., *Loving With a Vengeance: Mass-produced Fantasies for Women* (London: Methuen, 1984).

Moretti, F., *Signs Taken for Wonders* (London: Verso, 1983).

Morris, V. B., 'Arsenic and blue lace: Sayers' criminal women', *Modern Fiction Studies*, vol. 29, no. 3 (Autumn 1983), pp. 485–95.

Nolan, W. F., *Hammett: A Life at the Edge* (London: Barker, 1983).

Palmer, J., *Thrillers: Genesis and Structure of a Popular Genre* (London: Edward Arnold, 1978).

Parker, R. B., 'The violent hero, wilderness heritage and urban reality: a study of the private eye in the novels of Dashiell Hammett, Raymond Chandler and Ross Macdonald', PhD thesis, Boston University, 1971.

Parker, R. B., *Ceremony* (Harmondsworth: Penguin, 1987).

Ponder, A., 'A dialogue with Robert B. Parker', *The Armchair Detective*, vol. 17, no. 4 (Fall 1984), pp. 340–8.

Porter, D., *The Pursuit of Crime: Art and Ideology in Detective Fiction* (New Haven, Conn.: Yale University Press, 1981).

Quayle, E., *The Collector's Book of Detective Fiction* (London: Studio Vista, 1972).

Sayers, D. L., 'The omnibus of crime', in R. Winks (ed.), *Detective Fiction: a Collection of Critical Essays* (Englewood Cliffs, NJ: Prentice-Hall, 1980).

Symons, J., *Bloody Murder: From the Detective Story to the Crime Novel* (Harmondsworth: Penguin, 1985).

Wilson, B., *Sisters of the Road* (London: Women's Press, 1987).

5

The masculine fiction of William McIlvanney

PETER HUMM AND PAUL STIGANT

POPULAR fiction ties genre to gender with a tight pink or blue knot. Readership surveys, which discover thirty female readers of romance for every male, eight male science fiction fans for every every woman, confirm the impression given by the iconographic covers displayed in the bookshop or supermarket.[1] There we have doctor/nurse romances, horse-riding epics, Regency masquerades for her; spy mysteries, sea adventures, prisoner of war escapism for him. Even within a category such as crime fiction which attracts almost equal numbers of male and female readers, there is an understood distinction between the feminine tradition of spillikins in the parlour and the tough world of mean streets down which a male reader must go.[2]

The three terms assembled in the title of this book are a further encouragement to admit rather than ignore the partiality of reading. Moving between questions of genre, gender and pleasure has encouraged us to examine our own experience as readers in ways that have only recently been readmitted within critical bounds.[3] We have tried to recognize those personal histories of reading which lie behind the choice of which books to read, or teach, or recommend to friends. Mixing the business of writing an article about popular fiction with the pleasure of reading and talking about it has taken us down a street narrowed between the remote traditions of previous dissections of the popular and the present temptation to sit back and celebrate the discovery of a new man hero – a kind of critics' male bonding. That temptation is a dangerous one because it can lead to an over-confident reliance on the traditional simplicities of masculine virtue. Masculinity, as I shall be arguing in the first two sections of this essay, is a more complicated, more deceptive matter than it is reputed to be.

Recognizing the uses and risks of such a subjective criticism has been an important part of the recent history of studying popular fiction. Janice Radway in *Reading the Romance* made the critical break from the literary, ideological analysis of the text to the anthropological study of how readers make use of their chosen fictions in their everyday lives.[4] Yet that may be to replace one form of distancing with another. However much we learn about the knowledge and critical habits of the readers interviewed in such a study, we remain outside observers of others' pleasure. There is still, we would argue, a need for critical readings of popular fiction which can include some self-examination of ways in which a text can be used.

This chapter attempts then to read the Laidlaw novels by William McIlvanney in ways which can serve to focus questions about masculinity and our own situation as male readers and critics. As the divided structure of the essay suggests, that situation cannot be viewed from any single perspective. Moving from my initial discussion of masculine difference to Paul Stigant's emphasis on issues of class and control demonstrates our complementary theoretical interests and our belief that popular masculine fictions warrant the multiplicity of critical approaches that are applied to the literary canon or to what is now distinguished as women's writing. For there is a dispiriting theoretical conjunction which has placed popular fiction and masculinity as simple unproblematic concepts, serving as the tuxedoed background for the rich complexities of literature and the feminine.

As the title of his most recent novel *The Big Man* suggests, McIlvanney's fiction has frequently examined the key rites in a man's life: the death of a father in *Remedy Is None* (1966) and *Docherty* (1975), the insecurities of middle age in *The Big Man* (1985). But it is in two crime fictions, *Laidlaw* (1977) and *The Papers of Tony Veitch* (1983), both rewarded by the Crime Writers Association, that McIlvanney makes most interesting use of the connection between genre and gender. There is a continuing tension in these novels between the conventions – narrative and thematic – of genre and McIlvanney's investigation of the nature and consequences of masculinity. McIlvanney is using these masculine narratives to question the cultural codes and practices through which masculinity has been constructed in fiction and in history.

In describing McIlvanney's work as men's writing, there remains the question of how to develop a corresponding gendered criticism. Explicitly theoretical definitions of masculine texts are still comparatively rare. The enormous and accelerating expansion in feminist criticism has not yet prompted any equivalent sustained investigation of what might be meant by a masculinist criticism. The very awkwardness of the term suggest how far we are from a criticism which can place questions of masculine difference in the foreground instead of leaving them to be worried out by feminist critics. The recent history of feminist criticism describes an instructive trajectory from resisting the authority of male reading to celebrating a continuing feminine tradition to a more open and intertextual investigation of difference. This suggests both a paradox and a strategy for male theorists interested in the questions we are raising in this essay. For a masculine criticism needs both to respond to the arguments of feminist theory and to move on to its own discoveries; to find, as feminist writers have done, definitions of sexual and textual difference free from the narrowing limitations of old oppositions.[5]

Mary Ellmann in *Thinking About Women* has identified the critical tradition which has not helped – the phallic criticism by which Norman Mailer or Anthony Burgess or Robert Lowell protect their heroic notion of masculinity by disparaging those women who threaten it.[6] But such by now notorious comments as William Gass's suggestion that women 'lack that blood congested genital drive which energizes every great style' set up a rigidity that most men would find too uncomfortable to sustain for very long.[7] Which may be why Jerry Palmer's discussion of the 'thriller's need for a climactic ending' moves so swiftly into the language of the Fleming and Spillane novels he is analysing: 'the purpose of the "big bang" ending is to provide for the reader the simultaneous experience of intensity and release'.[8] As Richard Dyer points out, 'there is a suggestive similarity in the way both male sexuality and narrative are commonly described. Male sexuality is said to be goal-orientated; seduction and foreplay are merely the means by which one gets to the "real thing", an orgasm, the great single climax'.[9]

The objection to this wham-bam treatment of the text is not only that it ignores everything men may slowly have learned about the subtleties of sexuality but that it forces masculinity back into the most reductive biological determinism. In this it provides an uncannily distorting echo of the most sharply defined account of feminine difference which has come from psychoanalytic criticism and particularly the work of French feminists such as Hélène Cixous and Luce Irigaray.[10] There is not the room here for an extended account of their highly influential theories of an *écriture feminine* but I want to examine one tension in this work which is important to my reading of masculine fiction. Their argument moves between literary and sexual style in asserting a contrast between women's diverse and plural textuality/sexuality and the monotony of the masculine narrative/sexual drive. The pun in Irigaray's *This Sex Which Is Not One* can be read by the unwary as a negative dismissal of women's sexuality but turns around to a celebration of women's sexual totality in contrast to the unified, merely single nature of phallic sexuality. This in turn leads to a view of women's writing as essentially discontinuous, open-ended, for ever resisting any constricting conclusion.[11]

This side-trip through the opposed extremes of sexual/textual criticism is worthwhile if it leads to a fuller sense of how a masculine criticism can be constructed. One important direction is signalled by Judith Kegan Gardiner:

> We must expand psychological feminist criticism so that it can clarify how gender works everywhere in literature – in texts by both men and women; in books about identity, work and politics as well as those concerning love, marriage and the family; and in both popular communal forms and elite self-referential meditations . . . We may well find buried 'maternal' and paternal subtexts in novels by men, relationships that challenge our exclusive focus on male autonomy, individuality and difference.[12]

This change in emphasis from sexuality to gender does not mean a relieved retreat from the dangerous revelations of the personal to the safe world of the social. Instead it means considering, as

Alison Light has argued,

> ways of articulating the production in literary texts of gendered
> subjectivities within and through those other historical discourses
> which go to make up 'a sense of self' like, for example, those of class
> or race. We need an analysis of the ways in which literatures offer
> fantasised resolutions and refusals of dominant gender definitions.[13]

The notion of 'gendered subjectivity' opens a way through
the tedious road-block of public versus private, social versus
personal, which has served too often to separate male and
female. It encourages male readers and critics to work through
their own definitions of masculinity free from the dragging unease
or over-immediate denial of individual responsibility which is one
frequent result of any sustained reading of feminist criticism.

For that is the other intellectual history which informs our
interest in the possibilities of a masculine criticism. We both belong
to that generation of academics which was the first to register the
professional influence of feminism and which, however unevenly
and slowly, has begun to think through the consequences of gender
as well as of class. And that process has not stopped within our
professional lives; one immediate point of contact with feminism
is that any attempt to restrict the discussion and re-examination of
gender to the occasional equal opportunities meeting is a shallow
denial of our own subjectivity and history. What has taken longer
to discover is how to construct our own agenda and not just respond
with easy good guy nods to the issues raised by those feminists
we live and work with.

How do two novels set in the hard underworld of Glasgow fit into
this attempt to think through changing definitions of masculinity?
As anybody who begins to recall their own history of reading
knows, books have always provided both an individual source of
images and identities to try on in front of a mirrored self and a
means to share those discoveries comfortably with others. Now
it's one thing to pass around favourite *Just William* stories among
other members of the eleven plus class equally anxious to learn
the ingenious scheming that meant street credibility in 1955; it's
supposed to be another when two Humanities lecturers meet after
work to plan their contribution to a seminar on popular fiction at

the conference for Higher Education Teachers of English.[14] But I guess I am more relaxed now in admitting the continuity between those two uses of popular fiction. Reading William McIlvanney, talking about his work with friends, having them read the first draft of this article has been a useful and pleasurable way to exchange ideas on what we now mean by masculinity.

Reading and discussing McIlvanney's representation of men's conflict with a dominant masculine culture has become one way to negotiate that complicated connection between sexuality and its social construction, between individual style and a more general questioning of the conventions of gender and genre. We have in our account of McIlvanney's two Laidlaw novels tried to keep moving between these terms and so establish the open possibilities of a masculine criticism.

II

Jack Laidlaw is introduced as someone caught in a 'wrack of paradox. He was potentially a violent man who hated violence, a believer in fidelity who was unfaithful, an active man who longed for understanding . . . He knew nothing to do but inhabit the paradoxes.'[15] This may seem a familiar duality for a detective hero, even for a detective inspector in Glasgow's Serious Crimes Squad. Yet what gives these novels their originality as critiques of masculinity is McIlvanney's exploration of the narrative as well as the thematic consequence of inhabiting paradox.

The key word in McIlvanney's fiction is 'connection'. Laidlaw as a detective investigating the rape and murder of a 17-year-old girl has to assume what the reader assumes – between these seemingly random and brutal events there is a connection. As he explains to his detective constable Harkness:

'Right. There are two basic assumptions you can make. Very basic. One is that it's a fruit-machine job. Sweet mystery of life and all that. That there was no connection between the villain and the victim. Except a time and a place. The lassie was the victim of a kind of sexual hit-and-run-job. All right. If that's the case, *we've* got no chance anyway. It's up to Milligan and his soldier-ants to take the situation apart leaf by leaf. Except that, for me, putting your faith in Milligan is just a fancy term for despair.'

Harkness was niggled by the reference to Milligan but he let it go.

'So for you and me to be any use at all, we have to take the second assumption. That there *is* a connection. What happened in the park didn't fall from out the sky one day. It's got roots. And we can find these roots. So we're going to make that assumption.'[16]

Earlier Laidlaw makes the same comparison between his reliance upon a narrative imagination and the mechanical reconstruction of events that is conventional professional practice.

'The commonest mistake people make when they think about a murder [is seeing] it as the culmination of an abnormal sequence of events. But it's only that for the victim. For everybody else – the murderer, the people connected with him, the people connected with the victim – it's the *beginning* of the sequence . . .

You were asking how we can connect. That's how. Milligan and his mob can reconstruct the crime if they want. We do something very simple. We just look for whoever did it. In the lives around him, what he's done must make ripples. That's what we're looking for.'[17]

Laidlaw then assumes the role of the narrator of a story that although presently uncertain is nevertheless already completed and waiting to be recognized. However horrific the crime, and this one involves the anal rape and killing of the daughter of a brutal and brutalized man known to him, Laidlaw acts as if there is a pattern which will make sense to those who can discover the connections. That confidence rests on Laidlaw's admission of his own connection to the characters in the narrative; it is this which sets him apart from the unregenerate masculine style represented by DI Milligan, whose brutal professionalism is constantly criticized by Laidlaw.

'Milligan has no doubt.'
'How do you mean?'
'I mean if everybody could waken up tomorrow morning and have the courage of their doubts, not their convictions, the Millennium would be here. I think false certainties are what destroy us. And Milligan's full of them. He's a walking absolute.'[18]

Set against this clenched certainty is a net of other meanings of connection which place Laidlaw not as a narrator of events but as someone trying to read them. Milligan is left in the separateness of authority while Laidlaw insists on his own and others' connection and relation to what has happened.

> 'I can't stop believing that there are always connections. The idea that the bad things happen somehow of their own accord, in isolation. Without having roots in the rest of us. I think that's just hypocrisy. I think we're all accessories.'[19]

That admission of commonality with the criminal is what leads Milligan to describe Laidlaw as an amateur and himself as 'a professional [who] knows what he is. I've got nothing in common with thieves and con-men and pimps and murderers. Nothing! They're another species.'[20] Laidlaw's amateur sympathy frequently risks a sentimental literalism as in these tributes to the murdered tout Eck Adamson in *The Papers of Tony Veitch*. 'Everybody's dying should matter to somebody. The more people who cared, the closer you came to some kind of humanist salvation.'[21] 'No death is irrelevant. It's part of the pain of all of us, even if we don't notice.'[22]

This Donneish credo is central to Laidlaw's sense of himself both as a man and as a policeman. For contrary to Milligan's brusque distinction – 'He's maybe a good man. Even kind to animals probably. But he's not a good polis-man' – McIlvanney is concerned to deny any such simple opposition.[23] Harkness recognizes that there are

> two basic kinds of professional . . . There's the professionalism that does something well enough to earn a living from it. And there's the professionalism that creates a commitment so intense that the earning of a living happens by the way . . . Laidlaw was the second kind . . . He thought of Laidlaw's capacity to bring constant doubt to what he was doing and still try to do it.[24]

Professional doubt then becomes part of McIlvanney's attack upon any singular notion of masculinity. Harkness's recognition that it is possible to be both a good man and a good policeman is more than an acknowledgement of the professional usefulness of the soft cop. McIlvanney's strategy is always to refuse any tight binary opposition which separates professional from amateur, hard from soft. Laidlaw, like the private eye heroes of classic American crime fiction, sets his own credibility, learned from the streets, against the black and white simplicities shared by the career detective and the professional criminal. In this way, McIlvanney constructs a more complicated notion of masculinity than the one celebrated in the pubs and police stations of Glasgow.

One of those pubs, owned by John Rhodes, the Don of McIlvanney's Glasgow, is called 'The Gay Laddie'. Going there to meet Rhodes, Laidlaw warns Harkness, 'Do yourself a favour, don't misinterpret the name.'[25] In reinterpreting the masculine conventions of the thriller, McIlvanney makes a continuing use of the homosexual whose otherness can define the distinctiveness of the Glasgow hard man. In *Laidlaw* and *The Papers of Tony Veitch*, McIlvanney makes homosexuality into a test of his characters' sense of themselves. The uncertainties of homosexual identity are crucial to the plot of *Laidlaw*. Tommy Bryson rapes and murders a 17-year-old woman in an attempt to escape the definition placed upon him by his homosexuality. As his lover Harry Rayburn remembers, their experience of sex had been 'so good that it had frightened Tommy by offering him definition. Finding himself one thing, he had rushed to prove himself another.'[26] Against that defeated and destructive acceptance of heterosexual values, Harry sets his own

> sense of himself. He wasn't a poof, taking his identity from a failure to be something else. He wasn't gay, publicly pretending to a uniformity that had no meaning in private. He was a homosexual, like everybody else one of a kind.[27]

This clearly raises serious issues of sexual politics. In his determination to give his homosexual characters an individuality free from the insults so readily offered by the hard men of the novel, McIlvanney is led to deny any collective resistance against that stereotyping. Tommy Bryson and Harry Rayburn remain frightened victims as well as murderer and protector: they exist to be offered sympathy by Laidlaw so that he can be distinguished from the narrow prejudices that confine his colleagues as well as the regulars at the 'Gay Laddie'.

Heterosexuality is also represented as an area of contest. Laidlaw's network rarely extends to women; when they are recognized it is for their courage in surviving the bitterness of marriage. This allows Laidlaw, and especially the unattached Harkness, the pleasure of condemning the brutality of husbands who do not deserve the women they themselves find attractively vulnerable. Laidlaw's own marriage is described as a 'maze nobody had ever mapped, an infinity of habit and hurt and betrayal'[28] and in both novels there is a running rejection of the domesticity which is the conventional retreat from the real world of the streets. John Rhodes, Laidlaw and Harkness all insist on this separation between the world of women and family and the world of men, but there is an important distinction between John Rhodes's godfatherly withdrawal into the insulated comfort of 'cardigan and slippers' – 'his family was the most important thing in his life. Everything else was just building fences around them' – and the two policemen's awkward and angry frustrations with the demands of family life.[29] The hard man's sentimentality about the home encourages the easy opposition that Laidlaw is seeking to challenge; that challenge in itself involves the risk of removing sympathy from anyone who cannot remain close to a constant questioning of masculine values.

III

We would now like to turn to what 'masculine values' are being questioned in the two Laidlaw novels, and suggest that that very questioning itself depends upon who is reading these novels. What follows, then, is an account of how far for one of us our 'masculine values' were challenged as a reader.

Important in the construction of a 'masculine' criticism, I would want to argue, is a recognition of the pleasure we get as male readers from any book we are reading. That, needless to say, is easier said than done. For while it might be relatively easy to say I enjoyed that book, or that bit of that book, and I enjoyed it for the following reasons, it is not always so easy to be truly honest about from where within the total social construction of yourself as a man that enjoyment comes. Here you are acting less as an 'objective' reader of the text, and more as an 'objective/subjective' reader of yourself and of the placing of yourself, of your masculinity, within a total social formation that in part relies upon division of gender and deeply powerful stereotyping. To recognize the way your own masculinity is constructed is one thing – and difficult enough – to begin to give some objective voice to it quite another, and properly very painful. But there are other problems, too, and not least for whom in reading any one text you are speaking *as a man*. It is not simply that the nature of masculinity will differ in terms of class, of race, of age, of education, of sexual orientation, but that how your own masculinity is evoked as a reader will differ depending on how you have been trained to 'read', why you read, when you read, or whatever other multitudes of experiences you bring to the act of reading. Yet despite these problems the task is still an essential one. I want, therefore, in this part of our essay to reflect upon the pleasure I derived, as a male reader, from reading McIlvanney's two 'Laidlaw' novels.

The first thing to say is how much I enjoyed both novels. The second is that I read them 'knowingly': aware that I should be looking for the ways in which McIlvanney raised issues of masculinity within the form of the detective thriller. But, thirdly, what I had not been prepared for was that I would ask myself why I had enjoyed both books so much, and how far that enjoyment was related to my own masculinity? And, following from that, how did McIlvanney's treatment of masculinity as a problem reinforce, disturb, or more generally allow conceptions of self to surface? In an attempt to try to answer these questions what I want to offer is a *general* 'reading' of both novels (and not a close textual analysis) in terms of how I believe for *some* male readers McIlvanney subverts yet ultimately celebrates male fantasies.

The character of Laidlaw is immediately recognizable to the reader of the tough detective thriller. Where Laidlaw differs from others of his kind is that, as Peter Humm has already argued, McIlvanney points constantly to his uncertainty, his awareness of the paradoxes that shape his own identity, his self-doubt. Moreover, McIlvanney sets this form of masculinity as a positive alongside the unquestioning masculinity of such characters as Milligan, Rhodes, or even Balleter, a Glaswegian 'hard man' who returns to the city in *The Papers of Tony Veitch*. Other male characters are more ambiguously positioned: Harkness torn between Laidlaw and Milligan; the student, Gus Hawkins, in search of an 'identity'; Lennie, the apprentice thug, caught in a world of gangster fantasies. In all this, however, Laidlaw and 'his world' remain immediately recognizable. Laidlaw is the 'rogue' cop, investigating crimes *his* way, against the rules; he is a detective who knows 'the streets'; who has a list of connections in or on the fringes of the criminal underworld; he has an empathy with, even an affection for, many of the characters of this world. Further, McIlvanney gives this world authenticity through such things as the specific detailing of the geography of Glasgow, and the constant use of dialect speech. These 'realities', as always in such fiction, lend reality to the characters.

Now, it is important and appropriate that an investigation of the contours, limits and nature of masculinity should be carried out within the framework of the tough detective thriller. First, because those issues have often been – unproblematically conceived – a central theme of the genre. Second, because the very ingredients of the genre invite such an investigation. And third, because the genre has a large male readership. Where better, then, politically to raise the issue? Yet to work 'politically' does it not also have to work as popular fiction? In McIlvanney's work it does. (Or, at least, it did for me.) McIlvanney's sense of the genre is excellent, and he writes to its format with great skill. Most importantly, I knew what I was reading and where I was being taken. As a reader I could comfortably position myself in relation to a 'world' and a set of characters that I 'knew' from a reading of the genre over the years, and accept the *narrative* journey I was being taken on through that 'world'. However, significantly, that sense of comfort was not disturbed by McIlvanney's use of the genre to raise issues around the nature and construction of masculinity. In that sense, I suppose, the novels might be said to have worked. But, equally, why was my own sense of masculinity not disturbed?

First, I came to realize as I read *Laidlaw* that it was because I was a heterosexual male reader. The crime Jack Laidlaw is investigating in that novel is the anal rape and murder of a young woman by a young man who is deeply disturbed by doubts as to his own sexuality. It can be argued that McIlvanney does not present this as Tommy Bryson's 'problem', rather the problem resides in a society that does not allow him to recognize and accept his sexuality. Tommy, then, and Jenny Lawson, the woman he brutally murders, both become *victims*. And that is a role too commonly ascribed to groups such as women and gay men. Hence, the question that raises is: if I were a woman or a gay man could I read *Laidlaw* in the comfortable, easy way that I did? McIlvanney's assumption, it seems to me, is that the reader will be able to identify with Laidlaw and 'his world' because the reader like Laidlaw is a heterosexual male. Indeed, that identification is, in some ways, made all the easier because of the presentation of Laidlaw as a complex personality, and in particular as a heterosexual male who refuses to make the easy judgements, that other men in the novel make, on the actions or motivations of people like Tommy Bryson.

The second major security the male reader is provided with, paradoxically enough, is the character of Laidlaw himself. Laidlaw may be constantly informed by his own uncertainty, but for the reader he always remains *in control*. In those few moments where he is not, at home for example, his wife Ena is presented as an unsympathetic character so that we men, along with Laidlaw, are pleased to escape. Again, it is worth asking, what would female readers make of Ena – the classic stereotype of the wife who does not understand her man? For the rest Laidlaw 'knows' the world he moves in, and he can survive in that world not, it is true, through his physical prowess but through his knowledge and understanding. Laidlaw's control is an intellectual control. Partly it has to do with language: he uses words like weapons – he uses them to hurt people, to puncture pomposity, to gain control in different situations. But in whatever way, language gives Laidlaw power. Laidlaw's control is further enhanced by the fact that despite his supposed uncertainty he has a 'philosophy', a worked-out view of the world. Laidlaw's philosophy sets him apart from the crowd, from other policemen, from other men. He is a real individual(ist).

There are some powerful masculine myths buried within these aspects of Laidlaw's personality; myths created and re-created in so many novels, films and TV programmes. He is the man alone, the 'Knight Errant of the Crime Squad' (Ena's bitter description in *Laidlaw*, p. 66); the man whose sharpness of intellect, whose control of words and ideas, whose 'knowledge', make him a power to be recognized on the mean streets of Glasgow. The masculine myth, then, embodied in Laidlaw is the individual power of *his* personality: his refusal to be shaped or determined by the world he inhabits. He does his 'own thing'. He constantly refuses to relinquish the power he has over others: he chooses when to be at home and when not; he chooses when to see his lover; he chooses to investigate crimes outside 'normal' police procedure. Laidlaw might 'inhabit the paradoxes', but he does it without giving up power. For a character who argues passionately for doubt as against conviction, Laidlaw is a remarkably uncompromising person.

Laidlaw's *control*, it seems to me, is important. Remove control from the male hero and what is created is a much more disturbing notion of masculinity. But it is also the nature of Laidlaw's control that is important. The character of Laidlaw, I believe, will hold a particular attraction for the male, middle-class reader. That attraction is, in part, based on his self-awareness and his understanding of the motivations of others and, in part, on his ability to move with ease through very differing 'class' worlds (something which is particularly marked in *The Papers of Tony Veitch*). To 'know' and be able to move through the world of the university, the suburb, the hard-men's pubs, or the 'mean streets' is something, I suspect, that appeals to many middle-class male readers. And to this, of course, we can add Laidlaw's intellect and 'philosophy', and, finally, his essential liberalism and humanity, his self-doubt and anxiety. The point I am making is that the character of Laidlaw reconciles liberal bourgeois '*Angst*' and self-doubt with the tough, street-wise cop. There is, I would suggest, something peculiarly male and middle-class about such a reconciliation; something that makes doubt and uncertainty into a positive set of values while crucially not allowing those values to undermine personal control. The bourgeois male can feel that he really does have control over the whole world, while at the same time priding himself on not being an unreconstituted male chauvinist pig.

Yet to argue this is, in some ways, to be unfair to McIlvanney, because it is important to raise questions about the readership of his detective fiction. Whose conception of masculinity is he putting at issue? McIlvanney himself is reported to have answered to the question 'Who are you writing for?', 'For those who don't read my books.'[30] So, if indeed McIlvanney has a particular audience in mind, is he seeking to unsettle a particular type of masculinity? I think he is, and does. And to understand how he does it we need to concentrate less on the character of Laidlaw himself, and more on the distinction that McIlvanney makes between tourists and travellers.

McIlvanney's distinction between tourists and travellers provides another route for the reader to negotiate the novels:

> 'Well, think of it this way,' Laidlaw said. 'There are tourists and travellers. Tourists spend their lives doing a Cook's Tour of their own reality. Ignoring their slums. Travellers make the journey more slowly, in greater detail. Mix with the natives. A lot of murderers are, among other things, travellers. They've become terrifyingly real for themselves. Their lives are no longer a hobby. Poor bastards. To come at them, you've got to become a traveller too.'[31]

Readers enter the world of McIlvanney's fiction as a tourist, recognizing the style but not the particular accent of his characters – the insistently phonetic Glaswegian is a constant reminder of difference for the non-Scot – and having to remain alert and open for the clues that allow them to become travellers. The reader is forced like Harkness to keep listening to the travel guide offered by Laidlaw. Yet what Harkness describes as the 'Laidlaw effect' is designed not to make things easy and familiar but to force a recognition of the 'strangeness of things'. . . . 'One day of [Laidlaw] was enough to baffle your preconceptions and make you unfamiliar with yourself.'[32]

'Making it strange', 'defamiliarization', are key terms in the critical theory of the Russian formalists who first described how the 'junior branch' of popular fiction might usefully disrupt notions of literature.[33] It is finally the formal effect of Laidlaw's insistence upon complication and uncertainty that makes McIlvanney's crime fiction a radical critique of masculine style. Those complications are to be discovered not only in the mysteries of male personality but within the narrative that describes them. Laidlaw insists that a case cannot be closed; McIlvanney works against the conventions of closure that have been the staple formula of crime fiction. Laidlaw rejects Harkness's congratulations on solving the crime:

> 'You don't solve crimes . . . you inter them in facts, don't you?'
> 'How do you mean?'
> 'A crime you're trying to solve is a temporary mystery. Solved it's permanent.'[34]

McIlvanney then resists the single-minded conclusion of conventional masculine narrative and moves instead towards a quieter, more open ending, which can be described as feminine but which we would prefer to call back into another masculine tradition – one which proves a proper respect for the difficult necessity of doubt. McIlvanney's work stands against or slips fluently around those paralysing polarities which have served to excuse the slow development of masculine criticism. Reading his fiction requires an equal attention to genre and gender but this cannot hide beneath a cautious neutrality. Whether we are reading popular fiction or within the canon, we need to be more aware of the gendered nature of that reading. That is one thing we can be sure about.

Notes

1 These figures come from Euromonitor, *The Book Report 1986*, Consumer Market Survey of Publishing Trends, Table Reference: RSGB/Euromonitor, p. 27. My thanks to Lorraine Gammon for telling me about them.

2 Raymond Chandler's own masculine criticism of the detective genre can be found in 'The simple art of murder', first published in 1944. It is reprinted in *The Second Chandler Omnibus* (London: Hamish Hamilton, 1973).

3 Elizabeth Freund's *The Return of the Reader: Reader-Response Criticism* (London: Methuen, 1987) is the most useful introduction. Jonathan Culler provides a more pointed analysis of 'stories of reading' in *On Deconstruction* (London: Routledge & Kegan Paul, 1983; originally published in the USA in 1982).

4 Janice Radway, *Reading the Romance: Women, Patriarchy and Popular Literature* (London: Verso, 1987; originally published in the USA in 1984).

5 A recent and very helpful collection of essays on these questions is Alice Jardine and Paul Smith (eds.), *Men in Feminism* (London: Methuen, 1987).
   Peter Schwenger's *Phallic Critiques: Masculinity and Twentieth-Century Literature* (London: Routledge & Kegan Paul, 1984; originally published in the USA in 1984) is an intelligent, pioneering work of masculine criticism.

6 Mary Ellmann, *Thinking About Women* (London: Virago, 1979; originally published in the USA in 1968).

7   William H. Gass, *New York Times Book Review*, 24 October 1976, p. 2. Quoted by Schwenger, *Phallic Critiques*, p. 75.
8   Jerry Palmer, *Thrillers: Genesis and Structure of a Popular Genre* (London: Edward Arnold, 1978), p. 65.
9   Richard Dyer, 'Male sexuality in the media', in Andy Metcalf and Martin Humphries (eds), *The Sexuality of Men* (London: Pluto, 1985), p. 41.
10 There are now two Readers which introduce the work of French feminists. Elaine Marks and Isabelle de Courtivron (eds), *New French Feminisms* (Brighton: Harvester, 1981; originally published in the USA in 1981) and Toril Moi (ed.), *French Feminist Thought* (Oxford: Blackwell, 1987). Toril Moi's *Sexual/Textual Politics* (London: Methuen, 1985) provides a good critical introduction.
11 Luce Irigaray, *Ce Sexe Qui N'Est Pas Un* has now been translated by Catherine Porter, *This Sex Which Is Not One* (Ithaca, NY: Cornell University Press, 1985).
12 Judith Kegan Gardiner, 'Mind mother: psychoanalysis and feminism', in Gayle Greene and Coppelia Kahn (eds), *Making a Difference: Feminist Literary Criticism* (London: Methuen, 1985), p. 139.
13 Alison Light, 'Writing fictions: femininity and the 1950s', in Jean Radford (ed.), *The Progress of Romance: the Politics of Popular Fiction* (London: Routledge & Kegan Paul, 1986), p. 147.
14 Two acknowledgements are due here. The first is to Dan Humm who has brought me back to the pleasures of Richmal Compton. The second is to the other members of the H.E.T.E. seminar, especially Roger Bromley, Peter Brooker and Derek Longhurst, who added so many ideas of their own to the discussion.
15 William McIlvanney, *Laidlaw* (London: Coronet, 1979; first published by Hodder & Stoughton, 1977), p. 9.
16 ibid., p. 105.
17 ibid., pp. 72 and 73.
18 ibid., p. 134.
19 ibid., p. 186.
20 ibid., p. 52.
21 William McIlvanney, *The Papers of Tony Veitch* (London: Coronet, 1983; first published by Hodder & Stoughton, 1983), p. 36.
22 ibid., p. 161.
23 McIlvanney, *Laidlaw*, p. 51.
24 ibid., p. 143.
25 ibid., p. 94.
26 ibid., p. 113.
27 ibid., p. 112.

28 ibid., p. 9.
29 ibid., p. 127.
30 cited at the H.E.T.E. conference seminar.
31 McIlvanney, *Laidlaw*, p. 104.
32 ibid., p. 142.
33 Tony Bennett's *Formalism and Marxism* (London: Methuen, 1979) is the most helpful introduction to their work.
34 McIlvanney, *Laidlaw*, p. 219.

6

Rewriting the masculine script:

The novels of Joseph Hansen

ROGER BROMLEY

ONE WAY in which myths of power are constructed is through the mediating codes of masculinity, inscribed in numerous cultural forms. In many popular fictions these codes are culturally dominant to the point where they have become naturalized and taken for granted.

The organizing of the male subject in the 'tough guy' tradition of crime fiction is through the construction of a 'libidinal economy' based upon an ideology of masculinity. The texts become a general 'battlefield' where the struggle for signifying supremacy is forever re-enacted. Victory is equated with activity, and defeat, ultimately, with passivity. I say 'ultimately' because, of course, figures like Brigid O'Shaughnessy in *The Maltese Falcon*, and others with comparable power, threaten 'masculinity' by their *activity* until they are finally eliminated. Women are constructed passively or they are not allowed to survive. Many classic crime fictions begin with the death or disappearance of a male figure, then proceed to eliminate women at the level of language and spatial/territorial significance. In *The Maltese Falcon* Sam Spade says at one point, 'This is my city and my game.' Public spaces are the only 'knowable community' and, it is implied, not available to the female who, to survive, must either mimic or defer to male power and inhabit the territory of the 'private'.

The basic gender model around which the genre is constructed is the symbolic opposition between the male body, self-enclosed and directed towards the outside world with everything projected away from self, and the female body, modest, restrained, reserved and directed towards the inside and the dark, damp house of the inevitably soiled woman. When not directed to the inside, the woman is threatening because she potentially becomes the object of male desire. The opposition between the centrifugal, male orientation with its movement upwards and outwards towards other men, and the centripetal, female orientation, which is the principle of the organization of domestic space, is also (ideologically) the basis of the relationship of each of the sexes to their mental being and their sexuality. Reason, logic, deduction are located in the sphere of maleness, distanced from the, possibly threatening and uncontrollable, realm of feeling and instinct, the sphere of the female. As I hinted earlier, often the most subversive female figure in crime fiction is the one who is able to stimulate and fake 'maleness'. The specifically male relation to sexuality is based upon sublimation and euphemization, ways of refusing any direct expressions of sexuality and encouraging its transfigured manifestation in the form of manly prowess; the affirmation of potency through repetition.[1]

The transgressive female (or the homosexual male, as in the case of Joel Cairo in *The Maltese Falcon*) threatens the self-enclosure and intimacy of the ever-vigilant male and refuses, or subverts, a discourse dominated by male values of virility. The paradigmatic case in crime fiction sets the male body and the world in a particular order by certain symbolic manoeuvres. The 'deadly' female invades this 'body-geography' (analogous to the city streets) and destabilizes the textual orderings of signification. In other words, the dispositions of gender in 'masculine' fictions are symbolically, not biologically, defined. They are based upon a determinate social definition of the functions of men and women in an ideologically defined vision of the sexual division of labour. In this division, more *power* (in terms of self and social imagery) is attributed to the male than to the female. So this opposition between the differential availability of symbolic capital to 'masculinity' and 'femininity' is the fundamental principle of the division of the social and cultural in crime fictions. Its potential destabilization is the principal narrative strategy.

In the 'Dave Brandstetter' novels of Joseph Hansen,[2] the death or disappearance of a father, son, or husband is almost always the precipitating moment of the text, as it is in the 'classic' mode, but what follows is an inquiry into the ideological bases of norms of gender and sexuality. In these texts, destabilization is not simply a matter of plot, but the basic ordering principle of the narrative.

The public and conventionally sublimated sexuality of the male is undermined by a domestication of maleness (where interiors are not retreats or recuperative spaces) and a 'speaking' of a previously secret and/or alienated sexuality. The texts mark a partial break with the ritual logic with which popular cultural forms help to organize the system of social/symbolic values of masculinity and femininity. They begin to trace lateral possibilities, bringing the 'deviant' and 'eccentric' into the centres of the cultural/social text, by constructing male bodies as subjects and objects of the sexual 'look', rather than as the conventional 'fighter' body shaped in, and for, violence.

Usually, gender language in the masculine genre is a vernacular/ideolectic form of euphemization and sublimation, locked inside normative gender categories as a way of not confronting the roots of desire and the economy, which are displaced and masked by the production of a defensive, symptomatic language, austere and object-like, based upon the 'pure, detached, aesthetic gaze'. The language constructs an illusion of male autonomy, with a tendency to formalism and the privileging of the constantly repeated signifier over the signified, particularly the female signified. It uses 'street language' as a *cover*, a literary code of masculinity, public and urban, driven by the fear of expropriation to establish power over women's sexuality by means of the appropriation of discursive space through violence as the medium of masculinity. It is a paranoid idiom, a form of verbal male bonding, exclusive, woman-less, and confined to surfaces, exteriors, and the extrinsics of language. This 'male' language is 'rational' and transcendent.

The 'pure' masculine language perceives as 'real' that which it nominates as *real* and involves the categorical assertion of the primacy of male form, given that the ideology of masculinity is partly based upon a fear of the inadequacy of the male sexual performance. These spare, controlled and self-enclosed narratives refuse excess, carnival, or any category inversion (although the edges of the text are often crowded with these) and equally refuse to celebrate the body (except for the stylized, demobilized female), the emotional and the sentimental. Any challenge to, or loss of, individuality either in relationships or the collective, is resisted. The primary male figure in the crime fiction supervises and polices the public spaces as a vigilante protecting the symbols of masculinity, shielding the male self and its rituals from the dissolving of gender boundaries.

If, as is often claimed, men are invited to recognize themselves in the different installations of the masculine myth, and popular cultural forms help to generate and circulate this myth, how do we make sense of a number of texts which take that myth, not as their centre of construction, but as their point of departure? Joseph Hansen's work leads us to consider how far the popular challenges or, more accurately perhaps, extends a culture of masculinity. The work does not subvert the ideologies of masculinity as such, but opens up their narrowly defined criteria to include thrillers constructed around the figure of a middle-aged gay insurance claims investigator.

Hansen extends the possibilities of the genre by imagining a range of male gender social roles with their own norms, particular identity and structure. In so doing, not only the sexuality but also the sociocultural realm of men is pushed beyond the dominant and limited images of masculinity which prevail in popular cultural forms and social experience. What Hansen does not really do is question the forms of patriarchy or the principal characteristics of the capitalist era which have together shaped many of the ideas and ideals of masculinity around competition, property, acquisition and violence. His is essentially a revisionist project, based upon a liberal-humanist, individualist premiss which constructs its critique of United States society in what I would describe as a cultural-ecological fashion. In other words, poverty, waste, corruption and violence are at the root of each of the fictions, but the possibilities of change are posed within an ethical and personal framework.

Hansen uses southern California as the background of his fictions, most of which are centred around the figure of Dave Brandstetter. In 1965, Hansen became a founder and editor with Don Slater of the pioneering homosexual journal, *Tangents*. He has said that his purpose in writing is 'to deal with homosexuals and homosexuality as an integral part of contemporary life, rather than something bizarre and alien'.[3] This ties in with certain moves in the 1950s and early 1960s to improve the image of homosexuals, to promote self-acceptance as part of what was known as the 'homophile' movement. Hansen's fictions are moderate and reformist, separate from the militant and radical gay consciousness of the post-1969 phase of liberation. Richard Stevenson's *Death Trick* (1981), on the other hand, has a central detective figure who is linguistically, culturally and sexually part of this consciousness, and the writing has a political cutting edge and insider-experiential quality lacking in Hansen.[4] It is, however, published by a 'minority' press and not easily accessible in the UK. Hansen's Brandstetter has few doubts or fears about his sexuality, nor any sense of stigma or self-hatred, although other characters in the texts are not free of these. In Brandstetter's role-modelling there is little specific reference to gay cultural norms (if such exist), with the exception of *Nightwork* and *The Man Everybody Was Afraid Of*.

In a deliberately quiet and restrained way, Hansen breaks the taboo on presenting homosexuality positively in popular fiction, and in the process questions family structures, gender categories and sexual codes. His preferred sexual model is a closed couple relationship based, in some ways, upon a duplication of heterosexual codes stressing that homosexuals are like anyone else. However, within the texts themselves, Brandstetter's father's own multiple marriages (nine) suggest the inappropriateness of the model by its parody of insecure and extravagant 'manliness'. Relationships in Hansen are structured around the traditional liberal idea of romantic love; there is no sense, as in Stevenson, of the hunt for sex or sexual adventure, but more of 'romance, intimacy and sustained partnership'[5] and serial monogamy (Brandstetter has three, live-in male partners in the seven novels to date).

Critics have frequently compared Hansen's work with Chandler, Hammett and Macdonald, but, except in certain respects, the links are mostly superficial. One link with Hammett and McIlvanney is the way in which 'tenderness', particularly between men, is the only form of love which seems to be *unconditional*. In writers like Spillane, Fleming and Robert Parker (and thousands of imitators in the thriller genre), the languages of 'masculinity' have an over-insistence which comes close to parody at times – defensive, brutalizing and territorial – and are alienating in the sense that they suggest their roots explicitly in the cultural and the ideological. They sound like 'quotations' from already existing, preconstructed roles, performances and linguistic presumptions: a common cultural framework. An excessive virility is evoked through fist and gun, to fortify and defend male autonomy (the characteristic form which insecurity takes). At their best, Hammett and Chandler simultaneously generate and distance these codes by registering the vulnerability of their heroes explicitly (as does McIlvanney who 'quotes' the codes and, in some ways, places them). Hansen 'quotes' the codes in order to deconstruct them. 'You a real, live private eye. I didn't know they had those. You don't look it, you don't act it.' And, 'He had never wanted a gun . . . for decades he managed without one. But times had changed. The game he loved had turned lethal.' And, ' "I don't want to shoot anybody," Cecil said'; and 'Because up in the kitchen, Cecil was crying. It was the saddest sound Dave ever heard.'[6]

Hansen is constructing an ethical symbolism around and through gay identities. His world is distinctively created out of middle-class ideology – art, classical music, tasteful commodities, economic 'liberty', combined with self-discipline and an internalized desire to work. Brandstetter has a 'designer' eye for colour, shape, structure, food, cars and other artefacts. This particular gay construction is part of a liberal bid for respectability and equal access to the male symbolic order, rather than a displacement of it. It is 'assimilationist', a process of normalization.

The private eye traditionally prefers to live alone, without social or family ties, which he finds as threatening to his integrity as the corrupt world in which he lives. Autonomy is identity. He must remain always hard, tough and dangerous, never soft or vulnerable. Brandstetter, on the other hand, has a series of monogamous relationships – the last one, with a young black media worker, is sustained over three novels. Often there is a stress on the domestic and on interiors. In *Skinflick*, for instance, there is a detailed, four-page description of Dave's washing up and tidying up in an alcoholic's motel room. In *The Man Everybody Was Afraid Of* the flat which Dave shares with his lover, Doug, is described in terms of its narrow, walled stairs, its awkward halls and its emptiness – semiotically producing the conditions of a dying relationship and signifying the generically alien sphere of the 'personal'.

By referring to three texts in particular I hope to indicate some of the main characteristics of the construction of sexuality, the placing of contesting ideologies of masculinity and the ways in which the thriller form is extended by Hansen's fictions. The three texts are *Troublemaker* (1975); *Skinflick* (1979); and *Nightwork* (1984). *Skinflick* is interesting, incidentally, because in it Hansen exposes the contradictions in the apocalyptic fears and harsh moralistic judgements of the Moral Majority – that very grouping which,

since AIDS, has generated a hysteria and scapegoating of the gay
community. It is their opposition to homosexuals which unites the
groups which make up the Moral Majority. The present wave of
fundamentalist anti-gay pressure is identified by Altman[7] as beginning in 1977, the year of Anita Bryant's Dade County campaign and
of a national scare against 'kiddie porn'. The vigilantes in *Skinflick*
regularly raid the aptly named Keyhole bookshop and condemn the
'kiddie porn' magazines, but one of their most zealous members,
the born-again Dawson, is found to be a paedophile. The murder
of Church stalwart Dawson and the subsequent discovery of his
infatuation for a child prostitute, Charlene, forms the basis of much
of the text. In each novel, the thriller enigma, or crisis, is built into
the principal moral/ethical problems; the detection/mystery element
is secondary to all the other complications thrown up. In fact, the
'presenting' mystery leads to a range of others, problematized around
certain paradigms: parenting, the family and heterosexual mores.

The texts centre on professional middle-class America and its
edges, repressions, absences. Its 'folk wisdom', common sense,
either/or propositions and essentialist categories are all questioned
and links are made with the underside of that milieu – racism,
poverty, bigotry, fear and hate. There are, the novels suggest, moral
ghettoes as well as social ones. In *Skinflick* a series of events links
the expensive Hillcrest neighbourhood with the drugs, prostitution
and destitution of Sunset Strip. The text proposes continuities, by
juxtaposition, which convention would separate.

In terms of the larger and earlier (pre-AIDS) moral debate about
gay 'promiscuity' versus 'monogamy', Hansen's position has always
been clearly in favour of the latter. The mainstream American gay
'life-style' or 'scene' – 'an unstable blend of trendiness, fellowship,
hedonism and sexual and romantic innovation'[8] – is explicitly
targeted for criticism in *Troublemaker*. The gay world of carnival,
insolence and improvization is far removed from the isolation and
repression of 'closet' homosexuals in *Gravedigger* (1982) and *Fade
Out* (1970). In the former text, Charles Westover is made to eat the
heart of his lover, Don, by his daughter and her Manson-like lover.
What Altman calls 'the psychic damages of social invisibility' for
pre-liberation homosexuals is a frequent theme in Hansen's fictions
– the trauma of masking and concealment. Hansen's narratives
form part of a 1970s cultural mediation of gay visibility beyond the

public stereotype of limp-wristed 'queen', particularly important to a generation (which Brandstetter symbolizes) confined by subterfuge and invisibility. Several of the characters are gay men lacking in self-worth and masquerading as 'straight' American family men. In the painful process of disengaging from the paradigmatic family, the tyrannies and deformation of the structure itself are exposed.

The Man Everybody Was Afraid Of (1978) focuses on conflicts within the politics of Gay Liberation, yet here the reformist figure, a wealthy man working with laws, resolutions and councillors, is contrasted negatively with the courage of those advocates of a radical style, a street presence and the collective affirmation of gayness. It is the only text which attempts to engage with the issue of gay rights and politics, but these are, nevertheless, secondary to the working-out of individualized conflicts. One of the gay radicals is held on a charge of murdering the homophobic police chief of a small town. In many of the texts, homophobia is traced beyond its symptomatic forms to its roots in male insecurities.

Brandstetter is not seen as a figure overwhelmed by the increasing demand to fulfil the specification of 'masculinity', nor is his gayness perceived as part of a deficit culture. In an article written in 1963 – 'The flight from masculinity' – the root problem of homosexuals was seen in the following way: 'They cannot compete. They always surrender in the face of impending combat.'[9] Maleness here is inscribed in the forms of competition and combat – the winner and the hero. If anything, the world of the novels is one which the indices of normative male sexuality have distorted and abused. The texts inhabit the boundaries of heterosexuality – Brandstetter's father's nine wives; the preoccupation with under-age and child sex in *Skinflick*; the Manson-like behaviour in *Gravedigger*. By this boundary analysis, the texts imply an analogy with the boundaries of homosexual desire which are always seen, in homophobic scenarios, as the centres. By establishing a continuum of heterosexual and homosexual 'deviance', a coexisting set of norms is proposed. Brandstetter behaves in a way – non-violent, unarmed, gentle, domestic – which refuses and shows the limits of the combat model of masculinity. Vietnam is often cited as the classic instance of the psychic damage inflicted by a warrior culture.[10]

Part of Hansen's achievement is that he has occupied one of the archetypal sites of popular masculinity – the private eye –

and emptied it of its classic content by a process of inversion and reversal, while still constructing effective thrillers. It is the violent, the tough and the insensitive who are seen as adaptive failures, unable to meet the requirements of a changing male gender role. He also breaks with another psychoanalytic cliché – homosexuals as aspirants to perpetual adolescence – by showing many 'normal' males caught in this posture. There is a recurring infantilization, disabling, or idealization of the female. The godlike father, with his nine wives, also suggests a parodying of the Oedipal obsession. Brandstetter does display some age and body anxiety but it does not manifest itself in adolescent-style fantasies. As well as writing mysteries (the heart of which is often heterosexualities) Hansen is also concerned with constructing positive images of homosexualities, with, admittedly, a fairly conventional, class-specific, *Gay News* set of possibilities. Nevertheless it has to be remembered that Hansen had published two Brandstetter novels while the American Psychiatric Association still listed homosexuality as a mental illness (this was changed in 1973).

Another factor in Hansen is that the 'evil' or 'negative' features are not simply constructed in relation to the positive moral image of the hero, but to a wider ethical symbolism, partly generated by the Vietnam experience which put into dispute a long tradition of aggressive masculinity ('we had met the enemy and they were us') now seen as gratuitous brutality. Vietnam, of course, is a war still being fought in popular cultural terms, as well as by figures like Colonel North and Admiral Poindexter. *Skinflick*, in particular, links the war-crazed Billy Jim Tackaberry with the ways of seeing associated with the Moral Majority, caught in their own myths of family and masculinity. Tackaberry retreats from the city and people, opening up another frontier; he is always styled in the western regalia of one of America's most enduring images of 'manhood'. His figure conflates and problematizes a number of archetypal representations of masculinity. The book is very much about *typecasting*; 'That's what Skinflick means – what you see ain't what you think, but it makes you think it is' (p. 88). This definition, interestingly, is given by Randy Van, a transvestite who constructs himself in and through camp discourse, and who says, at one point, 'The make-up makes me sweat too much. My identity runs' (p. 137). In a sense, this identity-running theme is at the centre of all Hansen's texts – transgressive figures and themes dispersing the dominant scripts, images and codes of masculinity and *textualizing* (by which I mean constructing narratives which install and recognize the culturally marginalized) homosexual relationships with their own authentications. The orientation of everything in the text around the image-industry deliberately addresses one of the central determinations in American society.

Brandstetter is also out of the 'greening' of America in some ways – the emphasis on the commodity spectacle; consumerism; the sensual immediacy of things; changes of clothes and consciousness to re-create the white, middle-class male. His life-style is, in a sense, shaped from the counter-culture but, essentially, is middle-class and style-oriented – *Brand*stetter: car, clothes, food, sophisticated sound system and taste in modernist music (Berg, etc.). In sum, Brandstetter resembles what Barbara Ehrenreich calls 'the seventies combination of pop psychology and men's liberation ideology', as much as he reflects any particular gay identity.[11] This male liberation was modelled, in many ways, upon women's liberation, and as a genuine response to feminism, as well as being a feature of American tolerance (by the mid-1970s) of people who rejected marriage as a way of life and gave rise to an entire 'singles industry'. Brandstetter is part of this wider internal and therapeutic change in the male, but, for Hansen, it is always a matter of psychology, rather than politics; it is a cultural transformation marked by a certain loss of defensiveness and the male fear of castration.

Hansen's writing, initially, was part of a new popular cultural vocabulary of the time, a rescripting of male gender roles. The texts explore a number of roles generated by, and against, received gender stereotypes. It marks a move towards 'self-authenticity' – a variable and fluid, mobile central figure contrasted with the static, blocked, competitive and repressed stereotypes in the text. At first, Hansen's construction of Brandstetter is close to a process of 'feminization' (as it is ideologically conceived). It also relates to the idea of an alternative life-style and of gay people as an ethnicized minority coded in terms of sexual orientation and life-style. Hansen is ambivalent about this – Brandstetter identifies with gay people, but never in any active or militant sense; the primary bond is that produced by the individual network. If anything, gay visibility in the late 1970s advertised its sexuality and constructed itself around a number of 'masculine' poses and image-styles. (This is an obvious over-simplification of a complex range of sexualities and styles, but Altman and others argue that this 'hyper-maleness' was a distinctive characteristic.)[12]

In *Troublemaker*, for instance, although shared positions are acknowledged among gay *professionals*, the notion of an identifiable community is rejected. At the 'Mr Marvellous' contest among the gay bars, the patrons are described as 'sad, ageing and interchangeable', and 'the clothes, the grooming varnished them to sameness' (an explicit distancing from a public 'scene' life-style). A critique is also offered of the gay appropriation of a cult of masculinity circulated through the 'macho' Western and reminiscent of the back lot of a defunct film studio, 'lariats coiled and lacquered into uselessness . . . strictly ornamental'. This draws attention to the ways in which 'masculinity', deliberate 'gender eccentricity', is constructed as a matter of style, of *forms* without function, but it misses the possible iconic wit and parody – campness – in these styles, given their origin in 'male bonding' and *their* appropriation by heterosexual, middle America. To Hansen, it is simply pastiche, but as Altman points out, 'the man dressed as a stereotypical man is also mocking the assumption that to be gay is to want to be a woman'.[13]

The gap between the world of baths, bars and cruising and Brandstetter's is articulated by the figure in *Troublemaker* (the troublemaker, in fact) who has lived a criminalized, derelict gay life far removed from the professional life-style of the central figures:

> I saw you [Brandstetter] come in and I was pretty surprised. I mean, I knew you were gay – I can always tell. But I didn't think you'd come for this. I thought your lifestyle would be different. You'd have a lover, somebody permanent. And you'd go places like ballets and operas and plays and art galleries. Together. You wouldn't cruise bars like this, and baths, and all that.[14]

The very 'syntax of envy' suggests professional, middle-class, heterosexual mimicry as the gay 'norm' set up by the homophile movement prior to the 1970s. Where McIlvanney constantly focuses on the social, political and cultural co-ordinates of crime, Hansen keeps much closer to the surfaces, the 'psychologies'. In the former writer, this quoted exchange would be part of a critical placing of a certain set of assumptions; in this text, it is coded in terms of what is seen as the characteristically self-pitying envy of this negatively constructed figure, Taylor. Nevertheless, the whole sequence is an important contradiction which points to Brandstetter's closeness to the liberation, fluidity and 'humanization' of middle-class discourse and consciousness-raising: personal growth. His relationships are outside the governing philosophy of the hedonism of gay Los Angeles. Even when he invites Cecil Harris to live with him there is little sense of his 'keeping a young man' as a pastime or for fashion's sake. In fact, Cecil is quite explicit about not wanting to be 'kept'; their relationship is based upon companionship – a marriage model – not sexual adventure, unlike the negatively constructed bi-sexual, Miles Edwards in *Gravedigger*, who wants to marry, and have sex with, both Brandstetter and Cecil.

The novels do, however, make public, *textualized* and 'speakable' certain features of gay desire which marked a quite radical departure in popular forms. With Brandstetter, Hansen has perhaps created part of a gay liberal 'fantasy' that all homosexuals are basically the same as everyone else – as we have seen, the 'suburban couple' image is certainly strong. However, the transvestite figures in both *Skinflick* and *Nightwork* are coded positively (in the former text, there is one of only two instances in all seven novels, of Brandstetter being involved in 'casual' sex). In *Nightwork*, the ageing, rich, closet transvestite is surrounded by high walls, pillars and iron gates behind which he lives out fantasies based on an early love affair with screen idol Ramon Novarro (in his portrait, Novarro is for ever young). This is an interesting perspective because of Novarro's marketing as a supreme icon of heterosexual masculinity. Linked with this is De Witt Gifford's (the transvestite) protection of the young Hispanic gang leader, a Novarro look-alike and also gay, but who is *publicly* meaningful only in terms of his 'macho' imaging. His name Silencio refers both to his hidden sexuality and also to Novarro – the silents star.

These positive codings are an important strategy, even if based upon fairly simple image reversals; as so often, fear/mocking of transvestitism is fear of homosexuality itself ('to be gay is to want to be a woman'). In a novel about the Moral Majority (*Skinflick*) this is significant because of the right's caricature of the homosexual as 'effeminate' and 'pederastic', and it is also critical of bourgeois gay attitudes of exclusion (of transvestites) and collusion with a form of homophobia. Hansen doesn't, however, while breaking with the internalized self-oppression represented by effeminacy, go along with the 'clone' masculinization of gay life (constructed around another set of stereotypes, perhaps, of the 'super macho'). For heterosexual men the 'enemy within' is especially the homosexual, and an idea of 'effeminacy' helps therefore to maintain a 'healthy' distance from 'real' masculinity.

The novels rarely explore male sexuality, although they show men desiring men and men as objects of sexual desire, but they do question and debate the rhetoric of masculinity, particularly the way in which violence is constructed; it is never lingered over. It is always minimized, either recorded sparingly, or made a matter of report. More often than not, Brandstetter is bested in a violent encounter. In challenging traditional roles, Hansen comes close, at times, to suggesting that living out a combination of elements from both female and male roles constitutes a form of gay liberation. At other times, the social constructions of masculinity are seen as so negative, that gayness is a simple reversal, a form of rejecting those constructions and their competitive norms. However, Hansen does not produce his central figures in terms of a series of styles drawn from an image-repository. Rather, he creates a definition of masculinity (gay in its specificity, but not specifically gay) which 'lays bare the emotions, so that we have an eroticized reality of men who are both gentle and strong, who give full expression to their feelings, listen to their hearts and allow their warmth to be taken, used and reciprocated'.[15]

In summary, what has Hansen tried to achieve in his fictions?

1 He has questioned some of the central images and archetypes of 'manliness', particularly those constructed around the private eye (the cynosure of 'hard-boiled' masculinity) seen as part of the cultural process of producing and foregrounding particular types and formulas of 'privileged' masculinity. Hansen's work is a first step in remediation or reculturation, even if limited by a tendency to romanticize its central figure. The texts complexify the received cultural images of masculinity, marginalizing its more stylized, yet influential, images which have for a long time 'thought' male perceptions and actions.

2   The fictions include, at their centres, the capacity for tenderness,
    emotional depth and aesthetic feeling – reclaiming these from
    their ideological location as culturally (naturally) 'feminine'.
    The texts introduce the idea of a fluid and variable masculinity
    and decentre the traditionally valued imagery of playground and
    battleground. They bring restraint, responsibility and reciprocity
    from their positions of marginality and subordination in male
    socialization. *Agency* and *power* are scripted in gentleness as a
    way of demystifying *the* male text – the classic ascriptions of male
    meaning systems. Confusion and misrecognition – the conditions
    of the crime thriller – are seen as part of meticulously observed
    surfaces, which become metaphors of the confusions of gender
    in the genre, in lived cultures and social relations.
3   Violence – of all kinds – is seen as part of the processes that
    produce conventional masculinity and is not simply an expression
    of it. Violence divides masculinities from each other and is seen as
    generated, at some levels, by role and performance anxieties.

Conclusion

At a time in which strongly competing images of the male as
violent, aggressive and macho are again current, Hansen's work
should not be minimized. It problematizes some aspects of male
identity and creates some space for a different version of masculinity
to be circulated in popular cultural forms (a television adaptation of
his novels would mark quite a significant challenge to the territory
customarily occupied by the 'popular'). The textual surfaces are
not just 'landscapes' of narrative but also sites of possible contradiction. Hansen offers a provisional contribution to a new cultural
imagery and definition in which men can 'think' themselves. I fully
acknowledge that, in Frank Mort's words, the fictions 'involve men
addressing the way they are written into the structure of sexual power
and taking active responsibility for their behaviour', a vision/version
of masculinity which, Mort argues, is associated with men's groups
and sections of the gay movement since the early 1970s (Hansen is
part of this 'moment').[16] This 'New Man' version of masculinity,
dismissed by Frank Mort for its middle-class specificity, is the
principal resource used by Hansen to construct Brandstetter. It

is both the strength and limitation of the fictions. Their humanist gloss on feeling and coherent identities *is* narrowly class-based and ethnocentric. Brandstetter's relationship with Cecil Harris is, in liberal terms, 'integrationist', but it is also 'assimilationist' as the latter's black culture/experience is never actively invoked, only in terms of gaining Brandstetter access to the 'ghetto'. Cecil becomes a partner not only in the sexual sense, however, as in two novels he is actively involved and by his presence makes possible the resolution of the mystery. This is a positive extension of the white, male hero, moral crusader and bringer of order, because Cecil is no sidekick, or innocent foil to the supermind, but *complementary*. The fact also that Cecil is legally under-age when he and Brandstetter first meet suggest that Hansen, although ultimately establishing a 'closed couple' relationship, is raising questions about the arbitrary and discriminatory use of law to regulate gay sexuality.

The 'identity-running' and gender slippages in Hansen's fictions now, perhaps, look somewhat dated in the face of a reassertion of sexual and gender boundaries among gays, but a gay culture which is constructed upon existing male/female ideological differences and stereotypes is not necessarily more positive. So, however limited Hansen's work may seem in the issues it addresses, given the existing cultural political climate in the United Kingdom and the USA and the swing towards conservatism and a new form of homophobia, his work does nevertheless offer a series of representations which touch upon deep, unconscious fears and challenge the tyranny of family, marital sex and the patriarchal system. Maybe every prime time 'soap' does have its token gay now, but a serialized genre fiction which disarticulated the gender categories of its originating codes would be a very different proposition.

Notes

This chapter is based on a paper given at the Higher Education Teachers of English conference on 1 April 1987 at the University of Kent, Canterbury. It was part of a joint session in which Peter Humm and Paul Stigant made a contribution on the work of William McIlvanney. To them and the others who participated in the discussion I am grateful for many helpful comments.

1   Much of the discussion in this, and the subsequent, paragraph is based upon Pierre Bourdieu's *Outline of a Theory of Practice* (Cambridge: Cambridge University Press, 1977), esp. pp. 92–5.

2   To date, there are seven 'Dave Brandstetter' novels: *Fade Out* (1970); *Death Claims* (1972); *Troublemaker* (1975); *The Man Everybody Was Afraid Of* (1978); *Skinflick* (1979); *Gravedigger* (1982); *Nightwork* (1984). The dates given are those of the original US publication. *Fade Out* and *Troublemaker* are published in the UK by Grafton, all the others (except *Death Claims* which is not yet available) by Granada, with distinctive covers designed around the identity of the hero.

3   Joseph Hansen, quoted in *The Mystery and Suspense Engagement Calendar 1987* (Pittstown, NJ: Main Street, 1987).

4   Richard Stevenson, *Death Trick* (Boston, Mass.: Alyson, 1981).

5   Edmund White, *States of Desire* (London: Picador, 1986; originally published in the USA in 1980), p. 279.

6   All these quotations are from *Nightwork* (1984).

7   Dennis Altman, *The Homosexualization of America, The Americanization of the Homosexual* (New York: St Martin's, 1982). Much of the discussion in this chapter has been shaped and informed by Altman's excellent book.

8   White, *States of Desire*, p. 340.

9   Abram Kardiner, 'The flight from masculinity', in Hendrik M. Ruitenbeek (ed.), *The Problem of Homosexuality in Modern America* (New York: Dutton, 1963), p. 27.

10 The BBC television programme *Haunted Heroes* (1985) dealt with the cases of hundreds of Vietnam veterans who were unable to return to 'civilization' and spend their lives in the woods and forests of Oregon and other states.

11 Barbara Ehrenreich, *The Hearts of Men* (London: Pluto, 1983), p. 116.

12 Altman, *Homosexualization . . . Americanization*. See also Frances Fitzgerald's subtle analysis of the Castro in *Cities on a Hill* (London: Picador, 1987), pp. 25–119. Several of the comments in this chapter are drawn from Fitzgerald's essay.

13 Altman, *Homosexualization . . . Americanization*, p. 13.

14 *Troublemaker* (1975), p. 162.

15 Martin Humphries, 'Gay machismo', in Andy Metcalf and Martin Humphries (eds), *The Sexuality of Men* (London: Pluto, 1985), p. 85.

16 Frank Mort, 'Images change: High Street style and the New Man', *New Socialist* (November 1986), pp. 6–8.

7

The divided gaze:

Reflections on the political thriller

TONY DAVIES

IN THRILLERS, men pursue, hide, threaten, fight, kill; but more than anything, they *look*. The timbre of the look will vary, from the apparently casual sizing up of colleague or adversary to the charged climactic stare that passes, at the moment of truth, between hero and villain. But more than fist or weapon, the true medium of exchange and authentic instrument of male combat, rivalry and conquest is the eye. Masculinity is grounded, in these texts, in the power of the gaze. In Buchan's *Thirty-Nine Steps* (1915), Richard Hannay, disguised and on the run, finds that he has unwittingly taken refuge in the home of the master criminal himself.

> Then he looked steadily at me, and that was the hardest ordeal of all. There was something weird and devilish in those eyes, cold, malignant, unearthly, and most devilishly clever. They fascinated me like the bright eyes of a snake. I had a strong impulse to throw myself on his mercy and offer to join his side, and if you consider the way I felt about the whole thing you will see that the impulse must have been purely physical, the weakness of a brain mesmerised and mastered by a stronger spirit. But I managed to stick it out and even to grin.
> 'You'll know me next time, guv'nor,' I said.[1]

Roszika Parker has noted, in a parallel context, that 'although men observe women constantly, they do not *see* us, do not perceive who we really are'.[2] Looking, in these situations, has less to do with seeing than with dominating; and though always involving a kind of recognition (Hannay and his host, both in disguise, have recognized one another for the first time), an encounter of masked and symbolic identities, the look exhibits some of the semiotic displacement and narcissistic absorption of a fetish. What is 'recognized' in the exchange of looks is less an individual face or particular danger than an occasion of primal fear and insecurity, anonymous and pervasive.

> The man came nearer. Now he was looking straight at Bond. With recognition? Bond searched his mind. Did he know this man? No. He would have remembered those eyes that stared out so coldly under the pale lashes. They were opaque, almost dead. The eyes of a drowned man. But they had some message for him. What was it? Recognition? Warning? Or just the defensive reaction to Bond's own stare?[3]

And just as the everyday language of masculine insecurity, forever on the alert to the danger of getting 'stuffed', 'fucked up', 'ripped off', or grabbed 'by the balls', betokens a ubiquitous apprehension of sexual assault and mutilation, so the imagery of these climactic *coups d'oeil*, where, literally, a look can kill, hints at a lethal eroticism of male pursuit and mastery. Forsyth's Jackal, on the point of making his kill, is finally cornered by the detective who has been patiently tracking him down through three hundred pages.

> Claude Lebel stared into the eyes of the other man. He had no trouble with his heart; it did not seem to be pumping any more.
>   'Chacal', he said. The other man said simply, 'Lebel'. He was fumbling with the gun, tearing open the breech. Lebel saw the glint as the cartridge case dropped onto the floor. The man swept something off the table and stuffed it into the breech. His grey eyes were still staring at Lebel.
>   He's trying to fix me rigid, thought Lebel with a sense of unrealism. He's going to shoot. He's going to kill me.[4]

It is at moments like this, with the hero transfixed in a state of psychological paralysis and ideological indecision, that the genre's characteristic *paranoia* emerges most clearly. Jerry Palmer has defined the classic thriller narrative as a contest between competitive individualism (the hero, embodying the value of the 'free world') and criminal conspiracy.[5] But given the equivocal character of the former (for 'competitive individualism' could as easily describe the master criminal or mad scientist as the detective or adventurer who unmasks and outwits him), and the protean elusiveness of the latter (for the conspirator can often pass as, even actually *is*, 'one of us'), their encounter is likely to take the form, in all but the most politically simple-minded thrillers (Sapper or Bond, perhaps), of a vertiginous doubling, a queasy slippage of psychic and ideological signifiers, for which paranoia suggests itself as the appropriate description.

In the *Introductory Lectures* Freud tells of a patient, a young doctor,

> who had to be expelled from the town in which he lived because he had threatened the life of the son of a university professor residing there, who had up till then been his greatest friend. He attributed really fiendish intentions and demonic power to his former friend, whom he regarded as responsible for all the misfortunes that had befallen his family in recent years, for every piece of ill-luck whether in his home or in his social life.[6]

The two friends had been close since schooldays, even, on one occasion, sexually intimate; and the case confirmed Freud's hypothesis that persecution manias like this resulted from the repression of homoerotic desire:

> Experiences of this kind in ever increasing numbers led us to conclude that *paranoia persecutoria* is the form of the disease in which a person is defending himself against a homosexual impulse which has become too powerful.

In this case, moreover, that 'anxiety which is the regular outcome of the process of repression' had elaborated a narrative of persecution extending well beyond a sense of personal grievance and insecurity, and the delusions that attributed to the former friend and lover 'fiendish intentions and demonic power' (itself a phrase worthy of Sax Rohmer or Edgar Wallace) also held him responsible for an international conspiracy in the classic mode:

> He believed that his bad friend and the friend's father, the Professor, had caused the war, too, and brought the Russians into the country (the case dates from 1916–17). His friend had forfeited his life a thousand times, and our patient was convinced that the criminal's death would put an end to every evil.

This is the archetypal thriller plot, with the patient in the role of the agent who, hunted down and misunderstood, must singlehandedly save the world from the machinations of a pair of conspirators (one of them the inevitable 'mad professor') whom everyone else believes deludedly to be respectable citizens like themselves. And as in the classic thriller, the hero is confronted at the climax by his own immobilizing ambivalence, 'fixed rigid':

> Yet his affection for him was still so strong that it had paralysed his hand when, on one occasion, he had an opportunity of shooting down his enemy at close range.

It would be easy to draw facile conclusions here. Freud himself, influenced by the anthropological speculations of his generation and perhaps too by Nietzschean notions of historical and psychic 'recurrence', was drawn in his most celebrated study of paranoia[7] to speculate that the condition might involve a regression not only to infantile but to historically primitive, even primal, relations of family and society. In a similar way, writers on the thriller have often taken the formulaic and intertextual character of the genre for evidence of its mythopoeic and transhistorical nature, so accounting for what Bruce Merry calls 'the universality of popular literature and the atemporality of its appeal'.[8] Such formulations mean little, combining as they do the 'eternal truths' of traditional bourgeois aesthetics with a weak structuralism that tends, in Tony Bennett's words, 'to deprive [texts] of their specificity (formal and historical) by regarding them as merely the manifestations of structures (the structures of language or myth) which have their central determination and provenance elsewhere'.[9]

A comparable caution should govern the application of psychoanalytic concepts to popular narratives, where their use may be largely heuristic and metaphorical, and their lack, indeed refusal, of historical differentiation may block a proper understanding of the dynamics of genre. True, the gaze that locks hero and villain into a moment of mutual recognition is charged with an ambiguous intensity that the texts both invite and forbid us to call erotic, and it is not difficult to find in the action and imagery of thrillers examples of displaced or sublimated homosexual interest. The opening chapter of Fleming's *From Russia With Love*, for instance, is little more than an erotic reverie about the 'perfect body' of the SMERSH assassin Donovan Grant. But the texts are not simple transcriptions of some invariant paradigm of male narcissism and paranoia, and the search for permanent underlying structures, whether of psychopathology or narrative, runs the risk of losing not only the specificity of text and genre but their entire historical meaning and interest. The structures of popular narratives are in reality *restructurings*, their formulae and recurrent figures continual reformulations and refigurings; and it is those processes, which can only be understood historically, that actually constitute a genre and its readership, not some imagined 'atemporality' of popular interests or 'universality' of narrative conventions.

The pertinent question, for the early thriller, is the one posed by Roger Bromley, properly emphasizing not the structural immobility of the genre but its historical determinacy and protean adaptability:

> How does a residual fraction of the ruling bloc *re-present* itself in the cultural/ideological formation; how does a class fraction survive when its original power and function is displaced?[10]

To which should be added only that the power of a class fraction is also, axiomatically, the power of men, and thus capable of hegemonic representation in terms far wider than those of the class itself; hence the importance, in articulating as in reading these epochal shifts in social power, of the 'gendered genres', thriller and romance, with their complex intrications of class, masculinity, Englishness, their steely heroes whose unflinching gaze can 'evaluate, dominate and control',[11] their reassuring certainties, their profound and disconcerting ambivalences.

There is of course an element of arbitrariness, even of opportunism, in locating the 'origin' of a genre in a single text; but there are strong reasons and a measure of agreement for dating the emergence of the English political thriller from the publication in 1903 of Erskine Childers's *The Riddle of the Sands*.[12] The word 'thriller', in the broad sense of an exciting story of adventure and suspense, is a few years older: *OED*'s first example is from 1889. But the particular concatenation of features that constitutes the genre in its classic form appears fully for the first time in this tale of two young Englishmen uncovering a German invasion plan during a sailing holiday in the Friesian islands. The text itself, with the conscious literary intertextuality that will become a persistent feature of the genre, indicates what some of those elements might be. 'I'm not cut out for a Sherlock Holmes,' remarks Davies, one of the protagonists; and his companion Carruthers, stowing away on an enemy boat, wishes in vain for 'an empty apple-barrel, such as Jim in *Treasure Island* found so useful'. The convergence of the domestic detective mystery (the first Holmes story had appeared in 1887, and the great detective's encounters with the demonic Moriarty are the prototype of later ocular confrontations) with the most famous and influential of all exotic adventure stories (*Treasure Island* was published in 1883) supplies the formal preconditions for the new genre, the resolution of a mystery in circumstances of physical danger and energetic activity. Indeed, the superimposition of the two genres provides, in the opening chapters of *Riddle*, both humour and suspense, as Carruthers's expectation of a bit of leisurely yachting and Davies's mysterious reluctance to disclose the true purpose of the expedition produce a series of comic enigmas and misapprehensions.

But the juxtaposition of formal elements will not by itself produce a major generic shift. For that, new ideological materials and circumstances are necessary; and the early thriller is distinguished from its generic antecedents less by its redeployment of narrative conventions than by its capacity, through that redeployment, to articulate and organize a particular historical juncture, the Edwardian crisis of economic stagnation, social instability and inter-imperialist rivalry. 'Britain', Eric Hobsbawm has written of the early years of the century,

> was becoming a parasitic rather than a competitive economy, living off the remains of world monopoly, the underdeveloped world, her past accumulations of wealth and the advance of her rivals.[13]

And the years immediately before the Great War he characterizes as a period 'of uneasiness, of disorientation, of tension, which contradicts the journalistic impression of a stable *belle époque* of ostrich-plumed ladies, country houses and music-hall stars'. Just such a contradiction, between a complacent assurance of untroubled security and a deep unease and menace stirring beneath the surface, gives *Riddle* both its plot and its constitutive ideological motivation. It appears at the outset in the contrast between the two protagonists, the bored, amiable clubman Carruthers and the eccentric solitary Davies, socially inept but strong, resourceful and intuitively shrewd – two versions of Englishness thrown into uneasy camaraderie. It frames the narrative in an authorial preface and epilogue in which the urgency of the 'German threat' is openly spelt out. It surfaces in the climactic disclosure, for Carruthers as for the reader, of the real purpose behind a fortnight's leisurely boating and wildfowling in the Schleswig fiords:

> In the end it came out quite quietly and suddenly, and left me in profound amazement. 'I wrote to you – that chap was a spy.' It was the close association of these two ideas that hit me hardest at the moment. For a second I was back in the dreary splendour of the London clubroom, spelling out that crabbed scrawl from Davies, and fastidiously criticising its proposal in the light of a holiday. Holiday! What was to be its issue? Chilling and opaque as the fog that filtered through the skylight there flooded my imagination a mist of doubt and fear.
> 'A spy!' I repeated blankly. 'What do you mean? A spy of what – of whom?'
> 'I'll tell you how I worked it out,' said Davies. 'I don't think "spy" is the right word; but I mean something pretty bad.'

What he means is that the German business man Dollman, actually a cashiered British naval officer, Lieutenant X—, is helping the German navy with a secret plan to invade Britain across the North Sea. German spy-fever and a panic about British unpreparedness for invasion by its technologically powerful and expansionist neighbour were widespread in these years. From the alarmist stories of William Le Queux (*The Great War in England*, 1893; *Spies for the Kaiser*, 1909) to the sinister *Schwarze Stein* organization outwitted by Richard Hannay in *The Thirty-Nine Steps*, the archetypal enemy is the German, both fiendishly clever and dangerously elusive. In these texts, the chauvinistic delusion is fully developed, has, as it were, covered its tracks: all Germans are diabolically malevolent and cunning, inalienably 'other'. *Riddle* is less resolved, more interesting than this, closer in ideological and narratological terms to the critical ambivalence that Freud identified as the dynamic root of paranoia:

> The person who is now hated and feared for being a persecutor was at one time loved and honoured. The main purpose of the persecution asserted by the patient's delusion is to justify the change in his emotional attitude.[14]

Not only is the 'German' Dollman actually 'one of us' – indeed, the very incarnation of incorruptible Englishness, a British naval officer – but the German invasion plot itself is presented less as a piece of devilish cunning and malice than as a justifiable response to British imperialist greed and complacency.

> 'I don't blame them,' said Davies, who, for all his patriotism, had not a particle of racial spleen in his composition. 'I don't blame them . . . *We* can't talk about conquest and grabbing. We've collared a fine share of the world, and they've every right to be jealous. Let them hate us, and say so; it'll teach us to buck up, and that's what really matters.'

As for individual Germans, though one of the leading conspirators, the civilian Böhme, is described conventionally as 'the embodiment of that systematized force which is congenital to the German people', his colleague, the naval officer von Brüning, evokes unstinting admiration in the guileless Davies ('a real good sort, and a splendid officer too – just the sort of chap I should have liked to be'), while even Carruthers's response, though more ambivalent, has none of the Boche-hating bigotry of Sapper, Buchan, or Le Queux:

> I am bound to say I liked him at once, as Davies had done; but I feared him too, for he had honest eyes, but abominably clever ones.

This looks like an anticipation of later developments in the spy thriller, drawing *Riddle* closer to the political agnosticism, if not to the weary disillusion, of Deighton and le Carré and distancing it from the strident jingoism of its more bellicose contemporaries. No doubt Childers's own anti-imperialism[15] situates him outside the hysteria that characterized the dominant response to the 'German menace'. But that hysteria itself was always inherently unstable, superimposed as it was upon an envious admiration of the Prussian virtues of efficiency and military discipline. Franklin Scudder, the American agent whose violent death in Hannay's flat precipitates the action of *The Thirty-Nine Steps*, provides, in a classically paranoid splitting manoeuvre, one all-too-familiar resolution of the dilemma of the good-and-bad German, a manoeuvre neither endorsed nor fully repudiated by the text itself:

> Take any big Teutonic business concern. If you have dealings with it the first man you meet is Prince *von und zu* Something, an elegant young man who talks Eton-and-Harrow English. But he cuts no ice. If your business is big, you get behind him and find a prognathous Westphalian with a retreating brow and the manners of a hog. He is the German business man that gives your papers the shakes. But if you're on the biggest kind of job and are bound to get to the real boss, ten to one you are brought up against a little white-faced Jew in a bathchair with an eye like a rattlesnake. Yes, sir, he is the man who is ruling the world just now.[16]

It is easy to see, here, how imperialist paranoia modulates effortlessly into racism, a racism expressed in the quasi-scientific physiology ('prognathous') of Gobineau and Lombroso,[17] but specifically in detailed physiognomies and modalities of gaze. Eliot's 'Chicago Semite Viennese' Bleistein, registered with languid Bostonian disdain, 'stares from the protozoic slime' with a 'lustreless protrusive eye'; but Buchan's 'little white-faced Jew' is more typical, with his 'eye like a rattlesnake'. Peter Ivanovitch, the leading revolutionary and 'great feminist' of Conrad's *Under Western Eyes*, conceals his own eyes behind dark glasses, but his aristocratic female companion exhibits 'the rigour of a corpse galvanised into harsh speech and glittering stare by the force of murderous hate', while Hannay's arch-enemy could 'hood his eyes like a hawk', and the text's – the genre's – ocular fetishism rises at the climax of *Thirty-Nine Steps* to a revelatory disclosure of recognition-in-otherness:

> The old man was looking at me with blazing eyes . . . There was more in those eyes than any common triumph. They had been hooded like a

bird of prey, and now they flamed with a hawk's pride. A white fanatic heat burned in them, and I realised for the first time the terrible thing I had been up against. This man was more than a spy; in his foul way he had been a patriot.[18]

Almost everything separates the melodramatic bravura of *The Thirty-Nine Steps*, which Buchan himself called 'an elementary type of tale',[19] from the glum complexities and anomic understatement of the contemporary spy thriller. Everything, that is, except the central motif: the final encounter, the look, the recognition of self and other in the familiar, inhospitable no man's land of a 'looking-glass war':

> They faced each other; they were perhaps a yard apart, as they had been in Delhi jail . . . They exchanged one more glance and perhaps each for that second did see in the other something of himself. He heard the crackle of car tyres and the sounds of doors opening, while the engine kept running. De Silsky and Skordeno moved towards it and Karla went with them . . . [Smiley] didn't watch them go. He felt Toby Esterhase fling his arms round his shoulders, and saw that his eyes were filled with tears.[20]

He has, George Smiley realizes wryly at this his second and final encounter with Karla, the Soviet master-spy, 'no real name by which to address his enemy: only a code-name and a woman's at that'. In thrillers, the enemy is frequently anonymous (*Thirty-Nine Steps*) or known only by a pseudonym ('Dollman' in *Riddle of the Sands*, 'Major Quive-Smith' in *Rogue Male*); but Smiley's realization that he cannot name the enemy he knows more intimately than any friend has a special significance. In one sense the Russian needs no name, since in the paranoid shadow-play of east and west, hunter and hunted are interchangeable, identical even, negative and positive of the same image. In another sense, though, the woman's name is profoundly appropriate, since Karla, who 'seemed to have acquired already the submissive manner of a prisoner', is no longer in any sense an 'agent'; he has surrendered his power of action, and thus, in the world of the thriller, his defining identity as a *man*. For the code that defines and determines these anagnoristic moments,[21] across deep gulfs of class, ideological antagonism, even physical revulsion, is masculinity, the master-discourse of the thriller and the ultimate referent of all its ambivalent and competitive solidarities. When hero and villain confront one another with a look that appraises, challenges, *recognizes*, they are engaged ·in something quite different from the man who, to complete the quotation from Roszika Parker, can 'evaluate, dominate and control women with his gaze'.[22] The look between men is a transaction, a moment of symbolic exchange. It accords to the other the status of a subject to the degree that it recognizes it as the obverse and mirror-image of itself; whereas the gaze that dominates women permits them no other existence than as objects.

Masculinity, the overriding ideology that binds hero and villain, hunter and hunted in a masonic solidarity of mutual rivalry, is at once a unified and a highly differentiated set of codes. Thus it can act as a solvent of other forms of difference: Davies can admire the stereotypical hated German as 'the sort of chap I should have liked to be', and Hannay, seeking a disguise in which to escape unobserved from his apartment, can appeal to a common code of masculine sportsmanship that subsumes secondary considerations of class, even as it promotes them to the foreground:

> 'I reckon you're a bit of a sportsman,' I said, 'and I want you to do me a service. Lend me your cap and overall for ten minutes, and here's a sovereign for you' . . . 'Right-oh!' he said cheerily. 'I ain't the man to spoil a bit of sport. 'Ere's the rig, guv'nor.'[23]

At the same time, sportsmanship is no synonym for an inert or sentimental classlessness, but a figure deeply marked with social accents and historical antagonisms. It both reflects a major social development – the rise of the professional and suburban petty bourgeoisie – and attempts to contain and oppose that development by recruiting the supposedly common interests of rural gentry and traditional working class against the 'feminized' and sedentary complacencies of the suburbs. Hannay himself is a figure for this neo-Disraelian enterprise.

> A man of my sort, who has travelled about the world in rough places, gets on perfectly well with two classes, what you may call the upper and the lower . . . But what fellows like me don't understand is the

great, comfortable, satisfied middle-class world, the folk that live in villas and suburbs.[24]

And Geoffrey Household's celebrated elaboration of the trope in *Rogue Male* (1939) brings out clearly its aggressively populist as well as its reactionary-masculine character:

> I wish there were some explanation of Class X. We are politically a democracy – or should I say that we are an oligarchy with its ranks ever open to talent? – and the least class-conscious of nations in the Marxian sense. The only class-conscious people are those who would like to belong to Class X and don't: the suburban old-school-tie brigade and their wives, especially their wives . . . I should like some socialist pundit to explain to me why it is that in England a man can be a member of the proletariat by every definition of the proletariat (that is, by the nature of his employment and his poverty) and yet obviously belong to Class X, and why another can be a bulging capitalist or cabinet minister or both and never get nearer to Class X than being directed to the Saloon Bar if he enters the Public.[25]

Rogue Male is itself a notably transitional text, and in passages like this it is possible to see the code of the sportsman – the clubman of Childers, Buchan, Sapper – undergoing a major transformation. The terms of that transformation ('class-conscious', 'proletariat') associate it topically with the 1930s – the passage could almost be from Priestley or Orwell – but they also look forward, within the genre, to the cool, rootless, urban professionals of the postwar thriller. The hero's first attempt to assassinate an unspecified Central-European dictator (the novel was published in the year of the Molotov-Ribbentrop Pact, and the ambiguity is clearly deliberate) has been a failure, conceived as it was in Buchanish terms as a hunt for big game across open terrain:

> It was a mistake to make use of my skill across the sort of country I understood. One should always hunt an animal in its natural habitat; and the natural habitat of man is – in these days – a town. Chimney-pots should be the cover, and the method, snapshots at two hundred yards.[26]

The shift of locale is also a shift of class and its associated gender-connotations. Ian Fleming made Bond an Eton-educated 'toff', in the tradition of Bulldog Drummond; but his tastes, though affluent, are tourist-class, and Fleming himself later acknowledged the sharper focus and greater appropriateness of Sean Connery's performance – a Scots Joe Lampton enjoying his life at the top with ironic ostentation – in the Salzmann-Broccoli films of his books. The steely gaze and the firm handshake retain their figurative status as indicators of normative heterosexual masculinity; but pipe-tobacco and damp tweed give way to Marlborough and Fabergé and, above all, to a technician's knowledge and control of machinery: cars, guns, planes.

Here again *Rogue Male* marks the shift, reworking generic formulae through a revised and shifting set of social codings. To take one example: Hannay's sporting milkman is the conventional Edwardian cockney 'sparrer' ('Right-oh, guv'nor!'); but in a structurally closely similar handling of the improvised-disguise-and-escape motif, Household's hero, posing as a suburban family man complete with 'missus' and 'nipper', acquires a tandem bicycle and sidecar from a young couple on holiday with their baby, and the husband, easily identified as proletarian Class X, proves to be a representative of the new order, neither sporting 'card' nor traditional artisan but skilled technician:

> He was a boy of about twenty-three or -four. He had the perfect self-possession and merry eyes of a craftsman. One can usually spot them, this new generation of craftsmen. They know the world is theirs, and are equally contemptuous of the professed radical and the genteel . . .
> 'Are you in the cycle trade?'
> 'Not me!' he answered with marked scorn for his present method of transport. 'Aircraft!'
> I should have guessed it. The aluminium plating and the curved, beautifully tooled ribs had the professional touch.[27]

Chance encounters like this, however they may strike readers as too conveniently serviceable to the narrative, perform an important referential function. As well as establishing the hero's Odyssean resourcefulness and effortless command of social codes, they situate the narrative of the thriller in a wider ideological space, a terrain of cultural representations not unlike the 'hierarchy of discourses' of classic realism,[28] but constituting not so much a social continuum and an illusionistic reality-effect as an allegorical typology of classes, genders and ethnicities. Popular narratives are often discussed in terms of fixed 'stereotypes' deployed within recurrent narrative formulae; but a historical reading of a genre like the thriller suggests that these character-types and their positions within the textual hierarchy are changing continually in small but significant ways, and that the visual, phonetic and cultural codes through which they are generated are engaged in an unceasing intertextual transaction between the already-constituted genre and the historically shifting registers of class, masculinity and Englishness. Indeed, it may be precisely this structured interaction between textual signifiers and changing historical meanings, rather than some immanent 'deep structure' of narrative components, that actually constitutes a genre as a historical and formal entity.

A definition of genre in these terms ought to imply a decisive break with the Aristotelian formalism that still dominates the discussion of popular fiction, in the academy at least; though even then a residual formalism will persist so long as the 'changing historical meanings' are themselves conceived simply as other 'textualities': discourses, or signifying practices, or the ephemeral contents of a persisting and self-servicing form. It ought to make it difficult, too, to talk about ideologies *in* the text, waiting patiently to be mechanically 'decoded' by successions of identical readers. Janice Radway has defined the important move, in her study of romance and its readers. 'The analytic focus', she argues,

> must shift from the text itself, taken in isolation, to the complex social event of reading where a woman actively attributes sense to lexical signs in a silent process carried on in the context of her ordinary life.[29]

To study a popular genre is to study lived social relations, not because popular fictions transparently 'reflect' those relations but because the meanings and structures of their narratives are 'actively attributed' by their readers – among whom, of course, must be numbered their writers, and ourselves, who study them.

Here once again a parallel with psychoanalysis suggests itself, this time an institutional one. The theory and practice of psychoanalysis originate in a moment of strategic refusal: the decision to interpret its patients' hysterical narratives of sexual molestation and assault not as memories but as remembered *fantasies*, requiring interpretation and theory beyond the lay capacities of the patients themselves.[30] All such moves are fraught with danger and ambiguity; for while without such a refusal of the self-evident, a moment of radical theorization, no new knowledge or practice is possible, it almost always implies, in societies grounded on inequality and the power of professional elites, a dispossession of valid experience (many of those patients, we can now be sure, *had* been sexually abused in infancy) and a monopolization of the means of understanding it. So professional literary criticism too begins with a refusal of the experience of the non-academic reader 'in the context of her ordinary life'. Actual readings, in all their variety, are subordinated to the authority of *a* reading; readers, with all their differences, are subsumed in the rhetorical figure of *the* reader, in reality little more than a euphemism for the textual authority of the critic and *his* reading. What is lost in this process, among much else, is the pleasure of reading, or rather its many pleasures: pleasures of identification and fantasy, to be sure, but pleasures of judgement, too, of distanciation and critique and contradiction (Janice Radway's collaborators demonstrate how cheaply inadequate is the usual knee-jerk dismissal of popular reading as uncritically escapist and addictive).

But the repression of pleasure in critical discourse points to another order of difficulty, one by no means confined to the orthodoxies of bourgeois criticism; for the pleasures of reading, in thrillers, seem inescapably predicated on an endorsement of patriarchal norms and oppressive masculine codes. I cannot escape the force of this in my own case: these narratives transfix me with a gaze as thrilling and as repellent, a fascinated self-recognition as ambivalently compulsive as the most devilish of villains, the most masterful of heroes. Of course a case can be made: the unravelling of mysteries and the exposure of conspiracies – the immediate locus of textual pleasure in the genre – have lost none of their pertinence in an age dominated by bureaucratic secrecy and transnational monopoly, and the lone adventurer-hero can still, as Gramsci remarked of Dumas, articulate the ordinary citizen's

Utopian hopes of justice. But while they can evoke those hopes, these texts can never truly answer them, for the unravellings and exposures of the classic thriller are accomplished entirely within the terms and along the grain of the dominant popular codes – sexist, imperialist, racist – of masculinity and Englishness; codes which the text can expose to view, even sometimes to question, but never – without breaking with the genre altogether – to fundamental challenge.

Meanwhile these texts return an image of the world at once profoundly deluded and compellingly true; for who will say which of the two seems, now, closer to the reality of their time and ours, the great rationalist and healer, Freud, or the young doctor, his psychotic patient? Reading his case now, we may be struck less by the irrationality of the doctor's delusions than by their timeliness and historical prescience, for his conviction that his erstwhile friend and lover was not only responsible for his own misfortunes but had actually 'brought the Russians into the country' and 'caused the war' anticipates so uncannily the normal domestic and foreign policy assumptions of the major capitalist powers that it might be read as a prophetic allegory of the last forty years. And as for his belief that 'the criminal's death would put an end to every evil', if that is evidence of homicidal lunacy, what shall we find to say about Vietnam, the Bay of Pigs, Nicaragua, the Malvinas?

If Freud's case, introduced almost casually into a lecture to illustrate a general point, can seem even now to follow us with its troubled and divided gaze, its unsettling questions about truth, interpretation and history, so too can the thrillers that it so closely resembles. Freud omits the therapeutic outcome; his account leaves the patient stranded amidst his delusions. Thrillers generally offer more narrative closure than that, but their resolutions are never more than partial and provisional. *Riddle of the Sands* ends with an odd, reticent offhandedness, its ominous question hanging in the air. *Thirty-Nine Steps* closes as war breaks over Europe. *Rogue Male* concludes with the hero's task still unaccomplished. Beyond the endings, the plot unfolds and thickens, out of the reach of narrative or therapeutic cure: the dramas and delusions of masculinity, the terrors and mysteries of contemporary life, the fear and the hope of change.

Notes

1   John Buchan, *The Thirty-Nine Steps* (London: Blackwood, 1915). The text used here is Pan, 1959, p. 79.
2   Roszika Parker, 'Images of men', in *No Turning Back* (London: Women's Press, 1981), pp. 236–7.
3   Ian Fleming, *From Russia With Love* (London: Cape, 1959). References are to the Triad, 1977 edition; here, p. 178.
4   Frederick Forsyth, *The Day of the Jackal* (London: Corgi, 1971), p. 380.
5   Jerry Palmer, *Thrillers: Genesis and Structure of a Popular Genre* (London: Edward Arnold, 1978).
6   Sigmund Freud, *Introductory Lectures in Psychoanalysis* (Harmondsworth: Penguin, 1974), p. 475.
7   Sigmund Freud, 'Notes on a case of paranoia' (1911), in the *Standard Edition*, Volume XII (London: Hogarth, 1958).
8   Bruce Merry, *Anatomy of the Spy Thriller* (London: Macmillan, 1977).
9   Tony Bennett, 'Marxism and popular fiction', in Peter Humm *et al.* (eds), *Popular Fictions* (London: Methuen, 1986), p. 260.
10 Roger Bromley, 'Hegemony and popular fiction', in ibid., p. 152.
11 Parker, op. cit., p. 237.
12 Erskine Childers, *The Riddle of the Sands* (London: Smith, Elder, 1903). Quotations are from the 1931 edition, published by Sidgwick & Jackson.
13 Eric Hobsbawm, *Industry and Empire* (Harmondsworth: Penguin, 1969), pp. 192–3.
14 Freud, 'Paranoia', p. 14.
15 An Ascendancy Protestant and Liberal MP, Childers campaigned for Irish nationhood, fought with the IRA during the Civil War and was shot by de Valera's Free State government in 1922 for armed opposition to the partition treaty.
16 Buchan, *Thirty-Nine Steps*, pp. 11–12. Anti–Semitic sentiments were not of course confined to popular literature in this period. A couple of years after this, T. S. Eliot was confiding to his highbrow readers that 'The rats are underneath the piles. The Jew is underneath the lot.' ('Burbank with a Baedeker: Bleistein with a cigar', *Collected Poems* (London: Faber, 1969), pp. 40–1.) After 1917, the evil German is partly supplanted in popular-imperialist folklore by the Bolshevik – a move adumbrated in Joseph Conrad's *Under Western Eyes* (1911).
17 Joseph-Arthur, comte de Gobineau (*The Inequality of Human Races*, 1853–5) and Cesare Lombroso (*The Criminal Man*, 1876) argued from

physiological and ethnological evidence for the immutably biological character of, respectively, racial difference and criminality. Both were immensely influential.

18 Buchan, *Thirty-Nine Steps*, p. 137.

19 ibid., author's note.

20 John le Carré, *Smiley's People* (London: Pan, 1980), pp. 334–5.

21 Aristotle used the term *anagnorisis* ('recognition') for the hero's realization of the true nature of things that marks the climax of the tragic action.

22 Parker, 'Images', p. 236.

23 Buchan, *Thirty-Nine Steps*, pp. 26–7.

24 ibid., p. 129.

25 Geoffrey Household, *Rogue Male* (London: Chatto & Windus, 1939). References are to the 1968 Penguin edition; here, p. 41.

26 ibid., p. 192.

27 ibid., p. 72.

28 'Hierarchy of discourses' is Colin MacCabe's term. See his *James Joyce and the Revolution of the Word* (London: Macmillan, 1979).

29 Janice Radway, *Reading the Romance* (Chapel Hill, NC: University of North Carolina Press, 1984), p. 8.

30 For an account of this crucial theoretical turn, see Ernest Jones, *The Life and Work of Sigmund Freud* (Harmondsworth: Penguin, 1964), pp. 278–80.

8

Gorky Park:

American dreams in Siberia

BARRY TAYLOR

> This realization of a great city as something wild . . . this romance
> of detail in civilization.
>> (G. K. Chesterton, 'A defence of detective stories')[1]

CHESTERTON'S paradoxical defensive formulation places detection as a primary agency in the advance of the city – of the rationality of civic organization – over the incoherence of nature. The paradox rests in the fact that as the city establishes itself in opposition to natural disorder, there opens within its organized spaces an effect of incoherence – an illegibility – which reiterates that of the wilderness outside. It is in this context that the working of detection upon detail appears as romance, a rendering of the contingent, the blankly organic into the patterns of significance:

> there is no stone in the street and no brick in the wall that is not
> actually a deliberate symbol – a message from some man.[2]

The growth of the city is an advance of structure and system that carries with it its own contradiction; an increase in complexity, density and diversity which renders civic space opaque and intractable to any systematic understanding. It is this internal wilderness of sub- and counter-culture, underworld and ghetto, which calls for the mobile and improvisational flair of a reader of signs; an interpreter ready to immerse the self in the material, to risk going native, to reclaim the blank reaches of the system through the exercise of knowledge and methods unavailable to the collective agencies of order.

The figure who emerges to satisfy this requirement in the work of Eugene Suë, Balzac, Dumas and Charles Brockden Brown, is that of the police agent, explicitly modelled in all these cases on the Red Indian guides and trackers of Fenimore Cooper.[3] A complex exchange between the opposed terms of nature and culture, America and Europe is initiated here; an exchange which will be of central importance to the development of the detective genre and which is a principal structuring agency in *Gorky Park*.

The enlistment of the skills of the American native by the forces of European civic order sets the pattern for the relationship between the fictional detective and government. The detective's usefulness is in his intimacy with the disorder he combats. The principle which he represents is that of inoculation, an enlistment of the eccentric and the extra-ordinary by the powers of centralization and conformity. This theme is consolidated in the chronicles of Vidocq, whose pre-eminence as a police agent is founded in his previous career as master-criminal.[4] Balzac emphasizes this ambiguity when he elaborates upon Vidocq in the character of Vautrin, whose criminality persists within his police career as at once the foundation and the undoing of his usefulness to the state. In *Père Goriot* the final arrest of Vautrin is met with his declaration of himself as a 'disciple' of Rousseau; the agent of civil order is also the militant child of nature.[5]

The licensed abnormality of the detective returns in the anti-social tendencies of Dupin and Holmes. The Dupin of the literary decadence, the Holmes who despises 'every form of society with his whole Bohemian soul';[6] it is this regulated alienation which allows the detective to infiltrate the city's counter-cultural spaces and decode their recalcitrant detail. The continuity between these blind spots of civic order and the external wilderness is carried over from the genre's origins in Conan Doyle's treatment of the marginal territories of suburbia, the country estate and the railway 'frontier', and beyond them the wilds of Dartmoor (*The Hound of the Baskervilles*) and the north (*Round the Fire Stories*) as the 'natural' milieux of crime.

The taming by the detective of the alien, both within and outside the city, amounts to a homogenization of social reality around dominant conceptions of the normal, the regular, the known. Crime disrupts these rules of plausibility, intruding a kink of disreality into the fabric of the understood. The detective's investigation begins with the 'impossibility' of the narrative offered him by the crime, the incompatibility of the clues with any accepted account of the real. The detective's imposition of order upon the deviant is then also a consolidation of the 'real' upon conventions of rationality and verisimilitude. The real is confirmed as that which is drawn within the meaningful configurations of civic order. The nature of the criminal, the criminality of nature – these derive from their perceived randomness and particularity, their refusal to signify within the codes of the dominant. The detective's aim is a reading of the signs of the alien which will discover in them the syntax of the familiar, the understood.

It is in this sense that detection exemplifies the hazard – and the threat – involved in any reading, if we take reading in its broadest sense as the soliciting of meaning from things. The detective breathes life into the inert material clue, spiriting it away from the silences of the natural into the redemptive order of the significant. By the same process he abducts that which falls outside systematization into the order of reason and the city. It is this crime of the detective, this theft in the name of the law, which is punished in the generic inversions and reversals of *Gorky Park*.

The opening up of America, and of its literary culture, involves a new orientation within the opposition between the wilderness and the city, and consequently a shift in the implications surrounding the detective as agent of civil order. Hawthorne suggests the nature of this development in *The New Adam and Eve*:

> We who are born into the world's artificial system can never adequately know how little in our present state and circumstances is natural, and how much is merely the interpolation of the perverted mind and heart of man . . . Art has become a second and stronger nature . . . It is only through the medium of the imagination that we can lessen those iron fetters, which we call truth and reality.[7]

This radical mistrust of any social order as the imposition of artificial constraints upon the spontaneity of the natural – nature here being both organic and human – becomes a central element in the developing American literary culture.[8] It is in the social structures of Europe, in their very density of social texture, that this tendency locates the full burden of repressive Law – an historically accumulated weight of governing discriminations and exclusions enforcing the rule of the *proper* across the territories of the psyche, of social relations, of political association and of cultural production.

The foundation of the American republic is imagined as opening the possibility of a polity and a social order which will have mitigated the grip of these repressive structures; which will, paradoxically, have given the libertarian critique of the social and institutional incarnation. So for Mark Twain, to produce the mechanisms and institutions of civil order is to risk reproducing Europe at the expense of America's original liberation potential. It is significant that Twain links the possibility of this betrayal to the American absorption of the realist novel as practised by Scott, Eliot, Stendhal and Balzac. In 1881 he could write that Scott was 'in great measure responsible for the Civil War' because his work encouraged in the South 'a reverence for rank and caste, and pride and pleasure in them'.[9] More generally, the libertarian impulse entails at least an unease in relation to the European realist novel, which in its nuanced notation of the rituals, mechanisms and discriminations through which social order is articulated, is readily seen as an agency for the maintenance and circulation of the forms of oppression.[10]

It is within this perspective that I want to situate *Gorky Park*. The ambiguity of the detective's positioning between nature and 'the world's artificial system'[11] and his privilege as an uncivil agent of social order place him at the centre of the libertarian problematic. Two manifestations of this tendency in American writing are of particular relevance to a consideration of *Gorky Park*. One is the attachment of writing to an order of detail and particularity which is believed to resist the abstract reductions and systemizing force of social classification – as in Hemingway's intended fidelity to 'concrete names'[12] or in this prescription of Emerson's:

the truthspeaker may dismiss all solitude as to the proportion and congruency of the aggregate of his thoughts, so long as he is a faithful reporter of particular impressions.[13]

The second is the location of authentic subjectivity, and with it the possibility of an uncompromised accession to the truth, in an alienation of the self from all social investment or interaction, a tendency embodied in the detached observer whose integrity is precisely in his or her powerlessness, an ironic detachment from the ensnarements of sociality. This figure, classically, is an American at loose in the Old World and at a tangent to European Law; what happens then when this exemplary American is a Russian agent of police?

In the Moscow of *Gorky Park* the streets are lined with the bad pastiche which constitutes 'Stalin Gothic'; egregious functionaries sip 'Soviet Sparkling' in their exclusive dining-clubs; investigator Belov retails the minutiae of convention and prejudice which go to make the rules of good form; and a junior detective complains of the privileges and exclusions of the class system:

> 'I know the KGB. Those prick-twisters. After we do all the work . . . They get twice the pay of detectives, their own special shops, fancy sports clubs.' Pasha rolled along on his own track. 'Can you tell me how they're better than I am, why I was never recruited? There's something wrong with me because my grandfather happened to be a prince? No, you have to have a pedigree, sweat and dirt for ten generations.'[14]

In this array of ersatz forms and protocols, the Soviet social system is represented as the nadir of Old World order – an artificially contrived and imposed regime of official ideology, mediated through monolithic institutions and an inflexible order of behavioural norms and 'good manners'. The synthetic and reductive nature of this system in relation to reality is presented synecdochically in the Operations Room of the Moscow Militia:

> One wall was an enormous map of Moscow divided into thirty borough divisions and studded with lights for one hundred thirty-five precinct stations. Ranks of radio switches surrounded a communications desk where officers contacted patrol cars . . . or . . . precincts. There was no other room in Moscow so ordered and restful, so planned, the creation of electronics and an elaborate winnowing process. There were quotas. A militiaman on the beat was expected to report only

so many crimes . . . then the precincts one by one trimmed their statistics to achieve the proper downturn in homicide, assault and rape. It was an officially optimistic system that demanded tranquillity and got it. (p. 15)

Here Soviet planning achieves the tranquillity of order through a systematic misrepresentation of reality; as we are informed later, 'Maps, at least in the Soviet Union, were deliberately inaccurate' (p. 318). This deliberately deficient mapping of the real identifies Sovietism as a system of *bad representation* – mendacious, reductive, clichéd, formalistic, dependent on moribund conventions and derivative themes.

This production of social order as a kind of representation is necessary in order to underwrite the representation which encloses and exceeds it, namely that embodied in the novel itself. If the Soviet system is shown to supply a contracted, selective image of reality, then *any* supplementation of that image by the novel, any filling in of gaps or enrichment of detail, is endorsed as a superior registration of the real. The evidential status of this supplementary content has no relation to any external criteria of accuracy; its 'truth' is the product of that surplus of novelistic representation which arises from a management of different 'levels' within the novel. The writing which enfolds and 'places' the bad writing of state socialism must by implication be a good representation of the real.

In producing this effect of the real, the novel has as its main agent its detective hero, Renko. It is through Renko's investigation that the 'truth' of the Soviet system is gradually produced, by the excavation of a counter-republic latent beneath the artificial accretions and encumbrances of 'scientific' socialism. If the system is named as synthetic, mechanical, constructed, then this level uncovered by the detective necessarily claims the status of the organic, the site of natural spontaneity and authenticity. In a reversal of their classical function of recuperating and consolidating social order, detection and the detective novel operate here in the name of *nature* – an intransigent asociality in the essence of the inorganic, the animal and the human. This opposition between social order and recalcitrant nature binds the novel structurally, but it is not a static binarism. It is crucial to the novel that the natural emerges in its 'truth' through a gradual unfolding by the processes of investigation and narrative development. If a principal characteristic of the social is an imperviousness to innovation and modification, then the very temporality of investigation and narrative endorses their integrity as procedures for disclosing the real.

The disclosure of the counter-republic proceeds across several interrelated spheres. The first is that of geography and ethnography. Here the official order is shown to function as an abstract and reductive grid mapped on to the 'natural' heterogeneity of territories and peoples. This official reduction is shown as operating at three geographical levels: civic, national and international.

In the case of Moscow, the novel opposes the official organization of city space into a grid of public squares, prospects and monumental buildings – a space disposed by the requirements of economics, policing and political regimentation – and the intimate geography of the street, the quarter, the city periphery and the suburbs. It is in these places that the tranquillity of planning is challenged by the unregulated rhythms of street-life, a local ecology of conviviality, recreation and delinquency:

> The street kiosk filled up, more men in overcoats using the beer kiosk as an excuse to stand around. Without any grand squares or a building high enough to hang a banner from, Novokuznetskaya had the air of a small town. The mayor and his planners had ploughed Kalinin Prospekt through the old Arbat neighbourhood to the west. The Kirov section to the east of the Kremlin would be the next to go, laid to rest under a new boulevard three times longer than Kalinin. But Novokuznetskaya, with its narrow streets and small shops, was the kind of place to which spring came first. Men with beer mugs greeted each other as if during the winter everyone had been invisible. (p. 104)

The space which represents this other geography – and its recreative energies – at the heart of the city and the system is Gorky Park itself, the site of a re-creation of the Soviet citizen outside official definitions and the reductions of public role:

> Gorky Park was the purest heart of the city. Even Pribluda [the KGB major] must have visited Gorky Park as a fat child, a gross picknicker, a grunting suitor. Even Pribluda should know that Gorky Park was for recreation, not education . . . He remembered when *The*

Magnificent Seven came to Moscow, and every male between the ages
of twelve and twenty started walking like Yul Brynner; Gorky Park
seemed to be full of stiff-legged cowboys looking for their mounts.
A time when everyone was a cowboy. Amazing! What were they
now? City planners, factory managers, Party members . . . *Krokodil*
readers . . . fathers and mothers . . . That was one of the things about
Gorky Park; it was the only place in the city where you could fantasize.
(pp. 35; 62–3)

The affiliation between the 'free' space of the park and the American
West; the recreation of the citizen, in *his* truth, as a frontier
American; these translations of geography and identity will recur
as a central theme of the novel.

At the national level, the novel opposes to the official map of
a Russianized USSR the 'real' heterogeneity of the Union. This
process is focused in the repression of Siberia, its redefinition as a
merely negative space of punishment and exile, a place where social
disenfranchisement is mapped on to geographical marginality:

Most of Russia was Siberia. The Russian language admitted only
two mongol words, *taiga* and *tundra*, and those two words expressed
a world of endless forest or treeless horizons. (p. 102)

My grandfather was the first Siberian in my family . . . he was put on
a train east to serve fifteen years hard labour in five different Siberian
camps before he was freed in perpetual exile – which is to say he had
to stay in Siberia . . . The Davidovs were from Minsk. Their block
committees had a quota of 'Jew sophisticates' to arrest. So off the
rabbi and his family went to be Siberians. (p. 198)

If the system attempts to exclude and deny the independent reality of
its peripheral states, then what the crime effects and the investigation
exposes is an eruption of the periphery into the centre, a rebellion
of geography over official cartography:

Leaving Siberia is the only real crime a Siberian can commit. That's
all your investigation is about. How did these wild Siberians get here?
How did they get out of the country? (p. 199)

At the international level this return of the repressed occurs in
the context of an official representation of the Soviet Union as sealed

at the borders in a righteous isolation from the geography of world capitalism. As in the previous case it is through the crime and its investigation that this representation is overturned, in a tracing of the routes of commercial and political complicity which links the USSR to capitalist America. Once again the excluded term – here, exteriority – emerges at the centre of the system, a process captured metonymically in the intimacy between the criminal Western individualism of the American entrepreneur, Osborne, and the motives of Soviet state policy.

If we move from geography to the ethnographical, we can trace a parallel movement in the novel's restoration to visibility of the ethnic diversity of its main characters – Renko a Ukrainian, Levin a Jew, Pasha a Tartar, Irina a Siberian – and of those marginalized and excluded ethnic groups whose existence compromises the official drive towards Russianization:

> Russians, procreate!! the article demanded. Fertilise a glorious roe of young Greater Russians lest all the inferior nationalities, the swarthy Turks and Armenians, sly Georgians and Jews . . . swarming hordes of ignorant yellow Kazaks, Tartars and Mongols . . . tip with their upraised organs the necessary population ratio between white, educated Russians and dark. (p. 33)

This is a silent reflection of Renko's, his sardonic rewriting of an official article; one of many examples in which the novel's uncovering of the repressed 'truth' of official representations is effected through the detective's alienated perceptions. This is one instance in which the novel's eliciting of natural heterogeneity and disruptive energies is accompanied by the detachment of the detective from his orthodox social role and socializing function.

The discourse of ethnic authenticity also finds its focus in Siberia as the sign of ethnic militancy and peripheral nationalism. If we add to this its signification of the other repressed geography of the Gulag, Siberia emerges as the focal point at which the novel assimilates dissidence, criminality, racial and geographical heterogeneity to the order of the real which it represents as persisting beneath the tendentious mapping of official ideology.

As the place where the state monopoly in sable meshes with the black economy of the bandits and icon traders and Osborne's

Faustian entrepreneurism, Siberia also witnesses the emergence inside the official order of socialist economics of the 'reality' of capitalist motive and initiative. From forensic scientist Lyubin's trade in chemicals to Golodkin's racketeering, to Prosecutor Iamskoy's dealings in luxury goods, Renko's investigation brings into visibility a level of officially criminalized activity which is represented as the real economic motor of the society. Golodkin's apartment represents the grounding of this entrepreneurial economy in the repressed consumerist appetites of the Soviet citizen:

> Golodkin's apartment, two and a half rooms of cartons of scotch, ciga-
> rettes, records and canned foods heaped on a floor thick with Oriental
> carpets laid one over the other . . . Arkady went through . . . throw-
> ing armloads of parkas and skis out of the closets, cutting open
> cartons of French soaps while the borough investigator watched,
> rooted to one spot not just by anxiety that he'd have to account
> for the damage but out of horror for an assault on such valuables.
> (pp. 113–14)

Here and in the equally emblematic incident of Misha's comically exploding washing machine (trademarked, tellingly, 'The Siberia'), the authenticity of repressed or unsatisfied desire finds its true object in the commodity, and in consequence socialist economy appears in its truth as merely an incompetent, parodic form of American consumer capitalism.

It is Renko's investigation which, in probing the interstices and tracking the margins of the official 'map', links the various dimensions of repressed geography and economy in a coherent network of oppositional sites and forms. What is also uncovered on this terrain of the 'real' is the corresponding counter-culture, a repressed commonality of the deviant and the excluded. Renko's own alienation allows a positive recognition of the officially invisible – the dissident student Irina, the literary dissident Viskovs, the gay criminal lovers Swan and Tsypin, the romantic bandit Kostia. The investigation reveals as endemic styles of subjectivity and modes of social relationship which are officially represented as individual pathology or simply as non-existent: 'By definition prostitutes did not exist, because prostitution has been eliminated by the revolution' (p. 236).

On the other side of this valorization of the deviant is the novel's representation of figures such as detective Fet and Renko's wife Zoya. The running joke about Fet is his robotic demeanour, and Zoya is shown as fixed in the official role and representation of her Youth Poster image and works her body into the state of seamless efficiency celebrated in the rolling musculature and radiant skin of socialist realist portraiture. Clearly to participate in social order and social role is to aspire to the condition of the automaton, to submit psychic and organic spontaneity to mechanization.

On the basis of this entirely conventional representation of the engulfment of human essence by collectivism, what emerges as the 'real' of social relations is the anarchic commonality of physical appetite and indulgence which undercuts the conformities of social and ideological propriety. Witness the secret binges of the elite; the private bathing-house where the truth beneath the uniform is revealed and the socialist economist obsessively constructs the perfect caviare open sandwich. Or Goladkin at the centre of an economy whose currency is vodka; from the vodka troika of the first page, to the bacchanalia at Misha's dacha, to the worker's pub with its illicit TV. This picture of endemic inebriation is central to the novel's ideology of bodily appetite; if the nation's insistent desire is to get out of its head, that is because it is in the head that ideology takes hold, where the codes of official rationality seize and atrophy consciousness. So resistance to the social is lodged in the incorrigibility of the body and its attachments – in Renko's paunch and nicotine addiction, in the murderer Tsypin's agitprop tattoos, in the blemish on Irina's cheek which confirms her authenticity by announcing the ungovernable specificity of her physical constitution. By positing the social as the scene of a systematic reduction and mechanization of human spontaneities, the novel necessarily locates authenticity in the untotalizable quirks, excesses and tics of the body. The novel admits no social articulation of the real – the human subject assumes its authenticity as it moves towards the entropy and heterogeneity of the organic.

It is on this trajectory towards the extra-social space of the deviant and the organic that the possibility of an approach to authentic knowledge is located by the novel. 'Trust the freak's eyes' (p. 135), Renko is advised by the reconstructor of heads, Andreev. As a dwarf who feels at home only in the circus, Andreev's authenticity is fulsomely endorsed. In the process of his investigation Renko penetrates the subculture of deviancy not in order to police it, to impose upon it the regime of official rationality, but to confirm his own affiliation with it. In the same movement, the progress of detection towards a state of achieved knowledge is a progressive disqualification of Renko from any official role or conventional social existence.

Classically in detective fiction the accession to knowledge is also the moment of a triumphal recomposition of the social order around the normalizing principle of official rationality whose bearer is the detective. Here, on the contrary, it produces a definitive invalidation of the social order and marks the detective's final dissociation from officialdom; a confirmation that the case has been pursued in the name of a rationality which is radically incompatible with the dominant ideology.

The condition of authentic vision, then, is powerlessness, a radical alienation whose figure is death – 'Now it all comes together, the man said as he climbed the gallows steps, Arkady thought' (p. 212). It is as he anticipates his imminent execution by Pribluda that Renko is presented as evading the enclosure of ideology and entering a state of autonomous, self-generated consciousness:

> 'I think that I never knew *how* to think. I feel as if I'm making it up as I go along. I don't know. At least, for the first time, it's not making *me* up.' He opened his eyes and grinned. (p. 256)

This redefinition of the relationship between the detective and knowledge involves also a re-evaluation of the investigative techniques and procedures through which knowledge is approached. Police procedure is endorsed in opposition to a representation of official legal ideology as a species of bad writing. Pasha's sarcasms about 'doing dialectic' summon up the bogey of a crude systematization which imposes upon the variety and unruliness of fact a pre-established code of artificial categories – Vronskyism, hooliganism, pathoheterodoxy, individualism. Detection opposes this because it is an *inductive* procedure, tentatively building up from the particularities and disorganization of detail its flexible and inclusive hypotheses. If theory arrests its objects in static categorizations, detection crucially takes time. If theory imposes upon the social the inflexible definitions of a 'science', then detection operates the artistic or humanistic model of interpretation, which actively elicits the ambiguity and contradiction which 'science' will not tolerate.

Perhaps most significantly detection, as a discipline of memory and reconstruction, restores the integrity of the human subject. The reflex of the official legal apparatus on the discovery of the Gorky Park corpses is to tidy them away in the categories of antisocial activity and hooliganism. Detection takes the faceless, fingerprintless corpses and restores in its full density and particularity the intimate history of each and the dramatic narrative which brought them together. The movement is from the 'scientific' abstractions of Renko's initial official reports to the intensity of detail and dramatic tension of the reconstruction he performs in front of Irina.

This process is underwritten by Andreev's reconstruction of the heads which (like detection) tempers scientific rigour with artistic flair and through a recuperation of detail reclaims the vitality and truth of the body. For Renko the deployment of his skills in the name of particularity and authenticity is grounded in the nature of the crime which moved him to take up police work. This is the suicide of his mother, a crime whose truth is to be traced not in the gross codifications of official legality, but in the specific drama of the family – a drama, appropriately enough, of psychic health dislocated by the forces of social inauthenticity and 'performance'.

Detection emerges then as a privileged art of the real; an art whose provenance is in its intimate registration of empirical detail, nuance and inflection. In this it is the accomplice of the novel's own procedures, whose effect of truth is achieved by just such a mobilization of detail. The novel typifies its own activity in a movement out from the organized spaces and events of the city centre and into the contingent detail of the suburbs and rural communities:

> Red May Day banners stretched across a ball-bearing plant, a tractor plant, an electric plant, a textile plant. On the banners were golden profiles, golden laurels, golden slogans . . . Southeast through the Lyublinsky district . . . an hour's worth of travelling through larger

factories thinning to smaller ones, to the prefabricated gray of workers'
flats, to old homes razed for development, to a country field mazed
by surveyor's strings . . . past the end of the autobus line, still in the
expanded city limits but beyond it to another world of low houses little
more than cabins, swaying picket fences and tethered goats, wash in
the arms of women dressed in sweaters and boots, a church of plaster,
a one-legged man doffing his hat, brown cows crossing the road, a
back yard chopping block and ax. (pp. 220–1)

From the uniformity of official signs to the quirkiness of rural
detail, from 'golden profiles' to one-leggedness – this is an exemplary
therapeutic journey towards the untidiness of the 'real'.

This movement of pastoral retreat is enacted in broader narrative
terms in Renko's removal to a country estate for interrogation.
Here, in the episode of the peat fire, the submerged stratum of
organic volatility bursts through its containment by the forces of
civil order, disordering and eventually consuming the regimented
firefighters. The enemy underground, random and unpredictable,
takes its revenge; its source is a substance which concentrates the
repressed forces of organic inertia and vital spontaneity:

Peat was anaerobic compost, organic decay so old that all its oxygen
had been used up. Few microbes survived in peat, perhaps twenty or
thirty a cubic metre. Exposed to air and water, the microbes instantly
reproduced to many millions, a voracious pool of starved life that
bored through flesh like lye . . . They continued across more burning
plains, more scenes of calamity and heroism strewn randomly with a
generous hand, deaths in a war that would never be reported in any
newspaper. (p. 262)

Alongside this eruption of repressed natural energies into violence,
the country-house episode sets a pastoral recuperation dramatized
in Renko and Pribluda's mushroom hunt. Here the routine of rural
labour necessitates an intimate focusing of vision so that what is collected along with the mushrooms is precisely the redeeming detail:

A mushroom hunt always focusses the eyes on the twist of a leaf,
the discolored bark of a tree, freshets of wild flowers, the industry
of beetles . . . they were best seen at the corner of the eye, a homely
brown one here, among the leaves a stationary herd of orange mushrooms, another with the ruffled gill of a small dinosaur . . . They

were called not so much by name as whether they were best pickled, salted, dried over a stove, fried . . . A man hunting mushrooms had a whole year ahead to think of. (pp. 263–4)

Against the transfixing gaze of official power the hunt elicits the look from the corner of the eye, an artistic obliqueness which generates metaphor, imaginative fecundity and a natural, ecologically attuned calendar of husbandry and consumption. The full therapeutic force of this return to nature is registered in its effect on Major Probluda, a character who has been attached so tenaciously to his status as a Stalinist cliché. Here he is drawn by the detective-therapist into an admission of his essential humanity and is granted a redemptively unique personal history grounded in an intimacy with the cycles and detail of the organic:

'I came from a farm . . . at heart I'm still from the country. You don't even have to think; you can feel a drought coming' . . . he stomped among the pails, delighting in a new-found ability to entertain . . . 'This is peasant science. Hear the earth? You can hear how dry its throat is. You thought you cosmopolitans knew everything.' (pp. 257–8)

The tendency of the novel, in all the interconnected planes I have been considering, is towards this excavation of this free space beyond ideology and the social; a site in which nature founds the authenticity of the subject, of knowledge, and of personal relations; the site too in which the detective assumes his full liberating criminality.

For Renko and the novel the possibility of this escape from the social is fixed and guaranteed in the image of Irina. It is consequently in the contradictions which emerge in this representation that an unravelling of the novel's discourse on natural authenticity and liberation begins.

Within an entirely conventional set of oppositions, marriage is figured in the novel as merely the most intimate of repressive social institutions, and the wife, Zoya, is fixed as the willing agent of coercive norms and expectations, attempting to manoeuvre the antisocial spouse into ever deeper complicities with the system. Articulated against this, the illicit romantic woman is invested as the negation of social constraint and ideological confinement. Irina comes to signify the elemental, the unclassifiable, the unknowable:

> In many ways she was not a person at all . . . He didn't understand
> Irina, and he suspected he might never penetrate vast areas of her
> unknowability . . . Now this image of her had appeared, and for one
> night, at least, he was alive, too. (p. 260)

The inevitable clinch between penetration and the unknowable is
precisely what this discourse of extra-marital authenticity revolves
around; heterosexual intercourse as a natural union of opposites,
an authentic salving of contradiction to be opposed to the artificial
syntheses of official ideology:

> He entered her standing up . . . At his first touch she was wet, an
> unfolded secret . . . He felt drunk on her taste through the vodka and
> blood in his mouth . . . 'It's a physical thing . . . I still hate what you
> do; I don't take anything back', she said. 'When you're in me, though,
> nothing else matters. In a way, I think you've been in me for a long
> time.' (pp. 203–4)

What comes together here are the maximum states of knowledge
and inebriation; vodka and blood, intoxication and the authenticity
of the body; the spontaneous 'fit' of gendered subjects; the insistence
of the physical overriding the contradictions of consciousness. If the
heterosexual clinch appears as the ground of authentic relationship,
it is because it is viewed, paradoxically, as eroding the very difference
in which relationship is founded. Renko and the novel collude in
projecting the woman as the image of the protagonist's alienation,
a projection in which difference is cancelled, and with it the
possibility of contradiction, of inauthenticity, of all the traps and
detours of the social.

I have already traced the movement by which the novel excavates
the 'reality' beneath the artificial constructions of the Soviet system,
and the persistence with which that reality reveals itself as Western,
and specifically American, capitalism. The repressed imagination
of the Soviet citizen, the hidden complicities of trade and political
interest, the underground economy and the appetites it serves; all
these are signified as denials of America. An imaginary America,
I should stress, which is produced in the same movement which

produces both Siberia and Irina – the Siberian who desires America – as signs of negation, of the zero degree of Soviet social order.

When the novel transports Renko and Irina to New York, however, it commits itself to a representation of America as a realized social order. As a result, Irina's desire has now to be shown as directed not towards America as an imaginary, solely differential term, but to the compromised forms of Osborne's America:

> The only present she'd accept was America . . . Only Osborne could give her America. (p. 187)

Osborne represents the point at which unfettered individual appetite and entrepreneurial flair mesh with the policies of Soviet collectivism; the point where America emerges not as Russia's innocent antithesis but as its accomplice and equivalent. This, for Renko, is Osborne's real crime – he steals the imaginary America. Through Osborne then the novel opens up a perspective in which there is no liberating scene of nature – 'America' – beyond the ensnarements of the social. This is confirmed as the novel progressively undercuts Renko's vision of freedom until it is a fantasy without any plausible geographical location:

> I want to go out West. I want to ride the range and be a bandit like Kostia Borodin. I want to learn from the Indians . . . Was there tundra in Maine? . . . What did Kirwill mean, 'like Siberia with beer cans'? . . . Their life would be two stories . . . They'd get some books. American authors. If he got a generator they could have lights, a radio, a record player. Seed for a garden: beets, potatoes, radishes. He could listen to music while he planted – Prokofiev, New Orleans blues. In hot weather they could go swimming, and in August there'd be mushrooms. (pp. 281, 318–19)

The dream of America contracts to a hideout in Maine. Pursued by the combined forces of America and Russia Renko fantasizes a pastoral Amerussia which combines the frontier independence of both the Wild West and Siberia. The idea of Siberia returns for Renko as the answer to the oppressiveness of America; back in Russia Viskov had imagined a liberated Siberia whose outlines are those of backwoods America before the fall, preparing its declaration of independence:

I'll start a new life, build a cabin in the woods, hunt and fish . . .
That's where the future is, out there. You'll see, when I have kids
they're going to grow up different. Maybe in a hundred years we'll tell
Moscow to fuck off and have our own country. What do you think of
that? (p. 202)

America redeems Siberia: Siberia redeems America – the promise of
natural liberation has been reduced to this oscillation of imaginary
terms.

With the disappearance of the imagined domain beyond contradiction all that is left is the ambiguous terrain of the social. Irina's
imaginary integrity is abolished in the same movement. If she is to
secure Renko's freedom it will not be by incarnating 'nature' but
by acknowledging her position as the object of contending powers,
by attempting to manoeuvre within the field of social forces which
objectify both her and Renko. Renko names this effort as complicity,
or prostitution; it is when his own fantasy of America evaporates and
only the America that is in Osborne's gift remains that the necessity
of Irina's stance is acknowledged.

Gorky Park proposes a critique of the Soviet Union in the name of
a repressed nature, an organic reality which resists the reductions
of ideology and social organization. This Other of Soviet social
confinement appears in the image of a free America compounded
from a variety of historical myths and Utopian projections; free
enterprise America and the freedom of the frontiersman and the
cowboy; the America of Thoreau, of civil disobedience grounded
in a union with nature; America as a true democracy of appetites
and instinctual gratifications; counter-cultural America, a republic
of the deviant, the oppressed and the marginal.

The emergence of the detective as counter-cultural hero in *Gorky
Park* sets a limit to the libertarian tendency in American detective
fiction. The work of Hammett, Chandler and Ross Macdonald
witnesses a fundamental departure from European conventions;
detection no longer affirms the integrity of the established social
and civic order, but uncovers the corruption of city government, its
complicity with the criminality it claims to oppose. The questioning
of any social articulation of the law leads to its reinvestment in the
personal ethic of the detective, who becomes another of American

literature's alienated truth-bearers. Renko's hideout in Maine and his dream of extraterritoriality mark the terminus of this individualist tradition; the point at which it faces the necessity of locating its oppositional discourse upon the terrain of the social where the inevitably promised agencies of collective politics are at work. *Gorky Park* also makes clear the centrality of a question which has emerged since the decades of Hammett and Chandler – the question of how we are to think and represent the issues of American legality and liberty outside an oscillation of imaginary terms in which the land of the free confronts a people in chains.

At the beginning of this essay I discussed detection as a kind of reading, and the 'theft in the name of the Law'[15] by which the detective, classically, converts the non-sense of the criminal 'text' into the coherent signifying structure of the closed case. This process, which assures the ultimate legibility of the world, has its motto in the triumphal cry which, in the police procedural, heralds judicial closure – 'Book him!'

Reflecting on my own inquiry into *Gorky Park* it seems clear that it conforms to this desire for a coherent closing of the case, a bringing of the text to book. The reading uncovers a structure of oppositions which arrests the dynamic signifying work of the novel into an intelligible static configuration, an object of secure intellectual possession. As the object is secured, so too is my self-possession as reading subject; detached from the object of inquiry, penetrating its deceptive surfaces to unveil its secreted truth. The epistemology is Platonic, addressing the text as a structure of deception, a cover-up. As this suggests, it is also the epistemology of the 'classical' detective, and in both cases it secures the subject-object relation by purging the operations of knowledge of any imaginative, affective, or libidinal investment.

In the field of detection, the exemplary agent of dispassionate inquiry, 'the most perfect reasoning machine that the world has ever seen', is Sherlock Holmes:

All emotions . . . were abhorrent to his cold, precise but admirably balanced mind . . . for the trained reasoner to admit such intrusions into his own delicate and finely adjusted temperament was to introduce a distracting factor which might throw a doubt upon his mental results.[16]

What this makes clear is the complicity of Holmesian epistemology with a certain culturally privileged image of the masculine. The discipline of rational investigation is grounded in a subjective economy which dismisses the claims of the body and the passions. It is this disavowal which secures the process by which reason enters into chaste possession of its object, undistracted by the doubt which accompanies desire.

Gorky Park attempts to move beyond this equation of knowledge and masculine self-discipline by admitting desire and imaginary projection into the subjective economy of the detective. My own investigative procedure, however, remains within the self-policed enclosure of Holmesian knowledge. The principal sign of this in my reading is its failure to accommodate any trace of my pleasure in the text of *Gorky Park*. The avowal of pleasure would complicate and unsettle the serene conclusiveness of the reading as it stands. It would recast my engagement with the text as a dynamic interplay of identification and analytical reflection, desire and disavowal, in which I am as much the object of the text's imaginary capture as it is the object of my rational possession.

The move to this second kind of reading would not only produce a more responsive account of the complex engagement between text and reader, as well as unsettling my imaginary security as 'trained reasoner'. It would also be a step beyond the hermeneutic of suspicion which has informed the analysis of popular fiction in the last century and more. Variously disguised, wielding a variety of investigative methodologies, the critical reader of the popular text has consistently constructed it as an agent of criminal deception to be tracked down and 'booked'. What is more, just as the epistemology which supports this kind of reading is culturally coded as masculine, the criminal pathology of the popular text has been diagnosed as 'feminine'. This emerges in a critical language which names the effects of the popular text as seductive or neuraesthenic, luring the reader from the 'masculine' sphere of reading as social apprenticeship and moral labour into a 'feminine' space of emotional indulgence, fantasy and escapism. Given this gendered ideology in the work of cultural critics, it is significant that the recent work which moves beyond this policing of the popular text should come from feminist critics working on romance, a genre which has attracted the most strenuous efforts of the culture cops.[17]

Any account of gender ideology in the text of detective fiction would have to describe the 'fixing' of gender representations in relation to an unsettling of identity and relationship – a threatened collapse of order – elsewhere in the ideological constellation of the text. The same dialectical or contextual address would be necessary in thinking about the encoding of gender in critical discourse. In my own case this would involve an analysis of 'masculine' style and method in relation to a desire for a secure identification as a professional reader, and of that desire as determined by a specific history of class displacement and mobility. That case is not closed.

Notes

1   Chesterton's 'Defence' (1902), in Howard Haycraft (ed.), *The Art of the Mystery Story* (London: Carroll & Graf, 1946), pp. 4–5.
2   ibid., p. 4.
3   See A. E. Murch, *The Development of the Detective Novel*, 2nd edn (Westport, Conn.: Greenwood Press, 1968).
4   ibid., p. 43.
5   See Julian Symons, *Bloody Murder*, revised edn (Harmondsworth: Penguin, 1985), p. 33.
6   'A Study in Scarlet', in Arthur Conan Doyle, *Sherlock Holmes: Selected Stories* (Oxford: Oxford University Press, 1985), p. 206.
7   Quoted in Richard Poirier, *A World Elsewhere* (New York: Oxford University Press, 1967), p. 92.
8   For this theme, see ibid., ch. 2.
9   ibid. p. 190.
10   Poirier discusses this concern in relation to James, Whitman and Faulkner; ibid., pp. 18–19, 102–3.
11   Hawthorne, above.
12   See Tony Tanner, *The Reign of Wonder* (Cambridge: Cambridge University Press, 1965), p. 234.
13   ibid., p. 230.
14   All page numbers in the text refer to the Pan Books edition (1982).
15   See above.
16   'A Study in Scarlet', p. 206.
17   For recent feminist work on romance, see Jean Radford (ed.), *The Progress of Romance* (London: Routledge & Kegan Paul, 1986), and Alison Light ' "Returning to Manderley" – romance fiction, female sexuality and class', *Feminist Review*, no. 16 (April 1984), pp. 7–25.

9

Bodily symbolism and the fiction of Stephen King

VERENA LOVETT

Bodily symbolism and the realist novel

In the complex social matrix of modern British Society, the individual is exposed to institutional, public and private discourses. Recent anthropological theory suggests that social structure determines the use of the body in cultural representations, thus identifying the physical body as both part and image of the social body:

> The physical experience of the body, always modified by the social categories through which it is known, sustains a particular view of society . . . The forms it adopts in movement and repose, express social pressures in manifold ways.[1]

Arguably, then, information about social structure is communicated symbolically through a culturally specific, constructed body where organic processes are brought under control through infant socialization, while other bodily 'noises' such as gestures must be controlled or used communicatively in discourse. These 'natural' expressions are nevertheless available for artificial or naïve insertion into discourse, and are then understood implicitly through a bodily hierarchy which, in Western culture, privileges front over back, upper body over lower body – a hierarchy represented in literature through the classical body and the grotesque.

The development of the realist novel in the context of industrialization, bureaucratic rationalization and professionalization was paralleled by the evolution of the Gothic novel in which the body's symbolic function was foregrounded and used narratively within a dominant symbolist mode.[2] Bodily symbolism is nevertheless important to the realist novel, which represents the social world within a reformist discourse (one which expresses concerns and contradictions deriving from a specific social order, but articulates history as a linear process from enigma to resolution, confirming that order as natural). The symbolist mode can incorporate, within the realist novel, symbolisms drawn from public and private discourses, using movement, gestures and extensions of the body (in costume, landscape and materials) as implicit social referents.[3]

Arguably, then, symbolist narrative can expose contradictions in realism by revealing the contextual sources out of which the text is produced, that is, the author's anxieties about the social structure which has occasioned her/his authorship and lived experience. It is evident that in a capitalist patriarchal society, much female and popular culture is defined in relation to regulatory institutions (medicine, law, education), but also finds self-expression through discourses such as body movement, play, illness and gossip. 'Unauthoritative' discourses, which may exist outside the art-form largely in 'private' or oral speech, can, however, be expressed through the symbolist narrative.[4] I suggest that it is from this perspective, the representation of the body and bodily symbolism, that Stephen King's fiction can be addressed.[5]

'Carrie': synopsis and form

Carrie White is a small-town American girl seeking acceptance by her peers; for her, home and school are two completely different environments – her widowed mother's repressed sexuality finds expression in fundamentalist religion, while at school Carrie is a joke figure in a female world constructed around the necessity of finding a man and 'graduating' into adulthood through the school prom.

The plot is constructed around Carrie and two 'couples' representing good and evil: Sue Snell and Tommy Ross, Chris Hargensen and Billy Nolan respectively. Their actions are influenced and defined by the educators, Grayle, Morton and Miss Desjardin, who vicariously sanction the events that lead to the destructive denouement.

While the female protagonists are seen to be decisive in instigating action, indicating weak or absent males, all except Carrie are controlled by the implicit knowledge that their power is ultimately centred in the male. Sue expects to 'conform' to a dull house-wife/mother role sugared by the Pill; Chris's power (her car) is given, and can therefore be taken away, by her father, as her surname signifies; Miss Desjardin is answerable to the male principal; Mrs White obeys a patriarchal religion which defines her as inferior and responsible for the 'sins' of her father(s), both in passing on a gene which produces telekinesis in Carrie, and in giving birth to a female, who will perpetuate the sin by becoming a woman.

The story moves from Carrie's early telekinetic experience, through her ignorant reaction to her first menstruation (she thinks she is dying); for this she is taunted by her peers, and consequently helped by Sue and Tommy (who takes her to the prom), and attacked by Chris and Billy, who, in a final joke, pour pig's blood on her as she is crowned prom queen. The 'plot' ends when Carrie uses her telekinetic ability to destroy all around her before dying of a heart attack.

In using the horror genre, Stephen King has available both realist and symbolist modes for narrative articulation; the physical body can be used symbolically to represent disorder, the 'unnatural', or 'supernatural', which threatens the social order described within the realist narrative. Conventionally, use of the grotesque body as a symbolist device complements the realist narrative, asserting the horrific quality of that which is not normal or understandable. However, King uses the symbolist mode narratively, not just to draw attention to Carrie's abnormality and threat, but to undermine realist narrative authority which asserts a 'natural' understanding of Carrie as deviant female (witch); and also to enable narrative continuation beyond the plot ending outlined above. Arguably, this narrative provides a challenging critique: it asserts the necessity of knowledge and practice articulated specifically within female domestic discourse in authorizing the destruction of patriarchal capitalist society, so as to create a new one based on different strategies.

The novel, then, is both an account of adolescent female sociali-zation incorporating the menarche (realism), and a narrative of the development and effects of self-knowledge, represented through menstruality and symbolized, by a male writer, through telekinesis (symbolism).[6] Menstruation is central to both modes, and its significance as unauthorized energy is arguably essential to the reading of the symbolist narrative (which may therefore be more accessible to women readers).

Carrie is formally divided into three parts, entitled 'Blood Sport', 'Prom Night' and 'Wreckage', and further subdivided through forms ranging from the popular (graffiti), or the public record (death certificate), to journalism and academic, medical and scientific discourses. The realist narrative relies for its 'realism' on the authority of document and scientific inquiry, while the symbolist explores, through Carrie's body, private languages and their knowledge (i.e. the subconscious of Carrie and of her peers) and articulation of the domestic landscape, the White house, giving access to Margaret White and the mother/daughter relationship. This in turn gives a meaning to part 3 which cannot be found in the realist narrative. Again, menstruality as female difference, in both realist expression (menstruation and mental energy) and symbolic form (telekinesis and social taboo), serves to unify the disparate forms and discourses, providing a textual coherence which simultaneously asserts the interdiscursive relationships of the novel.

The importance of bodily symbolism in 'Carrie'

The symbolist mode fragments the realist, thereby calling into question its naturalism. It forces a reassessment of 'realistic' stereotypes by articulating an account of their construction process, i.e. by exposing the elements of social structure for which the body or body fragment is a symbol.

In the film of Carrie, the stereotypical 'unruly woman' is used to explain and condemn Carrie's unchannelled energy. This sanctions her removal from society, inviting audience consent while allowing for sympathy. This reading can be found in the book, but the literary text is more complex: the narrative construction itself immediately draws attention to interdiscursive relationships as a source of knowledge, foregrounding fragmentation and specialization through varied, punctuating, writing styles. A reading based on established evaluation of writing modes in Western literary culture prescribes the authoritative dominance of educational, religious and medical discourses, which provide the 'unruly' denomination. In this narrative hierarchy, the recorded gossip, slogans and intuitions which suggest a wider body-knowledge, can be ignored, and the 'story' read as an account of the inevitable self-destruction of a biological freak. Thus, the film text serves a ritual function, enacting and enabling removal of the undesirable, while highlighting the destructive threat Carrie's body presents to society.

The literary text does not, however, end with Carrie's death. The title of the final section, 'Wreckage', redefines what is contained there: the 'waste' deposits must be examined, not for the purposes of the 'story', since that finishes adequately at the end of part 2, but for their contribution to the restoration of order, or reordering, of society after the disaster of 'Prom Night'. Nor is this simply an appendix, since part 2 closes with Sue's sudden menstruation at a moment of acute sympathetic awareness of Carrie. This symbol of continuity, the shedding of waste material, establishing a site for new growth, subverts the text's ritual function, and part 3 then asserts a definition of death as simply the physical end of an individual body, while the social concerns which that body 'carried' exist beyond death in verbal deposits occasioned by Carrie's bodily narrative.

The sequential recording of this waste moves from an impersonal record of death and the effects of Carrie's destruction ('a town waiting to die', p. 86), towards an account of the existence of her body-type, not as a unique abnormality, but as a possible known formation, a recurrent historical event. However, the discourses used to identify this knowledge are private and thus unavailable as reference for the 1988 telekinesis occurrence referred to in the final 'deposit', a family letter.

Analysis of this letter, its textual significance determined by its placing at the end of the book, is important for an understanding of the text's structure and meaning, particularly the use of the symbolist mode. It is only the foregrounding of body and movement, fulfilling a realist function within the 'family correspondence' form, which makes sense of the letter's inclusion in the text. Here is a condensed version of the life of someone like Carrie, given in an exchange between two women, and written in a 'gossip' mode, denoting sub-literacy. It includes dirt uncritically within its social world ('she was playing in the dirt', p. 189). This is reiterated in the signing of 'Melia', an abbreviation synonymous with the Greek word for 'ash' – ambiguously available for classification as 'life' within the pre-social world, or necessary waste within the text's specific culture, a consumer-celebrating society ('butts and flakes of Morton's pipe tobacco scattered on the pale green nylon rug', p. 19).

The knowledge present in this letter is that of the historical formation of a Carrie-like body, known within women's domestic culture as something inexplicable within social norms, and therefore accommodated and denied through humour. Humour is used throughout the text in this ritual way, from the taunting of Carrie which makes her distrust laughter, to the significance of carnival and the grotesque in 'normalizing' the everyday. This body, then, is known in female domestic culture to occur in women, and is self-regulatory, not an uncontrollable energy source. It is recognized as of social importance ('I bet she'll be a world beater someday', p. 189), and the energy is used both in resistance to and for pleasure. As with the menstrual body symbolization, to be discussed later, there is a split of features across two bodies: the girl and her great-grandmother. Here, in a realist space, is a symbolic account of the socializing process of women, which selects certain features, and denies, in order to contain, others; the knowledge of denied energy remains with the individual adult, its source unrecognized, and is only recorded within women's culture. Though the couple split, it is a condensation of the Carrie 'story', written by a sub-literate narrator who shows no awareness of the concept of menstruality (to be examined further in the next section).

As noted earlier, King uses telekinesis to symbolize menstruality. This suggests, from a male perspective, an expression of a female physiological experience which reveals a use of energy not determined by external social patterns of economic production. This perception of the gender-specific menstruation phenomenon, narrated through Carrie's body in all its formations, provides a source of knowledge for social use. It may be that by symbolizing the concept and an experience of menstruation through taboo and telekinesis, King makes it accessible to both female and male readers, who can follow either trajectory, aware of their interrelationship, for an understanding of the potential social significance of a misrecognized energy source. A reassessment of the 'unruly woman' stereotype is thus argued for, implicitly questioning through the body/society relationship the control of human energy imposed by the economic order.

In *Carrie*, terms such as 'flow', 'flex', 'plug' and 'sweep', which occur differentially in the realist and symbolist modes, can be investigated through the figuration of Carrie provoking a potential critique of the realist and extra-textual social discourses in which such terms are commonly conventionalized, and which tend to prescribe meaning in the realist narrative.[7]

Flow: The menstrual symbol

Once . . . in New York, I saw an old drunk leading a little girl in a blue dress by the hand. The girl had cried herself into a bloody nose. The drunk had goitre and his neck looked like an inner tube. There was a red bump in the middle of his forehead, and a long white string on the blue serge jacket he was wearing. Everyone kept going and coming because if you did, then pretty soon you wouldn't see them any more. That was real too. (p. 31)

Through the use of Gothicist/realist literary conventions as a frame for the realist novel, the human body in *Carrie* is foregrounded and functions as a device around which the themes of the fiction are constructed. Body description in each narrative and in the text as a whole, the relative importance of body fragments and products to concepts of waste and use-value, and the possibility of reading the body as image and object of social control, are important to an understanding of *Carrie* as a cultural representation of late-twentieth-century society. Arguably, in its specific foregrounding of the female body and menstruation practice, and their articulation in the complementary spaces of carnival and everyday, the text sets up a critique of the social structure which it describes.

Despite a hierarchy of 'specialist' discourses, ranging from the litter of graffiti and folk memory, to the institutional knowledge of medicine, academy and government, bodily symbolism unifies and comments on this fragmentation in its narrative dispersal throughout the text. This is expressed syntactically in body parts, movement, energy production and dispersal, colour and relation to materials found in the urban landscape. For instance, the grotesque imagery of the above quotation follows soon after the realist description of Carrie's first menstrual flow in the shower (pp. 11–14). There is a reversal and splitting of bodies and body parts: Carrie's exposed menstrual body is transformed into the girl-with-bloody-nose/drunk-with-goitre 'couple' (thyroid enlargement is a feature of puberty, menstruation and pregnancy). While neither body is classical, blood can be validly exposed as it is relocated to the upper body. The girl's flow is 'unplugged', while the drunk's red bump is on his forehead (a sign of vampire intercourse). The white string on his jacket, being visible, is remarked on as being out of order, suggesting its 'proper' place on the end of a tampon for easy disposal, a symbol crucial to the plot to expose and dispose of Carrie at the end ('I think I'm gonna let you pull the string, Billy', p. 109). Both of these scenes cause disturbance: the primitive cat-calls and laughter of the first ('plug it up') paralleled by the 'civilized' response in New York: 'everyone kept going and coming . . . then pretty soon you wouldn't see them any more'. If the waste cannot be disposed of or ordered, then it must become invisible, non-real.

Since its invention in the USA in 1933, the tampon has been marketed as an effective and convenient form of sanitary protection, a euphemism indicating its relationship to social convention and order. By the 1940s, myths about spoiled virginity were less effective and the tampon was presented as an improvement on the sanitary towel, which, despite constant modifications, was difficult to conceal and more liable to leak blood and odour.[8] In the United States and Britain, despite the re-emergence of feminist activity in the 1960s, menstruation continued to be seen as a physical process which women suffered guiltily, conditioned by other women to regard it at best as a nuisance, but essentially as part of a taboo from which 'society' must be protected: the authority for discursive knowledge was medical, supported by residual religious articulations in popular culture. Medical discourse intervened in consideration of the effects of menstrual women on society, defining and prescribing drugs to cure 'pre-menstrual tension', a phenomenon described as the pathological manifestation of internal bodily mechanisms (nature), rather than arising out of problems experienced by women in accepting and adjusting to patterns of patriarchal society (culture).[9]

Meanwhile, the sanitary products industry was responding to women's practical need for a more efficient waste disposal method in terms of hygiene and cleanliness, common to the discourse of domesticity, a determinant of women's role within Western culture since the nineteenth century. The tampon was marketed as an attractive refinement of the towel, a device which could render the experience of blood flow invisible, even to the user; Tampax, the highest seller, even removed the possibility of touching the blood. While the tampon undoubtedly gave women more 'freedom' (e.g. to swim on *every* day of the month – a common ad. enticement) and made disposal easier, it nevertheless contributed to an even greater awareness of menstruation as socially taboo and reinforced the need to conceal/deny an aspect of female difference.[10]

At the time of *Carrie*'s publication in 1974 then, the production of menstrual blood was dominantly categorized as waste and negatively defined within the long-established taboo on 'unruly women' institutionalized by Western religion in the witch-hunt. Technology had developed a convenient and commercially successful disposal device which rendered the process invisible. Such knowledge of menstruality can be seen as contributing to the myth of female unpredictability and strangeness. Even today, tampon and towel ads avoid the menstrual process and its occurrence within a pattern of physical and psychical difference articulating concern for freedom from physiological constraints, and purified femininity.[11]

Menstruation does appear in media representations in the 1970s, where there is either insult, celebration, or more commonly a seemingly nonchalant acceptance. Audience response, however, indicates the danger of breaking taboos: most of the profusion of letters generated by the 'Battle of the Month' episode of US television's *All in the Family* (24 March 1973) objected to Gloria's accounting to her father for her bad temper as menstrual.[12] In 'women's' or juvenile girls' fiction, menstruation is regarded as problematic and specifically a part of female culture – a separate sphere.[13]

In this context, the use of the menstrual symbol in *Carrie* is significant not just for its effect in the realist mode of a horror novel as shock device, a breaking of taboo, but also in the way it is used as part of the symbolist mode to expose and define female experience through Carrie, in a dialectical relationship with domestic and public spheres. Additionally, its questioning of the connotative symbolic value of uncontrolled, unauthorized power ('Thou shalt not suffer a witch to live', p. 116), modifies the authenticity of scientific and medical discourses in the realist mode, exposing wider meanings of energy production, channel, waste and surplus, both mechanical and physical.

Arguably, the issue of blood from a female body in *Carrie* functions symbolically in three ways:

1 as a condensation and displacement of anxiety about definitions of waste and control of boundaries in a consumer-celebrating society; whereas classificatory practices can name and control surplus, profit, or waste in machine production, there is a threat to order from spontaneity and irrationality in human activity, where 'excess' energy may be produced in and for pleasure (anxiety about Carrie's telekinetic energy, p. 189);
2 as an available narrative articulation, linking parts already fragmented by the tripartite structure of the book, and its subdivision into 'specialist' discourses;
3 as part and image of the social body, defining boundaries and threats to patriarchal and capitalist order, through a critique of the purity role assigned to the female body in the domestic sphere.

Margaret and Carrie White express and expose bodily products as part of their domestic discourse, described in grotesque detail within the 'story' narrative, which also gives access to the domestic landscape:

> Weeping and snuffling, Carrie bowed her head. A runner of snot hung pendulously from her nose and she wiped it away . . . with the back of her hand. (p. 47)

> Her eyes bulged crazily, her mouth filled with spit, opened wide. (p. 48)

> [in the closet] Carrie had once fainted from the lack of food and the smell of her own waste. (p. 49)

Mikhail Bakhtin has noted the grotesque body's threat to classical order in that it extends beyond its boundaries through emissions

and protuberances.[14] The disinterested tone of the last extract
uncritically 'recognizes', through the symbolist narrative, a different and grotesque set of practices in the domestic space, the
White house.

Carrie produces and exposes her menstrual blood in ignorant
fear, unaware of social taboos. When she ignores the injunction from
disgusted classmates to 'plug it up', the plot develops around the
resolution of this transgression by using the 'normal' deviant, Billy,
to return the 'pig's blood' to the 'pig'. Thus, control of transgression
shifts from those delegated to the socializing role (women and
female peer group), to the dominant group around whom the social
structure operates. In containing Carrie's threat, attack is justified
by transforming her body to pig, a known literary convention.[15]
The realist narrative authorizes this through the pig kill:

> The flow of blood was immediate and startling. Several of the boys
> were splattered and jumped back with little cries of disgust. (p. 91)

> A rank, coppery smell hung in the air. Billy found he was slimed in
> pig blood to the forearms . . . Pig blood. That was good. Chris was
> right . . . Pig blood for a pig. (p. 91)

Billy's action in this vicarious menstruation ritual evokes comparison with Margaret White's definitions of the dirt of economic
production.

While Margaret White can be dismissed by the community as a
relatively harmless religious maniac, living in self-imposed seclusion,
Carrie is a danger not only as producer but also as consumer of dirt, a
fact publicly known through graffiti ('Carrie White eats shit', p. 9).
The theme of dirt and disorder is common to all of the narratives:
they articulate a description of a hierarchically ordered clean society.
Their difference lies in the manner in which they deal with bodily
wastes, the type of waste selected and the taboos that surround
them. Throughout the fiction, discourses are used to evacuate waste
from the surface. The waste that is Carrie's menstruality-knowledge
is variously manifested as primitive and trained telekinetic energy,
menstrual blood flow and disturbing bodily 'otherness'. While the
carnivalesque 'Prom Night' section allows for a reversal of values

through Carrie's point of view (laughter as violence, carnival as 'real'), it also creates a site for *containment* of the other and its self-generated physical destruction. However, as noted earlier, the text is carried through to a record of 'Wreckage' and potential 'revolution' through Sue's menstruation – the symbolic site of life-potential – as Carrie dies. After their psychical intercourse, Sue, infused with Carrie's knowledge, stands

> waiting for realization. Her rapid breathing slowed . . . and suddenly vented itself in one howling, cheated scream. As she felt the slow course of dark, menstrual blood down her thighs. (p. 180)[16]

The waste flows on after the carnival; Carrie's energy has prevented it from being washed away.

Flex: energy source and channel

> Her mind had . . . she groped for a word. Had flexed . . . not just right, but very close . . . a curious mental bending, almost like an elbow curling a dumb-bell . . . An elbow with no strength, a weak, baby muscle. (p. 25)

Carrie's inability to express verbally her sensual awareness of telekinetic power as knowledge, indicates both her social difference, and the lack of recognition by dominant institutional discourses of female knowledge as power. That knowledge is denied by allowing the 'muscle' to atrophy, remain inert, until the body's own vigorous development in puberty reacts to friction by exciting the electrical charge which produces telekinetic energy.

The signifier *flex*, identifying Carrie's energy, is linked to the text's discussion of energy production and control. Carrie, Billy and Chris all express bodily the energy of resistance, but for Billy and Chris it is within the convention of teenage rebellion and thus accessible to control by school and family (Billy also misrecognizes his 'flex', a potentially creative energy, through displacement into machine power: his car gives him 'mana').

Where Carrie's energy is variously seen as destructive, evil and uncontrolled, electrical energy is a necessary part of civilized social order, channelled through *flex*, a material for energy transmission to power essential machines (vacuum cleaners, lighting circuits, musical instruments, alarm systems). In Carrie's narrative, the verb flex describes the activation of energy which can be channelled and is self-controlled in the interests of survival. Carrie knows her power privately as intensely draining on physical resources, causing heart stress and headaches; with practice she finds an optimum level. It is suggested in the academic narrative that 'a doctor might have been interested' (p. 64); it is doubtful, however, whether Carrie would have survived such 'interest', given an extra-textual reference to the 'treatment' of women in modern American medical practice (as in Britain, radical surgery has been an effective 'cure' for female problems, whether breast cancer or mental instability); thus, the 'expert' prescription: 'We have no treatment except a bullet in the head' (p. 174).

Implicit references to electricity can be found in the terms 'amber' and 'orange', expressed through the 'purifier', Margaret White; and in 'neon' and yellow', indicating Carrie as a positive social influence through Sue and Estelle. Thus, Margaret's religious tracts are orange, and the tea she throws in Carrie's face is 'an amber fluid'.[17] Estelle, the witness of Carrie's childhood telekinesis, wears a yellow dress; Sue's sense of charm during Carrie's menstruation flows like 'neon'; her contraceptive pills are in yellow cases; and the light in the living-room, site of Carrie's economic production (where she makes clothes for sale), is also yellow. As adjectives, these uses of 'yellowness' are of course restricted in their semantic mobility across discourses. Rhetorically, however, they are used to identify and conduct Carrie's critical energy through narrative channels to which she has access. A yellow pill-case, then, symbolically questions the middle-class housewife role projected by Sue, which promises 'freedom' through sexual availability, aided by medical practice. Again, in 1974, much was known in public discourses of the pill's contribution to women's social and sexual freedom; little was said about such long-term bodily effects as cancer and thrombosis.

For this society, electricity is a controlled, clean, invisible energy; waste and its disposal are not problematic, since this is a necessary power source. For Carrie, electricity is a bodily energy, activated through mental flexing, and accessible through menstrual awareness. Her body determines production and use, and it is experienced sensually as an invisible flow out of the body (as thought), subverting the menstrual taboo by leaving no waste to be plugged up or swept away. Telekinesis can be seen as symbolic of the positive and socially necessary aspects of menstruality.

Plug: repression and containment

> Perhaps a complete study of Carrie's mother will be undertaken someday . . . I myself might attempt it, if only to gain access to the Brigham family tree.
>
> (*Carrie*, Academic Research Discourse, p. 115)

Margaret White is a female grotesque, described through body shape, movement and gestures, her dialogue with Carrie illustrated with vivid bodily images. She knows her pregnancy only as 'a cancer of the womanly parts' and is unaware of being anything but the carrier of a curse, a bodily knowledge displaced within religious norms as reparation for transgressive sexual consumption. This 'knowledge' issues from a Christian patriarchal view of women based on a well-internalized theory of cause and effect:

> And God made Eve from the rib of Adam . . . and Eve was weak and loosed the raven on the world. (pp. 46–7)

Margaret's repressed knowledge is recognized by the 'expert' narratives:

> Margaret . . . also carried the outlaw gene sign, but we may be fairly confident that it was recessive, as no information has ever been found. (p. 82)

But then it isn't sought: in another TK report, it is significantly 'one of Andrea's *brothers*' (my italics) who gives authoritative evidence of 'familiar witness-ship'. In this case the only possible witness is

'Margaret White, and she of course is dead' (p. 54). Even before this, however, 'Mrs White could not be reached for comment' (p. 9). Yet if Margaret's unspoken knowledge is read across the narratives, a clear critique of social norms and the invalidity of specialist knowledge is revealed: Margaret carries both physical genes and social norms to her child; while the first is predetermined, she is active in exercising choice over Carrie's socialization process. She creates her own order within the domestic sphere, teaching labour skills and a range of bodily expression unavailable to Carrie's peers. This provides Carrie with both economic independence and a sense of body/mind integrity, enabling her ultimately to understand her telekinetic energy as power-knowledge, contributing to a redefinition of femininity.

The symbolist narrative articulates Margaret's repressed knowledge of 'some great revelation which might destroy her'. Physical characteristics narrate a bodily mutilation occasioned by both her fear of sexual pleasure, *and* her paid work:

> a big woman with massive upper arms . . . but her head was surprisingly small on her strong, corded neck. It had once been a beautiful face. (p. 117)

> Lately her legs had begun to swell. (p. 45)

There is explicit reference to the deforming labour practice as she hits Carrie:

> behind it all was the heavy muscle developed by eleven years of slinging heavy laundry bags and trucking piles of wet sheets. (p. 47)

As noted, the grotesque body is not confined within its own boundary; Mikhail Bakhtin has also identified its regenerative function – a site for renewal out of waste and decay.[18] Margaret White fulfils this role in the symbolist mode, while acting as a purifier in the realist mode, cleansing dirt and returning material to society. The latter function finally dominates in Margaret. When Carrie rejects her mother's sterile purity, Margaret, like Billy, colludes with social norms to plug up the threat of Carrie's female energy: 'Thou shalt not suffer a witch to live' (p. 116). Throughout patriarchal history, women have been pressed into complicity in curing female 'deviance' to fit norms of femininity, whether mutilating the body as in footbinding, or destroying it completely as in Indian suttee.

The telekinesis phenomenon is important here: it can be seen as a textual device giving Carrie access to authoritative discourses in the realist mode, but also as a displacement of the author's own anxieties about the repression and social control caused by menstrual taboos and classifications of waste. It provides a critique of a system which denies female experience and corrupts human energy (Carrie's and Margaret's bodies, Billy's body and car) in its refusal to recognize that energy as a valued source of cultural production.

Sweep: order and waste

> [The Coorgs] treat the body as if it were a beleaguered town, every ingress and exit guarded for spies and traitors . . . The most dangerous pollution is for anything which has once emerged, gaining re-entry.
>
> (Mary Douglas, *Purity and Danger*, p. 123) [19]

There are two symbolic sites of conspicuous waste consumption and production in *Carrie*: the closet in the Whites' house, and Billy's car. Each articulates a concern with the effects of social contradictions. The closet is both sacramental and excremental; its location to the right of the bedroom, 'the place of the altar', suggests an inner sanctum where spiritual purity is attained through mental purging, but it is also a site for production and preservation of bodily waste as a sign of that purging. Purity is known through waste production. Only Carrie is upset by the 'smell of her own waste', 'the overpowering stench of sweat and her own sin'; for Margaret, these are signs of women's spiritual and social freedom, a release from polluting conventional sexual practice.

Billy's car is 'someone to be reckoned with . . . his slave and his god', and evokes the importance of the car in American teenage culture, perpetuating the illusion of authentic power vested especially in the individual male, regardless of class. It is also negatively signed as a symbol of otherness, 'dark, somehow sinister', with dirty tool-kit and greasy smell. It is this which attracts Chris: 'Feel me all over. Get me dirty' (p. 104). As a site of sexual activity, it represents middle-class exploitation of the working class, which is necessary to the realist plot. Despite his intellectual and biomechanical skills, his 'flex', Billy is cynically aware of his social impotence: 'plump, glistening daddies' cars. He felt the familiar gorge of distrust . . . rise in his throat' (p. 109).

Social order is defined in the realist mode through forms of dirt which can be disposed of as effects of consumption, and through the school, where Grayle embodies these definitions. Morton, who 'eats class-cutters for lunch' (while Miss Desjardin 'rips them down one side and up the other'), reveals the ordering of necessary dirt as he struggles to resist the disturbance of the menstruating Carrie and her lack of place in that order:

> Morton hunkered down carefully and began to sweep together the debris from the fallen ash-tray . . . his cheeks went pink . . . the little brush with the legend, Chamberlain Hardware and Lumber Co. NEVER Brushes You Off . . . 'There's going to be some left for the vacuum cleaner, I guess . . . ' He funnelled the ashes and butts into the waste-basket . . . 'I've placed her, I think.' (p. 20)

Carrie's telekinetic movement which destroys the ash-tray, highlights its textual significance as representative of the corruption of education through social control and oppressive discipline:

> (Rodin's Thinker with his head turned into a receptacle for cigarette butts.) (p. 19)

Other waste is observed by Carrie as she walks home after the shock of menstruation:

> Wads of gum . . . Pieces of tin-foil and penny-candy wrappers . . . A penny lodged in a crack . . . A dog-turd with a foot-track in the middle of it . . . a roll of blackened caps . . . Cigarette butts. (pp. 22–3)

The inventorial account prevents any sense of disgust, in contrast to the grotesque articulation of the Whites' waste products. The pavement waste, both economic and organic, can of course be swept up and disposed of, can be ordered.

Conclusion

The phenomenon of female energy is central to much of Stephen King's fiction, defined as supernatural, mythical, or animal. It can, of course, be argued that the 'horror' genre commonly exploits threats to – and violence upon – women's bodies; consistently, too, women are signified in relation to 'nature' and as 'mystery'. But I would like to argue that, in *Carrie* at least, the symbolic representation of female energy through the issue of blood allows for a relationship between reader, text and society within which the strength and validity of marginalized social discourses can be articulated.[20] And, in foregrounding the construction of 'texts' through fragmented narratives, puns and references to the demands of the publishing process, King identifies genre fiction as both object and image of capitalist production which is persistently signified as waste and corruption.

Carrie is the first of King's novels and I would argue that none of the later novels offers a comparable complexity, either formally or discursively. *Salem's Lot* (1976) is a classic Gothic vampire text, like its source, *Dracula* (1897),[21] explicitly concerned with dangers to purity and arguably homophobic; *The Body* (1982) addresses the nostalgia-fiction audience and maps a male 'rite of passage' from childhood to adolescence; *Christine* (1983) exploits the modern mythical significance of the motor car as power symbol and can be seen in relation to misogynistic pulp fiction, more interesting for its potentiality for readings concerned with the tensions of masculinity. Clearly, King's novels are hugely popular with both female and male readers – and, of course, that 'success' needs to be understood in relation to the escalation of the genre since the 1970s – but since *Carrie* their appeal seems less open to readings which permit progressive and positive images of female energy and power.

Notes

1 Mary Douglas, *Natural Symbols* (Harmondsworth: Penguin, 1970), p. 93.

2 e.g. Mary Shelley, *Frankenstein*, 1816; whereas the realist novel became part of the 'canon' of English literature, the Gothic novel was consigned as waste to the rubbish dump of popular fiction, to be recycled in the new twentieth-century cinematic art form as the horror film.

3 The continuing importance of realism as a literary, cinematic and televisual form cannot be simply due to institutional security; with the development of film, producing audiences variably skilled at reading a range of narratives articulated across verbal and non-verbal channels, it is conceivable that complementary practices would be applied to literary texts by modern readers.

4 e.g. the 'domestic' novels of Sarah Grand, Kate Chopin, May Sinclair, where illness, costume and landscape are narrative extensions of the body.

5 Stephen King has written: *Carrie* (London: NEL, 1974); *Salem's Lot* (London: NEL, 1974); *Different Seasons* (London: Macdonald, 1982); *Christine* (London: NEL, 1983).

6 Menstruality defined as the *experience*, in infancy, puberty and maturity, of physiological and intellectual movement and energy, which is specifically female.

7 In the realist mode they denote processes of production, consumption and waste disposal of electrical energy, connoting capitalist order, while in the symbolist mode they signify similar aspects of human energy, and patriarchal capitalism's control of socially marginal groups represented by Carrie, Margaret and Billy.

8 Arguably, since menstrual blood has no inherently harmful properties, it is likely that the smell and sight of it would be considered valid (as order), by a culture which valued menstruation as symbolic of female difference. It is in fact variously categorized across cultures as magical, contaminating, or enriching. See Mary Douglas, *Implicit Meanings* (London: Routledge & Kegan Paul, 1975); K. E. and J. M. Paige, *The Politics of Reproductive Ritual* (University of California, 1981); R. Snowden and B. Christian (eds), *Patterns and Perceptions of Menstruation* (London: Croom Helm, 1983).

9 Psychoanalysis has recognized the connection between acceptance of feminine role and stressful menstrual symptoms; this, however, from a 'normalizing', curative point of view, uncritical of the need for environmental change: Mandy *et al.* (1955), 'Many women seeking aid for female troubles are instead troubled females', cited in *The Practitioner* (May 1983), p. 855.

10 It is worth noting here that in a WEA discussion series (1984–5) on the effects of menstruality as a part of women's experience, group members (age range 30–50) spoke of denying that aspect of the female, because of negative definitions of 'cursed' and 'cursing'; of the relief of using tampons; of a sense of inferiority compounded by the inability to 'control' either bodies or emotions during menstruation; and of the negative social response to their primitive expressions of energy and creativity during the paramenstruum.

11 In magazine ads, well-groomed 'girls' at leisure are common images from the 1960s on, often participating in 'dangerous' sports such as parachuting and diving. Security and comfort are common pre-occupations. See also strict censorship rules on television ads which are on a two-year trial period, having been banned after negative audience response to the initial trial in 1980; the product cannot be shown, and no suggestion of women's sexuality is allowed (*Guardian*, 10 March 1986).

12 J. Delaney, *The Curse* (London: NEL, 1976), p. 116.

13 e.g. C. McCullers, *A Member of the Wedding* (1946); R. Godden, *The Greengage Summer* (1958); J. Blume, *Are You There, God? It's Me, Margaret* (1972).

14 M. Bakhtin, *Rabelais and his World* (Cambridge, Mass.: MIT Press, 1968), p. 26.

15 e.g. W. Golding, *Lord of the Flies* (London: Faber, 1952), where attack moves from female pig to 'effeminate' boy: 'Kill the pig – stick her in'.

16 Little is known at present about psychical control of menstruation, but research has acknowledged women's ability to synchronize menstruation when living together in groups, which would suggest some kind of unconscious ability to affect cyclical process. See P. Shuttle and P. Redgrove, *The Wise Wound* (London: Gollancz, 1978), p. 173; Snowden and Christian, *Patterns and Perceptions*, p. 161; also personal experience with family and group members.

17 Dictionary definition of 'amber': it 'does not conduct electricity, but can be used to store or excite an electric charge'.

18 Bakhtin, *Rabelais*, p. 26ff.

19 Mary Douglas, *Purity and Danger* (London: Routledge & Kegan Paul, 1966).

20 See reference to the writer/publisher/reader relationship (demands over length, form, content) in the Afterword in *Different Seasons*, and through the narrator in *The Body*.

21 Bram Stoker, *Dracula*, 1913 edn (William Rider).

10

Popular writing and feminist intervention in science fiction

SARAH LEFANU

Go little book, trot through Texas and Vermont and Alaska and Maryland and Washington and Florida and Canada and England and France . . . take your place bravely on the book racks of bus terminals and drug stores. Do not scream when you are ignored, for that will alarm people, and do not fume when you are heisted by persons who will not pay, rather rejoice that you have become so popular . . . Do not complain when at last you become quaint and old-fashioned, when you grow as outworn as the crinolines of a generation ago and are classed with *Spicy Western Stories*, *Elsie Dinsmore*, and *The Son of the Sheik*; do not mutter angrily to yourself when young persons read you to hrooch and hrch and guffaw, wondering what the dickens you were all about. Do not get glum when you are no longer understood, little book. Do not curse your fate. Do not reach up from readers' laps and punch the readers' noses.
Rejoice, little book!
For on that day, we will be free.
(Joanna Russ, *The Female Man*, pp. 213–14)

WHY ARE many women writers turning to science fiction? Does science fiction offer something to women writers that is not open to them elsewhere? Can feminist ideas, presented as science fiction, achieve a wider popularity than is now available to other types of 'feminist fiction'?

Science fiction offers certain obvious freedoms: unconstrained by the parameters of the realist mode it allows a writer to imagine other worlds and other times, making space for visions of a better world – in the Utopian tradition – or, in the dystopian, a worse one. Both Utopian and dystopian writings reflect on a present reality, the first created out of a felt lack, the second extrapolated from the perception of hidden or not so hidden inequalities and injustices. As the science fiction writer Suzy McKee Charnas has put it, science fiction allows us to write our dreams as well as our nightmares.

In terms of content, then, science fiction offers space for the flowering of ideas into landscapes and peoples; and I will look at Marge Piercy's Mattapoisett in *Woman on the Edge of Time*, where women and men live and work together in equality and happiness, Joan Slonczewski's Shora in *A Door Into Ocean*, an ocean-world where the all-female race of Sharers practise the arts of biogenetics and of healing, promulgating and defending their social system of pacific Sharing, and Zoe Fairbairns's Europea, the monstrous twenty-first century bureaucratic state in *Benefits*.

These examples will serve to illustrate what is open to women writers who turn to science fiction. I am not offering anything definitive here, only a suggestion as to why it is an attractive form for women to work in. But science fiction offers more than just the possibility of creating other worlds; it offers the opportunity to reflect on and explore the questions of writing and reading as women, that is, the position of the gendered subject. It offers this through its own central conventions: the alternate universes, black holes, folds and bends in the space/time continuum that litter the genre. For while these may be mere props for tales of swashbuckling space adventurers, they are also the means of examining and picking apart the apparently seamless narrative ideology that defines us as women and men in relation to each other and the world. This is apparent in the work of Joanna Russ.

In the extract quoted above, the final paragraph of Joanna Russ's *The Female Man*, the author plays with the idea of how a popular work of fiction is placed in time, how it reflects, or is a part of, a prevailing current of opinion. In this sense a work that challenges current ideologies, that stands against them, cannot achieve popularity. Russ gloriously imagines a time when feminism is so much a part of the social fabric that the arguments of its ideas can be simply ignored, or misunderstood, as no longer being in opposition and so no longer needing arguing. Can this really be envisaged, or is this an ironic Utopian vision? Whatever it may be, I would argue that it is possible to have popular political fictions, works that use a traditional popular framework but that require some agency on the part of the reader, that cannot be simply passively consumed and assimilated without any felt challenge. And this, I think, is what science fiction offers. Science fiction is not monolithic, and despite the refusal of many of its practitioners to question the sexual status quo, it has from the beginnings been a literature of inquiry, allowing comment and critique through the processes of defamiliarization and estrangement, embracing other narrative forms such as satire, myth, legend, historical reconstruction and straight polemic. Which is not to say that an awful lot of trash has not been written and published as science fiction; but it has shown itself to be a popular form, with a mass market audience, that by its nature encourages an interrogation of 'what is'.

I hope to show here how some women writers are using science fiction to explore the question of sexual politics, and how this might be seen as the beginnings of a popular feminist fiction; and I hope to show too, and here I will look particularly at the work of Ursula Le Guin and Joanna Russ, how such an undertaking is not free of contradictions and difficulties.

The feminist intervention into science fiction in the 1970s was concurrent with an emphasis made by critics and anthologists that despite the preponderance of male writers of science fiction there always had been women writers. This is reflected in the three anthologies edited by Pamela Sargent, *Women of Wonder*, *More Women of Wonder* and *New Women of Wonder*, which include women writers from the 1930s and 1940s such as C. L. Moore, Leigh Brackett and Judith Merril. The non-gender-specific pen-names chosen by some of these writers are indicative of the contradictions within which they worked; and the content of their fictions seems at times to be constrained by a dominant male ideology that, at work within science fiction, peripheralizes the role of female characters. When these latter are allowed to be protagonists, sexual stereotypes are challenged, and in more recent women's writing, in the work, for example, of Mary Gentle and Gwyneth Jones, worlds are created in which gender roles appear not to exist.

These early writers were published alongside their male contemporaries in the popular science fiction magazines of the day, *Astounding Science Fiction*, *Thrilling Wonder Stories*, *Amazing Stories*. The 1970s saw an incursion into the field of new women writers and writers who had not previously worked within science fiction, recognizing the possibilities that science fiction opened up for the exploration in fiction of political ideas, and in particular those of the developing women's liberation movement. A classic of this period is Marge Piercy's *Woman on the Edge of Time*, which is rich, detailed, passionate, politically engaged and imbued with the visionary idealism of the feminist thought of the time.

Woman on the Edge of Time is the story of Connie (Consuela) struggling to survive in the twentieth century under the weight of the oppression and exploitation she suffers on account of her class, her race and her sex. Her daughter is taken from her 'into care', her lover, who is black and blind, falls victim to a medical experiment in prison and dies of hepatitis, and, as the story opens, Connie is about to be incarcerated in a mental hospital once again. She is put there by her brother Luis and her niece Dolly's pimp, Geraldo, after she has witnessed Dolly's forced abortion. Questions of power and powerlessness are central to the depiction of twentieth-century life in *Woman on the Edge of Time*; white middle-class men – and in particular, in this instance, the medical establishment – wield power almost effortlessly, supported as they are by the policing activities of those lower in the hierarchy, by men like Luis and Geraldo, who, as Connie sees, strike some kind of bargain between themselves over the bodies of their women.

Powerlessness is not, however, a rigidly defined state of being. The driving force of the book, and what differentiates it from much previous Utopian writing, is Connie's refusal of passivity, her stretching out for the future and the assent she gives to a Utopian society. Process is prioritized; the future is seen quite clearly to be predicated upon the present, upon the choices made by the weak, the vulnerable, the oppressed.

Connie is a 'catcher': she is receptive to the time-traveller Luciente, from the future community of Mattapoisett, and with her help goes with her there. Mattapoisett is the future to which she assents, one of a variety of possible futures. It is a society in which there is no racial, sexual, or class oppression, where communal responsibility – for work, for children, for government – guarantees individual, but not privatized, freedoms. Marge Piercy portrays this society with subtlety, using the traditional science fictional formula of the culture clash, or human/alien interface (the people of Mattapoisett are of course human, but so different are they from all that Connie has learnt of 'human nature' that they might as well be aliens). Connie's own experience has made her mistrustful, doubting. In one of the most powerful scenes in the book she reacts with horror and revulsion to the sight of a man (and not an androgynous-looking man, but one with a bushy red beard) breastfeeding a baby. She sees it as an indication of men stealing from women the last and only power that women have left to them; a power and joy that in her own life were taken from her. Connie's final assent to Mattapoisett is made not for herself, but for Angelina, the daughter that she lost.

Woman on the Edge of Time explores and illustrates ideas that were central to the developing women's liberation movement in the 1970s: ideas that challenged women's traditional roles as childbearers and child-rearers, that broke down distinctions between the private and the public spheres, that questioned the dominance of nature over culture in the forming of an adult person. It questions other hierarchies of power besides that of men over women, showing a society in which children are empowered. Mattapoisett gives flesh to Shulamith Firestone's theories, expressed in an early text of the second wave of feminism, *The Dialectic of Sex*, of the potentially liberating effects of technology. The release of women from their reproductive functions is presented by Piercy as a premiss for the transformation of social relations that govern not just the division of labour around child-care but the wider division of labour throughout the society. The concomitant separation of sexuality from reproduction liberates women from sexual oppression; there is no sexual coercion in Mattapoisett.

Similar concerns are explored by Suzy McKee Charnas in *Motherlines*; this represents a women-only society, one in which, as in Mattapoisett, the child goes through a period of separation from its biological mother and where, again, child-rearing is seen as a communal rather than an individualized responsibility. Behind these visions of, in one instance, a society of women and men living communally without the constraints of gender roles and, in the other, of strong, loving women, lie analyses of the relationships between private property, the nuclear family and patriarchy. The Utopian tradition in science fiction lends itself to these explorations of feminist concerns.

Another concern of the feminist Utopia of the 1970s was ecology and the relation of people to the world they live in. This is central to such novels as Sally Miller Gearhart's *The Wanderground*, where the earth itself has turned against men's destructive exploitation of the land, and the post-holocaust *Dreamsnake* by Vonda McIntyre. More recently this has been explored by Joan Slonczewski, in *A Door Into Ocean*, where the ocean-world of Shora with its delicate ecological balance is threatened by a military invasion from its mother-planet Valadon. Slonczewski uses her setting for a profound examination of the philosophy and practice of non-violent direct action. The narrative is driven forward by the actual conflict: can the women of Shora survive a military-imperialistic onslaught without fighting back in kind?

A Door Into Ocean shows a continuation of what Joanna Russ has described as the 'extraordinary phenomenon' of the 1970s: the number of feminist Utopias that were written. In one way or another these books are all concerned with sexual politics: they foreground the conflict between women and men (even although in some cases men are absent, as in *Motherlines*, or Russ's 'When it Changed', or almost absent as in *The Wanderground*) and broaden it to include questions of class, race, economics, or, as in *A Door Into Ocean*, different forms of political action. Interestingly, science fiction has a long but not exactly distinguished history of dealing with the theme of sexual conflict: a variety of male-authored texts that show corrupt and crumbling matriarchies and women trying unsuccessfully to live without men. The differences between these two types of portrayal of 'the battle of the sexes' are illuminating. Where feminist writing expresses a concern with wide social and political issues, presented, often, as a vision of a better world, the male-authored men vs women stories seem to express private fears and fantasies about women and are almost without exception punitive in tone. They are moral tales, in which women are shown to get no more than they deserve. Joanna Russ has described these as 'Flasher books', for the way that their authors invest the phallus with extraordinary almost supernatural power, and compares them very interestingly with the feminist works that foreground sexual politics:

> The feminist utopias, to the degree that they are concerned with the 'battle of the sexes' (and most are) see it as a long, one-sided

massacre whose cause (not cure) is male supremacy. They are explicit
about economics and politics, sexually permissive, demystifying about
biology, emphatic about the necessity for female bonding, concerned
with children (who hardly exist in the Flasher books), non-urban,
classless, communal, relatively peaceful while allowing room for female
rage and female self-defense, and serious about the emotional and
physical consequences of violence. The Flasher books perceive conflict
between the sexes as private and opt for a magical solution *via* a
mystified biology. The feminist utopias see such conflict as a public,
class conflict, so the solutions advocated are economic, social, and
political. (Russ, 1980, pp. 13–14)

But to what extent can the feminist Utopian writing of the
1970s and 1980s be seen as popular writing? Although many
women writers have recognized the possibilities that science fiction
narratives open up, the science fiction market itself – perhaps
nurtured for too long on fearful fantasies of dominant women –
has not been wildly welcoming. Some of these works have been
widely disseminated, but I think it would be true to say that
they do not find much of a market beyond the not inconsiderable
feminist one.

On the reverse side of feminist Utopian writing we find a growing
body of feminist dystopian literature, which holds within it, I would
maintain, a Utopian streak. Cassandra was, if not the first, then
probably the most famous producer of prodromic utterances; but
whereas Cassandra was fated to be ignored, contemporary women
writers do achieve an audience, even if their works are not accorded
the 'classic' status of male-authored twentieth-century dystopias,
such as George Orwell's *Nineteen Eighty-Four* and Aldous Huxley's
Brave New World. In both, the model for 'humanity' is a male one
(which in part at least explains the institutional and cultural status
they have achieved). Feminist dystopias, on the other hand, are quite
explicit about their sexual politics. They offer another means for the
expression and exploration of the social and political consequences of
male supremacy. Again, as well as the work of science fiction writers
like Suzy McKee Charnas, Ursula Le Guin and Joanna Russ, we find
women who are not primarily science fiction writers exploring the
genre: Zoe Fairbairns with *Benefits*, Michele Roberts with a future
dystopian sequence in *The Book of Mrs Noah* and Margaret Atwood
with *The Handmaid's Tale*.

A common theme of these works is the reduction of women to their function as females, that is, their function as sexual, reproductive beings within an institutionalized heterosexuality. The female protagonists of these works speak out of an imposed silence, for the denial of speech is a denial of subjecthood. It is within the creation of a narrative that the Utopian element is found, as the protagonists seek to build an autonomy for themselves as social beings, denying the non-being imposed on them by male supremacy.

The lamentations of Margaret Atwood's nameless handmaid are powerful and haunting and frightening, but they do at least speak to a future world in which her text, the inscription of herself, as it were, is held up to academic/historical scrutiny. While the authenticity of her tale is questioned, this questioning reflects ironically on those who are doing it, those who have not suffered the excesses of Gilead.

For a feminist work *The Handmaid's Tale* has been remarkably successful, being shortlisted for the Booker Prize in 1986, and even more significantly (though I suspect with less repercussions in terms of sales) it won the first Arthur C. Clarke Award for science fiction. Is this a sign that feminism can infiltrate science fiction and be seen as reader-friendly? Will we see these authors lines up on station bookstalls between 'blockbusters' from Stephen Donaldson and L. Ron Hubbard?

Zoe Fairbairns's *Benefits* grew directly out of a debate within the British women's liberation movement around the question of 'wages for housework'. Zoe Fairbairns has described how, in 1976, her head was spinning with the arguments for and against women getting paid by the state for their work in the home, and how she found herself holding mutually contradictory opinions. She wrote: 'The question that I wrote *Benefits* to examine (though perhaps not answer) was this: what would actually happen to you, me·and the woman next door, if a British government introduced a wage for mothers? Inevitably, because I did not want to avoid the challenge of asking how such a thing might come to be, in what circumstances might a British government do it?' (Fairbairns, 1981, p. 255)

As in the feminist Utopian writing of the time, questions of reproduction and mothering are central. In *Benefits* we see this in personal terms – through the desire of one of the protagonists, Lynn Byers, for a baby, and how it affects her when that baby is born with cystic fibrosis, and then through the daughter Jane's own desire for a baby – and in wider political terms as the role and status and economic power allowed to a mother are seen to change over the years.

The novel illustrates an interesting shift in the social position of women. It opens with a group of women squatting in an abandoned tower block. Their marginality is self-chosen, a political as well as, for most of them, an individual decision. They are living outside the laws of state and family. Lynn, with both a career and a husband, is an uneasy visitor. As the story progresses and the 'position of women' is regularized and regulated by governmental decree, what little autonomy the women have is taken from them: incorporated into an enormous bureaucracy, they remain marginalized, but their marginalization is imposed upon them. Finally, however, the government policy crumbles as the monstrous consequences of state-planned motherhood are revealed, and Lynn, her daughter Jane and the other women begin to take tentative steps towards rediscovering a sense of themselves as female subjects.

This, perhaps, is why science fiction is so attractive to women writers: it offers a variety of ways in which women can place themselves as subjects of their own stories. Even in the dystopias just mentioned, women are shown struggling out of an imposed marginality, or silence, to achieve speech and subjecthood (whereas subjecthood is denied them by Orwell and Huxley, which is perhaps why these novels are so portentously gloomy!). Science fiction seems not just to offer a means of exploring 'women's issues', but to show how those issues cannot be marginalized. Questions of reproduction, of mothering, of sexuality, of desiring and dreaming, are shown to be central political questions. If science fiction lets writers create new worlds, then it also lets them set the political priorities within them.

But science fiction does have a strong male tradition. This is apparent not just in the male-authored 'battle of the sexes' literature, in which women are punished for stepping out of line, but more generally in its common narrative forms: the heroic quest and the tale of the lonely individual struggling against the universe. Women writers have to contend with this. It is not that these forms are inherently sexist, but that within them women have either been peripheralized or been ignored as women.

I would like now to look at two important writers of science fiction, Ursula Le Guin and Joanna Russ, in whose works we see an illustration of the difficulties in science fiction for feminist writers. For it seems to me that Ursula Le Guin does not challenge those traditional forms just mentioned, while such a challenge is apparent in all of Russ's work; and that from this certain tentative conclusions can be drawn about the accessibility of their work and the ease or difficulty with which sexual politics can be presented in a popular form.

Ursula Le Guin is one of the most popular of science fiction writers and one whose writing, perhaps more than anyone else's, is read by people who 'don't like' science fiction. She is passionate about the art of writing, and is enormously concerned that popularity should not be in conflict with quality. In an essay describing her development as a science fiction writer ('A citizen of Mondath', *Foundation*, no. 4, 1973) she tells a delightful story about herself and her brother Karl when they were young children:

> we looked for the trashiest magazines, mostly, because we *liked* trash. I recall one story that began, 'In the beginning was the Bird.' We really dug that bird. And the closing line from another (or the same?) – 'Back to the saurian ooze from whence it sprung!' Karl made that into a useful chant: The saurian ooze from which it sprung/Unwept, unhonour'd, and unsung. – I wonder how many hack writers who think they are writing down to 'naive kids' and 'teenagers' realise the *kind* of pleasure they sometimes give their readers. If they did, they would sink back into the saurian ooze from whence they sprung. (pp. 21–2)

Ursula Le Guin's two most widely known novels are probably *The Left Hand of Darkness* and *The Dispossessed*. *The Left Hand of Darkness* is set on a planet, Gethen, of which the inhabitants are androgynes, able to assume either female or male characteristics. This produces some startling consequences for the unwary reader; *The Left Hand of Darkness* must be one of the few novels in which a king is pregnant. None the less, apart from such biological anomalies all the characters are presented as male. There are no women on Gethen, only men. This is compounded by the author's use of the generic 'he' throughout. Ursula Le Guin, who I think is remarkable for her openness to criticism and self-criticism, has suggested that this pro-male bias merely reflects the bias, or indeed the prejudices, of the narrator of the story, Genly Ai, an envoy (male) from earth; and further that the sexual political element is only a minor part of the novel. The first response begs a variety of questions (what does it say, for example, about a future earth society?); the second, while it may be true, shows a conflict between authorial intent and the stubbornness of her readers. For it is the sexual political element that arouses readers' passions; perhaps because both science fiction and non-science fiction readers alike find it remarkable that such a possibility is explored with seriousness. (On certain levels the ramifications are explored, not least in the thesis of the book that one of the consequences of a non-polarized sexuality is the lack of wider social, indeed institutionalized, aggression.)

Although the socialist/anarchist society of Anarres in *The Dispossessed* is said to have been set up by a woman, female characters in this book play a distinctly secondary role to the male protagonist, the physicist Shevek. Sexual politics is a topic in *The Dispossessed*: the sexually egalitarian nature of the society on Anarres is set against the social structure of the capitalist bloc on Urras, where women are seen as commodities. But, as other critics have noted, there is a noticeable gap between what the reader is *told* about the organization of society and what the text reveals. Shevek, for instance, seems strangely unformed by the society in which he has been brought up. He is, in fact, the traditional solitary male hero, standing outside society, on a quest for self-knowledge.

The search for harmony is a theme that runs through all Le Guin's work, and is undoubtedly related to her interest in Taoism. In *The Dispossessed*, the different social systems are presented, finally, as having relative merits and demerits. Utopia, it seems, is a matter of perception. Shevek returns home a sadder and a wiser man; his discovery of the simultaneity principle (which was what pushed him into leaving Anarres in the first place) will not now be hijacked by one government or another to further its own ends. Shevek has achieved what he set out to do. But other areas of political conflict have faded into the background, not least the area of sexual politics.

As Genly Ai's mental horizons are broadened by his stay on Gethen, so are Shevek's by his journeyings abroad. Shevek's 'maleness' is never challenged, nor is the narrative structure that places him as hero. And so the uncomfortable questions that are raised about political, and in particular sexual political, conflict, are subsumed within an attractive traditional resolution: the achievements of and maturation of the male hero. I would suggest that this is one of the reasons why Ursula Le Guin is such a popular writer: she writes seriously about political concerns, but her fictional resolutions, striving for harmony out of conflict, allow the reader to escape with beliefs unchallenged and position as reader left secure.

There are other women writers exploring the SF genre, like C. J. Cherryh, Mary Gentle, Octavia Butler, who do much to subvert the sexual and racial stereotypes that, alas, abound in science fiction. But while in their work authority is shifted from male to female, from white to non-white characters, the wider political structures often remain unchanged. This may be due to their use of traditional narrative frameworks. But again this can work to good effect, because these popular forms have a guaranteed market which feminist writers can exploit by subverting the readers' expectations of what SF should be. It would be idealistic to imagine that the weight of dominant male values that has accrued around SF over the years can simply be swept aside; indeed the tension in much popular SF written by women reflects a tension in the real world between new ideas and established forms.

Now, finally, I would like to turn to Joanna Russ, whose work seems to me to exemplify the tension between form and idea that many feminist writers are struggling with. Joanna Russ is as well established in science fiction as Ursula Le Guin but, unlike Le Guin, she attempts to deconstruct the formal paradigms of SF and in so doing challenges both the masculine tradition and the notion of the reader as a passive consumer. Her books are therefore not as easy to read, and so, although she is respected by SF fans, she is not so widely popular. Her work constantly challenges the notion of what is 'natural'; contradictions are teased out and explored and are not necessarily resolved. She has described what science fiction offers her as a writer (Russ, 1975, p. 47):

> One of the best things (for me) about science fiction is that – at least theoretically – it is a place where the ancient dualities disappear. Day and night, up and down, 'masculine' and 'feminine' are purely specific, limited phenomena which have been mythologised by people. They are man-made (not women-made). Excepting up and down, night and day (maybe). Out in space there is no up or down, no day or night, and in the point of view space can give us, I think there is no 'opposite' sex – what a word! Opposite what? The Eternal Feminine and the Eternal Masculine become the poetic fancies of a weakly dimorphic

species trying to imitate every other species in a vain search for what is 'natural'.

(*Khatru*, ed. Jeffrey D. Smith, 1975)

Joanna Russ is very much at ease with the different forms of science fiction. Her *Alyx* stories, for example, play marvellously with the subgenre of sword-and-sorcery, with the tough street-wise Alyx, as swift with her wit as with her sword, in a role seldom permitted to female characters.

But it is in her later novels, and in particular *The Female Man*, that the possible contradictions between a political and a popular literature are most apparent. Like many other SF works, *The Female Man* is set in various time streams, a present, a past, various futures. The novel has multiple protagonists and multiple narrators, and the author herself is inscribed as a character. The narrative consists of description, polemic, meditation, dialogue set out as a play. There is a constant friction between the different selves who are the protagonists, and between the author and the reader. It is not a book that takes the reader by the hand to lead her from beginning to end with adventures on the way but with the ultimate certainty that all is fiction. Rather, it takes the reader by the scruff of the neck, shakes her, enrages her and makes her laugh. No easy identification is allowed between reader and author, or reader and protagonist. A similar refusal is apparent too in *We Who Are About To . . .* , where there is, it seems, a single central narrator protagonist. But during the course of this short and passionate novel (which opens with a crash-landing on an unknown planet, and eight people who must decide how, and if, to survive) the narrator's consciousness fragments. She becomes inhabited by ghosts of other fictions. As in *The Female Man*, the reader is forced to look at the different ways in which a woman is constructed as a woman, the ways in which she is placed by a patriarchal order and the ways in which she can struggle against that, both as writer and as reader. Russ does not allow her characters to be simple heroes or heroines.

Joanna Russ's work makes demands upon the reader, but while her politics may be distressingly overt to many a male science fiction reader, her ease with the conventions of the form is unmistakable. Her aim is not so much to subvert stereotypes of character, as to subvert the uses to which a science fictional narrative can be put.

As I hope I have shown, there are difficulties in reaching a mass audience with political fiction, but the first steps have been taken. Strong female characters now appear regularly in science fiction without any necessarily feminist political intent. And now that science fiction is being seen as something that women can write, too, there is hope that there will be a gradual changing of the structure and narrative conventions of the genre.

Bibliography

Atwood, Margaret (1986), *The Handmaid's Tale* (London: Cape; Virago edn, 1987).

Charnas, Suzy McKee (1978/1980), *Motherlines* (New York/London: Berkley/Gollancz).

Fairbairns, Zoe (1979), *Benefits* (London: Virago).

—— (1981), 'On writing *Benefits*', *Women and Writing Newsletter*; reprinted in Feminist Anthology Collective (ed.) *No Turning Back* (London: Women's Press, 1981), pp. 255–8.

Firestone, Shulamith (1970/1979), *The Dialectic of Sex* (New York/London: Morrow/Women's Press).

Gearhart, Sally Miller (1979/1985), *The Wanderground* (Watertown, Mass./London: Persephone/Women's Press).

Le Guin, Ursula K. (1969), *The Left Hand of Darkness* (New York/London: Ace/Macdonald).

—— (1974), *The Dispossessed* (New York/London: Harper & Row/ Gollancz).

—— (July 1973), 'A citizen of Mondath', *Foundation*, no. 4, pp. 20–4.

McIntyre, Vonda N. (1978), *Dreamsnake* (New York/London: Houghton Mifflin/Gollancz).

Piercy, Marge (1976/1979), *Woman on the Edge of Time* (New York/London: Knopf/Women's Press).

Roberts, Michele (1987), *The Book of Mrs Noah* (London: Methuen).

Russ, Joanna (1983/1985), *The Adventures of Alyx* (New York/London: Pocket Books/Women's Press).

—— (1975/1985), *The Female Man* (New York/London: Bantam/Women's Press).

—— (1975/1987), *We Who Are About To . . .* (New York/London: Dell/Women's Press).

—— (1980), '*Amor vincit feminam*: the battle of the sexes in science fiction', *Science Fiction Studies*, vol. 7, pp. 2–15.

—— (November 1975), contribution to symposium, in Jeffrey D. Smith (ed.), *Khatru*, nos 3 and 4 (Baltimore, Md: Phantasmicon).

Sargent, Pamela (ed.) (1974/1978), *Women of Wonder: Science Fiction Stories by Women about Women* (New York/Harmondsworth: Vintage/Penguin).

—— (1976/1979), *More Women of Wonder: Science Fiction Novelettes by Women about Women* (New York/Harmondsworth: Vintage/Penguin).

—— (1978), *The New Women of Wonder: Recent Science Fiction Stories by Women about Women* (New York: Vintage).

Slonczewski, Joan (1986/1987), *A Door Into Ocean* (New York/London: Arbor House/Women's Press).

11

Science fiction:

The dreams of men

DEREK LONGHURST

LAUNCHING his second science fiction magazine, *Science Wonder Stories*, in 1929 Hugo Gernsback declared his optimistic vision of the future of technological progress, describing it as the dawn of a new era in which

> dreams of men reach out to other worlds of space and time. The new unknown of science is calling. The ships of man will follow his dreams as caravans followed the dreams of Columbus. Science will answer the call, with a thousand new inventions – inspired by science fiction.[1]

It would be mistaken either to take such statements too seriously or to dismiss them as the mere ravings of one of the early SF entrepreneurs. The historical moment of Gernsback's venture, however, may be of considerable significance as his paean of praise to the 'new unknown' of science constitutes the potential of new dreams when so many of the old American dreams were preparing to cast themselves out of the top-floor windows of that paradigm of futuristic architectural technology, the skyscraper. When the 'logic' of capitalist progress in *this* world suffers internal combustion, fantasies of alternative worlds to be discovered and conquered take on a new edge. The model of Columbus and the discourse of power inscribed in the genuflection to a pioneer, frontier spirit registers the appeal to a mythic past as verificatory framework within which the future will be embraced. It is not, of course, specific to the 'history' of science fiction that there is no space within which to call into consciousness any knowledge of the consequences for those 'alien others', the native American peoples, of the caravans following Columbus's dreams. Yet, we may ask, how often has masculine science fiction rewritten that 'history' around conquest of primitive, hostile, nature-oriented societies resistant to the 'natural' patriarchal, ethnically harmonious family of American civilization/democracy/imperialism?

One central operation of Gernsback's formulation – and a common strategy – is to dehistoricize and depoliticize 'science' and 'technology' as signifiers within science fiction. Rendered socially and economically autonomous, science and technology are conceptualized – and in the process, of course, repoliticized – as having their own logic, history and evolution as the result of pure discovery, invention and progress. And as with the genre of science fiction itself, the motor force lies in the restless imagination and genius of men.

Clearly we are dealing here with complex issues, which stretch far beyond the scope of this essay, concerning male dominance within the social and economic institutions of education as well as in the public spheres of work and power. For the moment I would like to restrict my objectives to an examination of the ways in which popular science fiction narratives 'address' male subjectivities.

Now it is obvious that, since Gernsback wrote his editorial, the genre of SF has developed in richly variegated forms interacting with specific historical formations. Clearly, too, some of these forms have proved powerfully attractive to both men and women as writers and readers (although the genre has been less open to cross-gendered pleasures, I would argue, than crime fiction). The sheer heterogeneity of science fiction and its subgenres would seem to preclude simplistic definition and categorization. Is the field of SF criticism in itself, littered as it is with the struggle for 'definition', a 'text' of masculine desire? In any case, it is clear that essentialist or formalist analyses of the genre will not do. Abstract conceptualizations of science fiction rooted in the search for common textual conventions or iconographic typologies are doomed either to vacuousness or bizarre proscriptiveness. The frequency with which the boundaries between genres and subgenres are disturbed precludes such strategies from addressing in any precise way the social relations of the production and consumption of SF narratives. The most influential attempt at locating the genre has been Darko Suvin's ascription, the literature of 'cognitive estrangement'.[2] Suvin's theory emphasizes the fictional construction of an 'alternative' world, necessarily distancing the reader from 'common sense' assumptions about reality, thereby undermining the bridge between depicted textual world and the reader's sociocultural consciousness across which meanings are negotiated. Simultaneously, however, SF 'proper' draws upon current scientific or technological laws and paradigms in order to posit the evolutionary history and constitution of the alternative world. Thus, SF can be differentiated from the modes of realism on the one hand and sheer fantasy on the other – although we should perhaps note in passing the proximity of this paradigm to Todorov's structuralist account of the quintessential characteristics of literature of the fantastic.

Suvin's thesis, while useful as *one* starting-point for the reading of science fiction, is also designed to constitute the genre as a literature of subversion – the influence of Brecht is evident – which arguably leads into an academic cul-de-sac. Within these boundaries it becomes possible to 'discover' *true* SF, characterized by the universal and fixed quality of estrangement which permeates and underlies historical change and cultural diversity. Not only does this analysis, in the end, seem very un-Brechtian in its formalism, it also leads to the extremely unmaterialist exclusion of many forms of the genre which are commonly produced, distributed and read as science fiction.

Far from pursuing the chimera of such definitions, then, my concern in this essay is to explore, with considerable feelings of tentativeness, the possibilities for a gendered approach to the understanding of narrative pleasure generated by a range of SF texts, chosen specifically for their 'cult' status, in an effort to get at some dimensions of the genre's sources of appeal to male fantasy.

The object of this experiment is not primarily to praise or blame – inevitably, and I hope overtly, certain principles of judgement will emerge – but to assess critically the articulation of the 'natural' associations of science, technology, adventure, discovery and conquest, the exercise of power, the struggle for control and dominance within representations of male cognitive and physical prowess. As Richard Dyer has argued,

> We look at the world through ideas of male sexuality. Even when not looking *at* male sexuality, we are looking at the world within its terms of reference.[3]

Concerning these 'ideas', the Hite report suggests that when men are attempting to describe their identities and fantasies, the gauze through which the male gaze peers both aggressively and anxiously is woven around notions of 'being' as strength, achievement, authority, control, reliability, self-sufficiency, self-assurance, leadership – and, we might add, 'performance'. It is the pervasiveness of masculinity and the normative institutionalized authority of male heterosexuality which renders its power structures so 'natural' and invisible to those of us who benefit from their dominance. Heterosexual masculinity, then, has been able to present itself *as* 'reality' regardless in many ways of the specific historical experience of men, inducing thereby not only oppression of astounding proportions in every sphere of social life but also repression, tension and contradiction. And, of course, masculinity has constantly to reproduce its meanings against threats from *within* as well as from *without*. Thus, homosexuality is commonly constituted as the alien negative of masculinity – the 'failure' to *be* and *act* like a man in a social narrative where male bonding is always in the service of some superior ideal such as the nation, law and order, justice and so on. Meanwhile, relations with women are understood and practised through *their* complementarity (ideally) or displacement, especially perhaps when transgressive of the 'natural' boundaries of 'femininity'. Masculine identity is forged in 'public' but this is a model which is very dependent on the absence of women from that domain, nurturing male (hidden) psychological needs in the privacy of the home. Obviously the women's movement and changes in the labour market since the 1960s have introduced new challenges for this male hegemony.

It may be argued, with some justice, that these are broad generalizations calling for some qualification. In terms of cultural representation, film noir comes to mind, for instance. But the fact that it does, not only is a measure of the dominance of masculine narratives and genres but also registers the extent to which gender has for too long been designated as a 'women's issue', critically located as of relevance to women's cultural production and representation in which shifts of gender roles – and consequently of social relations – are foregrounded. What needs to be addressed – in addition to the ideological co-ordinates of class, nation and ethnicity where we white male critics have found ourselves more at ease – are the complex and covert processes through which narratives signify, articulate and reproduce masculine subjectivities and sexuality. This is not just a matter of differentiating a 'bad' from a 'good' representation – a strategy based on an assumption that there can be an objective norm against which significations of sexuality and gender are to be assessed – but more crucially it is a matter of questioning the ways in which narrative structure may be rooted *in* masculine discourses and how such discourses are nurtured through both the socioeconomic structures of patriarchy *and* the pleasures of its cultural representation within narratives.

These problems seem to be worth consideration in any analysis of the genre of science fiction and not just to the 'soft' social scientific end of the spectrum associated with Ursula Le Guin or Ian Watson; nor should they be ghettoized in relation to fantasy while the imagined future worlds of Asimov, Clarke, Heinlein *et al.* are seen as representations of the 'universal' conflicts of 'man' against nature, the 'drive' towards progress and rationality, the 'great questions' of mankind's [*sic*] evolution and so on.[4] Rather we have to ask how, as gendered readers, do these texts offer to position us in the processes of 'making sense' of the narrative? How, too, do they interact with the historically specific discourses which run through us as readers and social beings?

Isaac Asimov's sequence of short stories *I, Robot* was published originally during the 1940s at the high point of optimism concerning technological progress and its beneficial, deterministic effects on human society. Perhaps we might identify this period of SF as the 'Gee Whiz' era of *Tomorrow's World* science before the second H-bomb test in 1954 blew apart not only Bikini Atoll but also public confidence that scientists fully understood and controlled the consequences of their experiments. Asimov's stories explore the tensions between humans and machine intelligence (robots with 'positronic brains') as well as *within* machine intelligence occasioned by the three immutable laws of robotics:

1 A robot may not injure a human being, or through inaction allow a human being to come to harm.
2 A robot must obey the orders given it by human beings except where such orders would conflict with the first law.

3   A robot must protect its own existence as long as such protection
does not conflict with the first or second law.

Handbook of Robotics, 56th edition, AD 2058.

(Asimov, 1968, frontispiece)

In the penultimate story, 'Evidence', the linking character of
the sequence, Dr Susan Calvin, a 'robopsychologist', outlines the
rationale behind these fundamental principles which govern the
'positronic' brain:

> the three rules of robotics are the essential guiding principles of a good
> many of the world's ethical systems, of course, every human being is
> supposed to have the instinct of self-preservation. That's Rule Three
> to a robot. Also every 'good' human being with a social conscience
> and a sense of responsibility, is supposed to defer to proper authority;
> to listen to his doctor, his boss, his government, his psychiatrist, his
> fellow man; to obey laws, to follow rules, to conform to custom –
> even when they interfere with his comfort or his safety. That's Rule
> Two to a robot. Also, every 'good' human being is supposed to love
> others as himself, protect his fellow man, risk his life to save another.
> That's Rule One to a robot.
>
> (Asimov, 1968, p. 169)

We need not pause here to analyse the bizarre naïvety of this
liberal-humanist account of the instincts and ideal social conduct of
human nature which, for Asimov, provides the controlling principle
for the future of the technological age. The same stories chart the
evolution of the robot from clumsy but lovable domestic nursemaid
('Robbie', 1940), through various experimental stages and 'acci-
dents' in the space programme (US) involving the use of robots, to
humanoid robot morally and mentally superior to human politicians
('Evidence', 1946). And, finally, at the height of McCarthyism and
the Cold War, Asimov posits a future world in which 'The Machine',
evolving to a sophistication far beyond human intelligence through
the internal logic of technological development, is able to co-ordinate
political and economic systems *and* deal non-aggressively with
human opposition to its decisions ('The Evitable Conflict', 1950). In
an era in which the technologies of warfare and genocide had taken
on new proportions, Asimov's narratives reconstitute technology as a
potentiality to transcend human limitations and adherence to 'belief'

systems whether of fundamentalist religion, nationalism, capitalism, or communism: with the development of the positronic brain

> It no longer seemed so important whether the world was Adam Smith or Karl Marx. Neither made very much sense under the new circumstances. Both had to adapt and they ended in almost the same place.
>
> (Asimov, 1968, p. 186)

But these societies and their citizens largely remain an 'absence' at the heart of the narratives. What we are 'told' is that the technological revolution has led to an earth divided into four peacefully coexisting regions and organized economically into competitive corporations – internationally responsible and subject to government authority – such as that for which Susan Calvin works, 'U.S. Robot and Mechanical Men, Inc.'.

It has seemed unnecessary to emphasize the masculine discourse which structures Asimov's 'world' of the twenty-first century. In the previous essay, Sarah Lefanu has argued that women are rendered 'peripheral' in male science fiction writing and this observation has provided one starting-point for my attempt to investigate how, precisely, this marginalization operates. At the most obvious level, in *I, Robot*, apart from Susan Calvin to whom I shall return later, there are only two minor women characters inhabiting the world of the nine stories stretching from 1996 to 2052, while women as a gender existing in society are represented only once:

> 'There was a work shortage somewhere in Mexico once on the question of women. There weren't enough women in the neighbourhood. It seemed no one had thought of feeding sexual data to the Machine.'
>
> He stopped to laugh, delightedly.
>
> (Asimov, 1968, p. 194)

Thus, despite the experience of the Second World War, women are constituted as remaining outside the labour process in 2052 except in so far as they support it by providing sexual pleasure for men!

In 'Robbie', the first of the stories and the only one to register directly the effects of technology on the 'private' world of the suburban nuclear family, woman is the 'enemy' because inimical to the value of the robot – characterized like a pet – through adherence to socially conventional notions of what is 'natural'. Thus, Mrs Weston has agreed to buy a robot-nursemaid while it was a 'fashionable thing to do' but when the neighbours become suspicious of 'Robbie' she is registered as the archetypal 'nagging' woman, foolishly and persistently trying to get rid of 'him'; her husband is, on the other hand, a 'genial and understanding person' who

> loved his wife – and what was worse, his wife knew it. George Weston, after all, was only a man – poor thing – and his wife made full use of every device which a clumsier and more scrupulous sex has learned, with reason and futility, to fear.
>
> (Asimov, 1968, p. 20)

This characteristically stereotypical representation of 'women' in 'private' should be borne in mind when we come to the final tale, 'The Evitable Conflict', in which a woman has become a world leader of one of the four regions – the weakest and most unproductive:

> She shrugged her delicate shoulders, and allowed a thin smile to cross her little face as she tamped out a cigarette with long fingers. 'Europe is a sleepy place. And such of our men as do not manage to emigrate to the Tropics are tired and sleepy along with it. You see for yourself that it is myself, a poor woman, to whom falls the task of being Vice-Co-ordinator. Well, fortunately, it is not a difficult job, and not much is expected of me.'
>
> (Asimov, 1968, p. 196)

Here, Europe is represented as a declining and decadent *culture* economically unproductive and therefore symbolically associated with 'femininity'.

Not only, then, is there not much support for Susan Calvin from the narrative signification of woman as a gender but she is represented in a mode which locates her as an 'object' for observation. Her body is, typically, one way in which this is encoded – plain, unattractive, cold, frosty, colourless, thin-lipped and so on – and it is repeatedly suggested that her 'cold enthusiasm' for science and rationality is conducted at the expense of her true nature as a woman (her ambivalent role as a robot psychologist who analyses the logic of emotions is significant). This reaches a crisis in 'Liar' when a mind-reading robot suggests that her secret love for another scientist may be reciprocated by him. When she discovers that the robot has merely conformed to what it thought she had wanted to hear, she drives it 'insane', taking out her 'pain, frustration and hate' on 'him', while two of her male colleagues, equally deceived by the robot concerning their *professional* rivalry, watch 'in frozen bewilderment'. They, however, do not lose their 'mental equilibrium' (Asimov, 1968, pp. 108–9).

If women are peripheral to fifty-six years of Asimov's 'history' – or occupy Susan Calvin's frigid, isolated and embittered consciousness preferring robots to humans – what are 'men' doing? It will have been noticed that all robots are masculine in consciousness because in Asimov's society all *knowledge* is masculine (e.g. 'the machine' of 'The Evitable Conflict') and knowledge is power – a central theme of all of the narratives. While robots are created with a slave mentality a tension is explored in that the machine intelligence gradually becomes superior to the humanity which it serves. An interesting story here is 'Little Lost Robot' (1947) in which the robots are addressed as 'Boy'(!) with its racial connotations and the narrative touches on anxieties that any slackening of the slave mentality (Rule Number One) could lead to uppity robots realizing their potential for equality and even superiority. The 'normal' robots are dangerously influenced by the rogue individualist, but the 'deviant' is eventually singled out and the status quo re-established.

The essential point to make, however, is that the articulation of this 'alternative world' is conducted through a range of narrative strategies directed towards male identification. To draw upon Barthes, the text's symbolic code is firmly that of white male heterosexuality as the subjectivity through which meanings may be most easily negotiated (Barthes, 1974).[5]

Similarly, this provides the aperture through which the 'world' is focused in Arthur C. Clarke's *2001: A Space Odyssey* (1968). The basic proposition of the novel is that 'man's' evolution has been an elaborately programmed experiment conducted by an alien and superior intelligence which has transcended space, time and organic matter. The world into which this intelligence, represented by a crystalline monolith, first intervenes – that of the 'Primeval Night' of man-apes – is already constituted around certain 'natural' patterns.

The two babies were already whimpering for food, but became silent when Moon-Watcher snarled at them. One of the mothers, defending the infant she could not properly feed, gave him an angry growl in return; he lacked the energy even to cuff her for her presumption.

(Clarke, 1968, p. 11)

His 'father' newly dead, Moon-Watcher is a leader of a tribe, 'almost a giant' among his species, and it is he who responds to the 'education' offered by the monolith. Failing tests of manual dexterity, he proves to have a more natural bent for pitching stones at a target imaged for him in the crystal slab:

At the fourth attempt he was only inches from the central bulls-eye. A feeling of indescribable pleasure, almost sexual in its intensity, flooded his mind.

(Clarke, 1968, p. 21)

Thus, the narrative draws upon that common cultural discourse which constitutes violence as interactive with male sexuality and characterizes each in terms of the other; the problem, however, is the silence on how or why violence is so endemic to male sexuality, desires and relationships. Or is it a silence? The implication in this representation of the links between vulnerability, the male body, aggression, power and sexuality is that the educative conditioning of the superior intelligence *pulls out* innate, animal, natural urges. The ultimate implication of *that* narrative is that 'man can't help himself'. Its Pavlovian experiments completed, the 'intelligence' enters Moon-Watcher's consciousness and creates what kind of vision for him?

He was looking at a peaceful family group, differing in only one respect from the scenes he knew. The male, female and two infants that had mysteriously appeared before him were gorged and replete, with sleek and glossy pelts – and this was a condition of life that Moon-Watcher had never imagined.

(Clarke, 1968, p. 22)

Stimulated by this vision of the well-fed nuclear family, 'discontent had come into his soul' and Moon-Watcher 'had taken one small step towards humanity' (Clarke, 1968, p. 23). Here Clarke is probably drawing on the Darwinian notion of the family – with the 'soft', nurturing role of the woman at its centre – as the model for civilization and progress interacting with, but also restraining and shaping, the male aggression which ensures the survival of the species. The reconstitution of Victorian values may, of course, be one reaction to the challenges of the 1960s as it has been, in different ways, in the 1980s.

In Kubrick's film the link forward to the year 2001 is forged through the ape's recognition of bones as 'symbols of power' (Clarke, 1968, p. 26). As this 'weapon' flies up into the air it is visually transformed into a space craft, homologous in shape and definition. Building, perhaps, on Moon-Watcher's sensation of the pleasure of violence as proximate to that of (male) sexuality, Kubrick's *mise-en-scène* persistently elaborates upon technological imagery of phallic power and penetration. (His film of *A Clockwork Orange* also comes to mind with its insistently pornographic and exploitative representation of these issues in a science fiction.) It is worth noting that Clarke's novel does offer some sense of ambivalence concerning the double-edged value of technology for future societies.

But what *kind* of society does Clarke construct as an 'alternative world' which might disturb the reader's 'common-sense' notions of contemporary reality?

> The *trim* stewardess greeted him as he entered the cabin . . . [she] *fussed* over him a while and then moved to her cubicle at the rear of the cabin.
> (Clarke, 1968, p. 42; my emphases)

And for in-flight entertainment on his journey to the moon what does Dr Heywood Floyd, the hero of Clarke's later sequels, receive?

> Only the charming little stewardess seemed completely at ease in his presence. As Floyd quickly discovered, she came from Bali, and had carried beyond the atmosphere some of the grace and mystery of that still largely unspoilt island. One of his strongest, and most enchanting, memories of the entire trip was her zero-gravity demonstration of some classical Balinese dance movements, with the lovely, blue-green crescent of the waning Earth as a backdrop.
> (Clarke, 1968, p. 57)

He telephones his housekeeper to give her directions and ruminates on his three motherless children – 'perhaps for *their* sake *he* should have remarried' (Clarke, 1968, p. 44; my emphases). Arriving on the moonbase we do find that the equal opportunities demands of the women's movement may have had some effect:

> The eleven hundred men and six hundred women who made up the personnel of the Base were all highly trained scientists and technicians, carefully selected before they had left Earth.
>
> (Clarke, 1968, p. 61)

The narrative, however, does not sustain this 'reality' as only male scientists materialize. And the highly trained women?

> Floyd found himself in the familiar environment of typewriters, office computers, girl assistants, wall charts and ringing telephones.
>
> (Clarke, 1968, p. 64)

Floyd's journey to the moon has been occasioned by the rediscovery of the 3-million-year-old crystalline monolith. When it beams a magnetic field towards Japetus, one of Saturn's moons, a team of astronauts and scientists, led by Dave Bowman, is launched into the uncharted frontiers of space to investigate. Here, of course, it is 'naturally' a man's world. Like all of his colleagues, Bowman is unmarried as it would not be 'fair to send *family men* on a mission of such duration' (my emphasis). As 'one of the penalties of an astronaut's, as it had once been of a mariner's way of life' they accept their loss of contact with 'their girls on Earth' but as there are no 'compensations' of 'tropical islands full of dusky maids' alternative solutions to this minor distracting irritant have been developed:

> The space medics . . . had tackled this problem with their usual enthusiasm; and the ship's pharmacopoeia provided adequate, though hardly glamorous substitutes.
>
> (Clarke, 1968, p. 102)

This sordid and dreary little portrait of male sexuality – biologically given, an urge, a nuisance distracting from man's real goals in the universe, a sexuality somehow separate from gender identity, the rebellious penis somehow autonomous from the rest of the male body – is crucial to the establishment of masculine invulnerability, distance, autonomy, commitment to 'goals' of a higher service to humanity than the need for psychological dependency and the emotions of sexuality.

That this is a matter of gender identity may be illustrated by what follows. Having got their little problem out of the way, Dave and Frank Poole, his partner, can concentrate on the integration of their 'mission' and their male bonding – 'they were too intelligent and well adjusted to quarrel' (Clarke, 1968, p. 102). And we also discover why this has to be a man's world:

> Space-pods were not the most elegant means of transport devised by man . . . They were usually christened with feminine names, perhaps in recognition of the fact that their personalities were sometimes slightly unpredictable. *Discovery's* trio were Anna, Betty and Clara.
> (Clarke, 1968, p. 124)

And *there*, of course, lies half-concealed a classic case of transference. Women are rendered as unpredictable and therefore 'absent' from this man's world in order to preserve masculine gender identity intact whereas an alternative narrative might suggest that what is at stake is the repression of the 'unpredictable' – emotion, tension, fear – in male identity which might have to be confronted if women were a 'presence'.

Unfortunately, for the mission, the unpredictable turns out to be HAL, the spaceship's computer whose artificial intelligence is warped by 'his' knowledge and 'psychological' responses to the real objectives of the flight which have been concealed from Bowman. HAL's 'panic' leads to the killing of Frank Poole and the three hibernating scientists, leaving Bowman no option but to murder the computer by removing the 'higher centres' of the 'brain'. This introduces a note of ambivalence concerning the powers and limitations of technology but more particularly it serves to isolate Bowman in his lone heroic battle with nature and space until he makes contact with the alien intelligence. Transformed by this 'contact' in matter and consciousness (Kubrick's imagery played into 1960s representations of psychedelic experience) Bowman as a 'Star-Child' broods menacingly over the next stage in Earth's evolutionary history. An omnipotent presence surveying the 'glittering toy' of the planet he waited, marshalling his thoughts and brooding over his still untested powers. For though he was master of the world, he was not quite sure what to do next.

But he would think of something.

(Clarke, 1968, p. 224)

What that 'something' is can be discovered in Clarke's sequels *2010: Odyssey Two* and *2061: Odyssey Three*.

The question I have been pursuing to this point, then, is the extent to which masculine desire for power, autonomy, conquest, adventure, the fearless resolution of enigmas is predicated on that very exclusion of women as subject. Can it be argued that certain dimensions of male pleasure may be constituted in reading women as absent, displaced, or 'alien'?

In Murray Leinster's story 'First Contact' Man meets Alien and after testing each other out they discover that their differences can be resolved by recognition of their fundamental psychological similarity. The apotheosis of this brotherly bond is registered when Tommy (the human) and Buck (the alien) tell each other dirty jokes.

In the narrative I have examined so far, threats to male power from *within* are displaced totally by threats from without. One of the common characteristics of the representations of heterosexual masculinity is its constitution simply as *being*, and that provides the source for acts of *performance* through which strength, leadership and power may be signified. Insecurity, fear, or emotional responses other than anger or manifestation of self-control are withheld in the process of mystifying a narrative of male authority. Clarke's fiction, for instance, depicts three million years of evolution but in one sense the journey is extremely short. From Moon-Watcher to Star-Child, from myths of the first hunter to fantasies of omnipotent Godhead, male power resides in the realm of 'nature'; *that* narrative leads, of course, to the representation of the social relations of a patriarchal culture alive and doing well in the year 2001.

I would not like to suggest that what is involved here is a simple process involving texts as hypodermic injections with readers mainlining their dosages to get a 'fix' on their identities. Nevertheless, fictional representations are among the signifying practices through which as men and women we 'recognize' and construct our gendered subjectivities which the social processes of 'reading' engage in both cognitive and in emotional negotiations. For the purposes of this essay, too, I have isolated sexuality and gender, both of which are inevitably inflected by class and ethnic identity. For instance, it would be possible to trace modes of identification for the educated middle-class readership of SF (Mellor, 1984) through the scientists and intelligentsia such as Dr Heywood Floyd while the astronauts who 'test' the technology (Dave Bowman; Mike Donovan and Greg Poole in *I, Robot*) are signified in relation to practical, applied manual labour skills.[6] Significantly, perhaps, while the former group inhabit power and authority and seek mental resolutions to enigmas the latter are commonly represented as having to pick up the pieces or bear the consequences of decision-making processes. It is *their* resourcefulness under trial, however, which provides the core of the presentation of men as initiators of action.

Of course women *have* been signified as central in male science fiction but arguably only in particular ways. In Frank Herbert's *Dune* published in 1965, belonging to the subgenre of the SF chronicle saga, a powerful network of women, characterized as 'witches', has schemed and plotted to produce the Kwisatz Haderach. This messianic leader can only be constituted in a male child who will combine the male and female principles in his psychological being. The central conflict is organized around the epic struggle of good against evil, represented by the liberal-democratic house of Atreides governing with a due sense of human worth and maintaining a proper relationship between economic exploitation and ecological balance as against the viciously homosexual, grossly fat Baron Harkonnen who rules through the corruption, treachery and power strategies of autocratic *Realpolitik*. The final grouping are the Fremen, primitive tribes who have adapted to the barren and dangerous ecology of the planet Arrakis in order to survive. Following the death of his father through treachery, Paul Atreides makes common cause with the Fremen and becomes their messiah-leader, undergoing a number of virility tests while also introducing new values in that he incorporates rather than killing their previous leader. Marshalling the Fremen 'natural' weapons of stealth and strength Paul overcomes the advanced technologies of warfare possessed by the Harkonnen. The underground existence of the Fremen, their customs and rituals, their harnessing of the natural forces of the environment, where sophisticated technologies are useless or inadequate, call to mind, perhaps, both the native Americans driven on to barren reservations and the tragic confrontation being waged in South-East Asia in 1965.

Within the immediate concerns of this essay I want to isolate the central *inner* drama of *Dune*. The construction of political, ethical and sexual conflicts are played out in the mind and on the body of Paul as he grows from boyhood to manhood, confronting the death of the Father and gradual separation from the Mother by whom he has been nurtured in self-discipline and understanding. Jessica is absolutely central to her son's growth and development but characteristically she relates to power only through her support for her men, first the Duke and then Paul. Gradually it emerges that he is the Kwisatz Haderach, endowed with extraordinary powers of foresight, knowledge, 'race consciousness' and the capacity to dive into the unconscious. This latter theme, a characteristic concern of SF in the 1960s particularly, is signified in Paul's power to 'read' the hidden, psychological motives of others as he learns to exercise control, detachment and 'separateness' in the process of establishing himself as successor to his father's authority. Within this trajectory, Herbert's narrative can be read as an exploration of the ways in which masculine identity often conceals conflict, uncertainty and ambivalence. On the one hand, the pull of aggression, competitiveness and desire for dominance and on the other the need and desire for tenderness, intimacy and sharing. This uneasy dichotomy of public identity and private self is registered in Herbert's fiction together with an examination of the relationship between militarism and masculinity.

One way in which this issue is registered is through the use of technology. Where the duplicitous Emperor constructs a repressive regime to stimulate conditioned savage aggression in his troops and both he and the Baron – who can only move his body with the aid of technology – employ advanced weaponry (atomics, etc.), the Fremen have evolved a body-technology in harmony with the ecology. Ultimately, the latter is represented as more versatile and triumphant, reinforcing the political and economic themes of the narrative. This offers a more persuasive 'account' of the social relations of technology in comparison to Asimov or Clarke who has argued in his non-fiction, *Profiles of the Future*,[7] that it is possible to extrapolate from 'general laws' of technology unlike politics and economics and, as the former evolves, the latter will decrease in significance (!). Somewhat like pastoral, then, certain science fictions offer space as a realm of 'nature' – into which humanity and its technology is launched, to be tried and tested, while 'normal' social relations are (ostensibly) suspended.

Other science fictions bring nature as 'alien' to the earth in order to disturb conventional human and social assumptions. Robert Heinlein's cult novel *Stranger in a Strange Land*, originally published in 1961, for instance, centres largely on sexuality as a 'liberating' force in its satire of the repressions of American society. As such, it can usefully be related to other fictions of the period (*One Flew over the Cuckoo's Nest*, 1962) and to the emergence of the psychoanalytical theories of Herbert Marcuse (*Eros and Civilization*, 1955) and Norman O. Brown (*Life Against Death*, 1959), all of which explore or challenge the Freudian analysis of the role of repression in sustaining social organization.

In Heinlein's novel the last remaining – physically existing – Martian is brought to earth. Rescued from the exploitative, bureaucratic tentacles of the political authorities by an intrepid journalist and the individual initiative of a 'plucky' nurse, Valentine Michael Smith is subsequently protected by the legal expertise, aided by boundless wealth and material resources, of the anarcho-individualist Jubal Harshaw (it does help that the Martian's powers over his consciousness give him the capacity to 'discorporate' with a gesture anyone who threatens him or his 'water brother'!). A common feature of Heinlein's fiction is the clear advocacy of individualism and private enterprise which arguably plays into widespread popular frustration with the incomprehensible forces of bureaucratic systems and government agencies. These institutions are satirized either as the recourse of pusillanimously ambitious time-servers or as run publicly by politicians whose decisions are shaped by their 'hen-pecked' private lives (the President's wife consults an astrologer about all decisions!). Into this society the Martian releases sexuality or, more precisely, heterosexuality as an unstoppable force of the unconscious which threatens many common pieties, rooted in the repressions especially of fundamentalist churches. Inevitably, women play central roles as signifiers of sexuality – even before

Smith's arrival it should be said. Experiencing his love-making with mind *and* body – unlike other men he gives it his *whole* attention – women are released from jealousy, possessiveness, the desire for monogamy; indeed, they can even become interchangeable in their identities. The posited consequences, then, of this 'sexual revolution' seem highly problematic. The central woman character, for instance, experiences the male gaze as empowering *her* – she has been transformed from nurse to 'stripper', begins to appreciate the values of pornography, expresses relief that her new experiences have revealed that she is not subject to 'lesbian tendencies', warns Smith how to avoid homosexual 'passes' and boasts:

> I was coping with wolves when you were still on Mars. Nine times out of ten, if a girl gets raped, it's partly her fault.
>
> (Heinlein, 1965, pp. 280–3)

Given that there is little possibility of reading this ironically within the structure of the narrative, how much of a male agenda is there here! Indeed, we might relate this representation of sexuality and 'permissiveness' to Barbara Ehrenreich's thesis (*The Hearts of Men*, 1983) that any understanding of 'the sexual revolution' of the 1960s needs to take account of male bachelor desire and rejection of commitment to the breadwinner role of sustaining the family.[8]

Eventually, Smith allows himself to be torn apart by outraged religious fundamentalists but the 'Temple' he has established continues through his converts. One of these 'converts', reputedly, was Charles Manson.

It would be sad and, indeed, unjust to what I described earlier as the heterogeneity of science fiction to leave the discussion on such a negative note. For instance, Theodore Sturgeon's *Venus Plus X*, published in 1960, admirably illustrates how the field of popular fiction is a terrain upon which a struggle can be forged between dominant and marginalized discourses of sexuality and gender identity. Sturgeon constructs two juxtaposed interlocking narratives, one in which Charlie Johns awakes to find himself, disoriented and terrified, in a 'future world' and the other which sensitively, precisely and satirically depicts the interaction between socialization, sexuality and competitive capitalism in contemporary suburban America. This latter narrative, in a series of 'snapshots', constructs a detached perspective on the social manners, inflected by gender roles and male insecurities particularly, of a 'reality' in which identity and sexuality are mediated through film and television representation, advertising and the possession of consumer goods. There follows from this a restless interrogation of some of the most deep-rooted aspects of the social construction of masculinity – the ways in which men construct women as the objects of sexual desire and the ways in which women are pressed towards complicity, the 'absences' at the heart of men's social relations with each other, the emptiness of 'men's talk', male inability to confront body-politics and the association of male identity with potency, the anxieties produced in men by pregnancy and parenting, the impact of parental confusion upon childhood gender identity, the consequences for the social relations of gender of male preoccupation with goal-orientation, achievement and 'work' and, finally, the roots of misogyny, hatred, aggression and anger in the male need to preserve the 'self' apart, the seeking-out of 'difference' defensively to undermine the woman's power and attraction in order to constitute her as 'other'.

Against that narrative is placed the 'testing' of the male consciousness of Charlie Johns in his attempt to understand the alternative world of Ledom. Each of its inhabitants is both man and woman and biological evolution has followed the social development of gender in terms of similarity rather than 'difference'.[9] Technology, too, has been redefined specifically in relation to human need around two essentials: the A-field, infinitely flexible in its shaping of 'matter', and the cerebrostyle through which the inhabitants of Ledom are 'educated' in the 'truth' as against the confusion and inanities of human socialization. Charlie Johns is, of course, suspicious of the power of the cerebrostyle to condition passive Ledomites but the technology cannot be so abused as it is only part of a totally lived culture. When Charlie Johns is confronted with this apparent Utopia, its strangeness induces fear, anger and aggression in his consciousness. In his attempts to hold on to his identity, his memory reconstructs his relations with women – his mother, his teacher, his first sexual experience, Laura whom he believes he loves in his own world. He fears the Ledomite androgyny with homophobic intensity but is gradually won over to acceptance when he witnesses their celebration of children, their participatory leisure-culture (contrasted to the sexuality/violence of Western/horror movies), their mutual respect for each other and their individual skills. Ultimately, however, he violently rejects what Ledom offers when he discovers that its construction, adjacent geographically and temporally to that of Homo sapiens which is in danger of extinction it is suggested, has involved some genetic engineering to supplement *natural* mutations:

> 'Tell me, Charlie Johns: what would homo sap. do if we shared the world with them and they knew our secrets?'
> 'We'd exterminate you down to the last queer kid,' said Charlie coldly, 'and stick that one in a side-show.'
>
> (Sturgeon, 1960, p. 202)

The experiment to test whether homo sap. is ready for the peaceful, playful, unaggressive androgyny of Ledom thus comes to a sad conclusion in Sturgeon's fiction. Fortunately, however, the Ledomites have constructed their world within the protective shield of an A-field roof. Perhaps there is no better way to conclude this discussion[10] than with the quietly sad note on which Sturgeon ends his novel:

> 'At loving . . . amateurs,' chuckled Philos . . .
> 'Oh!' he cried, looking up.
> The sky began to shimmer, then to sparkle.
> 'Oh, pretty!' cried Froure.
> 'Fallout,' said Philos. 'They're at it again, the idiots.' They began to wait.

Notes

1 Cited in William Simms Bainbridge, *Dimensions of Science Fiction* (Cambridge, Mass.: Harvard University Press, 1986), p. 53. Bainbridge's analysis includes some attempt to register readerships for SF in social scientific terms.

2 Darko Suvin, *Metamorphoses of Science Fiction* (New Haven, Conn.: Yale University Press, 1979). For a more detailed discussion of these issues, see Martin Jordin, 'Science Fiction, genre and a new battle

of the books' in Asher Cashdan and Martin Jordin (eds), *Studies in Communication* (Oxford: Blackwell, 1988), pp. 157–65.

3 Richard Dyer, 'Male sexuality in the media', in Andy Metcalf and Martin Humphries (eds), *The Sexuality of Men* (London: Pluto, 1985), p. 28. For more contemporary – and British – evidence than the Hite Reports, see Yvette Walczak, *He and She: Men in the eighties* (London: Routledge, 1988).

4 See, for instance, Brian Aldiss's introduction to *The Penguin Science Fiction Omnibus* (Harmondsworth: Penguin, 1973), p. 11.

5 Roland Barthes, *S/Z* (New York: Hill & Wang, 1974).

6 See G. Klein, 'Discontent in American science fiction', *Science Fiction Studies*, IV, no. 1, part I (March 1977), pp. 3–13. Also useful is Adrian Mellor, 'Science fiction and the crisis of the educated middle class' in Christopher Pawling (ed.), *Popular Fiction and Social Change* (London: Macmillan, 1984). It is worth noting, however, that there are only two rather casual references to gender issues within this analysis of the class orientations of postwar science fiction.

7 See Arthur C. Clarke, *Profiles of the Future* (London: Pan, 1983), p. 9.

8 Barbara Ehrenreich, *The Hearts of Men* (London: Pluto, 1983).

9 Sturgeon acknowledges the influences of Ruth Benedict and Margaret Mead but it is possible that he also drew upon the Kinsey reports. It need hardly be said that there has been much critical debate concerning their work and the question of sexual difference.

10 I am very aware that my discussion of these fictions has only 'spoken' of pleasure insofar as my 'readings' have tried to unearth some of the more covert gendered appeals of SF to a male reader. In pursuing this strategy I am also aware that it may be argued, with some justice, that there is a danger of (a) viewing these texts from a position of ideological disdain and (b) reconstituting the power of the academic reader as an assessor of 'other' male readers. I can only declare that this has been far from my intention and that my project was to address critically my own experience and processes of reading and to turn same spotlight onto those 'movements' in reading which otherwise the male reader may slide easily over.

Quotations in the text are drawn from the following editions:

Asimov, Isaac (1968), *I, Robot* (London: Grafton).
Clarke, Arthur C. (1968), *2001: A Space Odyssey* (London: Arrow).
Heinlein, Robert (1965), *Stranger in a Strange Land* (London: New English Library).
Herbert, Frank (1977), *Dune* (New York: Berkley).
Sturgeon, Theodore (1984), *Venus Plus X* (New York: Bluejay).

Index

214 Index